Bella and Chaim

Bella and Chaim

The Story of Beauty and Life

Sara Rena Vidal

'Bella', meaning beautiful in French and Latin, is also God's Promise, from Isabelle, in Hebrew. The rose symbolises Beauty. 'Chaim' means life and *l'chaim* is a Jewish toast 'to life'. The symbol is the Hebrew letter *chai* which means life and is also the number eighteen.

Published by Hybrid Publishers

Melbourne Victoria Australia

First published 2017

National Library of Australia Cataloguing-in-Publication entry (paperback)
Creator: Vidal, Sara, author.
Title: Bella and Chaim: the story of beauty and life / Sara Vidal.

ISBN 9781925272659 paperback
ISBN 9781925281453 ebook

Notes: Includes bibliographical references and index.
Subjects: Heber, Bella.
Heber, Chaim.
Immigrants – Victoria – Melbourne – Biography.
Children of Holocaust survivors – Victoria – Melbourne – Biography.
World War, 1939-1945 – Poland – Biography.
World War, 1939-1945 – Atrocities – Poland.
World War, 1939-1945 – Refugees – Anecdotes.
World War, 1939-1945 – Refugees – History.
Warsaw (Poland) – History – 1943.

CONTENTS

AUTHOR'S NOTE REGARDING THE ELEMENTS

This telling – a mingling of voices that flow such that past becomes ever-present – is guided by a structure that, while not obvious, is deliberate.

MY MEMORY FRAGMENTS

Parts One, Three, Five, Seven, Nine, Eleven and Thirteen are comprised of extracts adapted from my childhood memoir: *The Making of Plans* (unpublished, 1949–59), journal entries (1992–99) and reflections (2006–16).

BASIA AND HENIEK'S STORY

Parts Two, Four, Six, Eight, Ten and Twelve (chapter 1–24) comprise Basia and Heniek's story of the pre-war period, the 1939–43 Warsaw Ghetto and the period 1944–49, as told to and uncovered by me. The whole contains selected memory fragments and is interspersed with:

- prose poems of longing and gratitude (mostly from 2009)
- inserts which include:

Basia's oft repeated phrases of recollection and longing.
Heniek's revealed insights

My thoughts, findings and reflections 2006-2016

HISTORICAL CONTEXT

These comprise two aspects:

Facts and Numbers with Hindsight: further factual information, post-event analysis and newspaper headlines;

Imagine Being in Their Shoes

These sections –
gleaned from the real-time journals of those who perished
and the recollections of those who survived –
offer detail and insight to things
my parents did not tell me,
of the events in the Warsaw Ghetto.

AFFIRMATION

Reflections on Living the Questions:

four instances of insight and a conclusion that is also a beginning.

Language: each section is written using the idiom of the time. Preference is given for the words used by victims and by survivors as found in the records and in their verbal testimonies. Also 'he', when used, if appropriate, includes 'she'.

And to them will I give in my house and within my walls
an (everlasting) memorial and a name …
that shall not be cut off.
Isaiah[2]

… the past is what is real and true,
while history is merely what someone recorded.
Andy Andrews[3]

Once upon a time there was a man.
He was and he is for we tell his story.
He has been because we are.
Once upon a time there will be a man since
we plant Olive groves for him
and we wish that he should enjoy their yield.
Agnes Heller[4]

In which my longing for that which is lost
as well as for that which might yet be
as told from memory fragments, journal jottings,
and delving into history past and present,
intertwining with my parents' stories of more than survival,
traverses despair to find transformation, home, and gratitude.
So the generations will know, and choose life
– after all it is a commandment.[5]

For Bella and Chaim. And for those to come.

PART ONE

LIGHT IN THE DARK

I AM THE LORD YOUR GOD

Bella's Longing for a White Cloth

We were lying there in the dark.
Me and your daddy. Unable to move.
Eighteen months in a hole in the ground ...
I thought I would go mad. But I saw a white tablecloth ...

Here is the hole in the ground,
the bunker with no space even to sit, let alone stand.
Lying down in this hole is a young man.
Next to him is a young woman.
With her eyes wide open,
stilling the images and daemons tearing her mind apart,
she holds back the enveloping dark by conjuring an image;
always the same scene, a *presque-vu* of anticipation.
A table laid out for the Sabbath.
A long table set with a crisp starched white cloth,
a golden plaited egg-loaf,
a pair of candlesticks with waiting-to-be-lit candles …
Hush; she listens for the tender sound of familiar footsteps …
Yes. Any moment her mother will come;

then will come her father and her sisters.
No. She knows that is not possible.
So she summons her God; the one whose name must not be spoken.
The one who declared as his First Commandment:
I am the Lord your G-d who has taken you out of the land of Egypt … [6]
Of this deity, in-whom-she-no-longer-believes,
having no other to take his place, she asks,
'Let it be at least I will one day have the white *Shabbos*[7] cloth.'

Must Not Wake My Mummy: Melbourne 1949

Dense dark.
A baby cries.
Is it me?
White light.

Ah-ah-ah, kotki dwa, szarobure obydwa,
nic nie będą robiły, tylko Sare bawiły …

Oh, oh, kittens two, grey and beige both,
nothing will they do, just with Sara play.

Black dots on the ground …
If I stand on one, I'll fall forever.
HELP!
Sha. Sha. Go back to sleep. *Frère Jacques … Frère Jacques …*
Dormez vous … Dormez vous. Sonnez les matines …
Sonnez les matines … Ding dang dong. Ding dang dong …

'WAKE UP MRS ROTSTEIN! IT'S SIX O'CLOCK!'

Morning sunlight makes a bright splash on the white door. I stand in the corridor and wait. A tired voice, the voice of the lady who will soon be my beloved godmother, comes from behind the closed door.

'Go awaay, Sara. It is too early.'

'I want to play.'

'Go and wake your muzzer.'

'My Mummy is asleep.'

'Go awaay, Sara.'

Let myself out of the big old house; on hands and knees I crawl
under tall trees through a carpet of spring flowers: blue forget-me-nots,
white lily-of-the-valley, and sweet-smelling pink flowers
which I will learn are called bergenia.

The street beckons. The gate opens easily. I am on the street.
The beach – just a few houses away; no one in sight. Hop, skip,
running and twirling on a long stretch of yellow sand in golden light.
All this space all to myself.

What is that moving speck in the distance? It is a lady. She walks a dog. She comes right up to me. Her voice is horrible to my ears.

'Little girl, how old are you? Nearly four?! Where is your mummy? Your mummy should not let you out by yourself. There are bad people, someone might hurt you. Go home.'

She glares at me so. She watches me.

So home I go, feet dragging, thinking …

My Mummy is so beautiful: her laugh, her rosy cheeks,
her round brown eyes and long, curling brown hair so soft to the touch,
silly yucky lady-from-the-beach, if she knew my Mummy she would
know that it is not my Mummy's fault.

Anyway, it is too early … my Mummy is asleep.

I Learn of Grandmothers: Melbourne 1952

'Wake up Mummy!'

Mummy stretches, sighs, opens her eyes. She sees me but, instead of giving me her usual good-morning smile, she looks puzzled and says, 'Why did you wake me? I was home, home with my mother …'

I reply, 'I'm sorry, Mummy.
It is time for you to get up. I will be late for school.'

She takes me in her arms. Holds me close. Questions fill my head:
Where are these people you long for?

When will we see them?

But I do not ask.

It is 1952, I am six, finished with the 'bubs'. I am in grade one at South Yarra Primary School, just a short walk through Domain Park from our flat in Park Street. I can read and write. The words in our readers tell many stories and we are writing with lead pencils now. No more chalk or crayons.

The twins, Cheryl and Laurel, with radiant smiles, dark brown ringlets, matching dresses, are definitely the most popular girls in the school; every day at play and lunchtimes in the concrete schoolyard their friends surround them. I want to join in, but I hang back.

One sunny day, after we have stood in queues to collect our small glass bottle of fresh milk – yummy with thick cream on top – and I am sitting alone in the shelter shed, one of the twins – I think it is Laurel – comes over and says, 'Sarena, come and play with us.'

I bask in the glow of their friendship. Then one day they invite me to come to their home in Prahran; Mummy says okay.

That is how, soon after, I find myself skipping with them through narrow streets, passing houses that share their sidewalls with their neighbours and have small garden behind low timber fences.

Their house, of wood with a corrugated iron roof, is cosy, dark, musty.

In an alcove, a lady with permed white hair sits at a sewing machine. They introduce me. 'Granny, this is Sara.'

She turns, smiles, keeps on fixing lace to a flouncy skirt.

Back home I look around our bright airy flat and I do not mind that we do not live in a house. As I inspect my mop of black curls in the mirror in Mummy's dressing table I think I would not be me with ringlets.

My plain clothes – hand-me-downs and often red – look fine.

But … But …

Now I know about grandmothers, oh how I want to have a grandmother. A mother for my Mummy.

My heart pounding, I ask Mummy,
'Where is my grandmother? Where is my twin?'

She gazes at me; she hesitates. I plead with her,
'Please Mummy tell me!'

Staring deep into my eyes, holding me by both hands,

Mummy Tells Me The Truth.

'Your grandparents are dead. Your cousins, aunts,
their husbands and children, all are dead.
Your twin is dead. I did not have enough for two.
You were born first. You are alive. You are a big girl – nearly seven.
You are the strong one; Daddy and I love you.'
'Mummy,' I whisper, afraid to ask, but asking,
'Why did they all die?'
Her reply is as if confiding a secret:
'Because of the war.
They are dead because of the war.'

So many questions unasked and unanswered,
but my need to tell is strong;
delving into Pandora boxes, setting memory in the record,
I bring you my parents' story,
as told to me in vignettes and dioramas;
words – being flawed and fragmented –
convey, even resonate in events unfolding today,
but they are not the thing.
It is the dark and light of my mother's longing
that both wakes me from deepest sleep
and motivates me through my days.

This feeling is more than Anemoia[8] –
longing for a time I've never known;
I've found no word or phrase as yet to encapsulates this longing.
The Welsh word Hiraeth (HEER-eyeth) is a starting point:

… a homesickness for a home to which you cannot return,
a home which maybe never was;
the nostalgia, the yearning, the grief for lost places.
To feel Hiraeth is to feel a deep incompleteness
and recognise it as familiar.[9]

Add to that:
immeasurable loss of entire family branches and trunks,
knowledge of what man can and does do, to, and for, his fellow man;
thus armed with courage to face the facts,
uncover immutable moments of treasured memories.
Hold onto belief that even in the darkest dark, you can find a light.
Mix well to make a brew potent and consoling
so long as memory persists.
Make a new word to encapsulate:
Atoh-dachaia.[10]

Thus armed with gratitude –
Come with me.

PART TWO

PICTURE (IM)PERFECT

Warsaw pre-September 1939

NO GOD BUT ME

'Why did you wake me? I was home with my mother.
My mother was such a nice lady. My father was so nice.
My sisters, the beautiful one and the clever one, were there.
Everything was so nice. Why did you wake me?
Oh how I want to be back home.
Home when the world was nice.'

'Did you buy and sell in good faith?
Did you have a set time for study?
Did you raise a family?'

A saying from The Talmud.[11]

CHAPTER 1: THE LAST SPRING

My mother's nice world is Poland. In the verdant forests of Świder, in a holiday cottage owned by her parents, she was born on 22 August 1923. Named Bella, known as Basia, she and her sisters, Zosia and Celina, immersed in the privileged life of a loving middle-class family living in a Jewish quarter, thrive in exciting, bustling Warsaw.

Basia's father is Pinkus Birenbaum. Pinkus comes from a village.

What was it called? I don't remember, but it was
so small that people would joke that if you gave
a yawn while travelling through you would miss it.
Oh, I remember now. Podelane – Wieś.

His father Eliakim has two sons[12] from a first marriage.

Pinkus is prosperous. A wholesaler in cotton and wool, he is of medium height, dark-haired, olive-skinned, portly, cosmopolitan; as a lover of good food, he even eats delicious forbidden ham when away on business. On ordinary days he sits at the table with his head uncovered without any hat or *yarmulke*, and on the Sabbath, as it is a bit far to walk, he catches a taxi to the Great Tłomackie Synagogue, but, as work of any kind on the Sabbath – which includes driving – breaks a commandment, he gets out a little before his destination, not to be seen.

Basia's mother is Rena Birenbaum nee Czosnek. Rena, pretty, capable, stylish, the youngest of fourteen children of which seven have survived childhood, came from Kraków, but was born in Działoszyce. She dresses in the latest fashion: delightful hats and berets, knee-length skirts, she even has a fine sable coat with a mink collar for winter. She manages her gracious home with the help of only one servant, Pola – a young Jewish girl from a small town – plus a washerwoman who comes in every fortnight. While Pola does general cleaning and cooking, Rena sees to all the shopping; in her kosher kitchen she ensures the dishes – one set for meat, the other for milk – are kept separate as laid down by *Halacha* – Jewish Law. For the minor and high holy days, she personally prepares the specialties: *challahs* (plaited egg loaf), chicken soup, *lockshen* (egg noodles), *kreplach* (dumplings), *gefilte* fish (fish patties), *kneidlech* (matzah balls), and *cholent* (bean and barley stew) for *Shabbos* lunch. The *cholent*, taken before the Sabbath to the communal bakery for slow cooking in pots that are numbered then put into the ovens on long paddles, is everyone's favourite. While waiting to collect their pot, people joke that the baker should mix the pots up so a poor man might get a rich man's pot filled with meat.

From the fragments of my mother's anecdotes
I build a Friday night in spring 1939,
forever the last spring of this time before War came to Poland.

With school finishing early on Fridays, the girls rush home to help in the kitchen and in the setting of the Sabbath table. When the first star in the night sky appears, the sign that joyful *Shabbos* can commence, Rena lights the two candles, covers her eyes, and blesses the candles with the traditional incantation.

Barukh atah Adonai Eloheinu, melekh ha'olam,
asher kid'shanu b'mitzvotav v'tzivanu l'hadlik ner shel Shabbat.
Blessed are You, Lord our God, King of the universe,
Who has made us holy through His Commandments
and commanded us to kindle the Sabbath light.

With everyone seated, there is silence while Pinkus intones further blessings sanctifying the wine and challah. Everyone says *omain* – amen; the challah cut into small pieces is passed around, the meal under way, tongues loosened by wine, speaking to each other in a Polish as fluent as that of any parallel Catholic home, the girls talk of many things while Pola serves the courses.

Rena surveys her brood. All is well. First, everyone is in good health. Second, tonight's meal has turned out delish. Perhaps a dash more salt in the soup? No, Pinkus assures her it is just scrumptious. Yes, she does love him, though without doubt she will have cause tomorrow to chastise him for playing cards on a Saturday, this being another irritating manifestation of his lack of respect for the many Mosaic rules. Thankfully, his irreverence pales beside his attributes: a caring husband, doting father, generous to her relatives, a good provider.

Not like her dear brother, Mayer Czosnek. Making money eludes Mayer yet neither he nor his wife Leah, known as Leyele, will accept anything from Rena. Despite abject poverty, Mayer radiates the soothing aura of a man of exalting faith. He is a sight in his full orthodox garb: a caftan and small brimmed hat.[13] And to pray he wears a *tallis (*a fringed shawl whose every tassel is prescribed) and bound to his head and arms the *tefillin* (black leather boxes), symbolic and mystical elements of the ritual. Pious Leyele, her head covered by the prescribed *sheitel* – that wig looking not at all becoming – keeps their one-roomed apartment spotless. In their crowded yet organised home, Leyele and Mayer earn a pittance by spending their days and nights overlocking knitted fabric for a manufacturer. In this building, they live, work, and even pray, because conveniently located on the ground floor is a *shteibel* – a prayer house. Their daughter Sara is still at home; how do they manage?

It would be nice if only Leyele and Mayer would come to partake of the Friday feast, or lunch on Saturday. However, her own brother will not eat in her home for, though she follows the Jewish dietary laws of *kashrut* with meticulous attention, he says it is *trayf,* not kosher enough for him. At least Leyele pops in for a cup of tea on Saturday. No, she would not like Pinkus to be religious like that. Give thanks to her dear blessed parents for making this *shiddach*. Make sure to emphasise to the girls the wisdom of this tradition of arranged marriages. Tell them: 'My parents told me I would learn to love him and I have.'

The gifts of her marriage multiply with the passage of time:

knowledge of continuance; delight in the present reality of watching her girls grows and mature. A son would have been a blessing to carry on the family name, but her princesses will bring sons to the family. *Peu, peu.* Out of custom she makes the spitting sound, to ward off the evil eye, and considers each daughter.

Zosia, the eldest, is named Sophia for wisdom. Just seventeen, charming, small, slim, graceful, a Dorothy Lamour look-alike; the young men flock, drinking in her charm. Of late, Zosia is favouring young Adam Poznanski, whose family came from Łódź. A nice boy, good family, well-off – it could be a match. But she is too young. Rena resolves to keep an eye on her daughter.

As for her middle one, while telling Basia that she is clever in her own way – that she will turn out best of all – Rena, with a mother's protective instinct, worries. Basia, though not as silly as she seems, in fact clever in a down-to-earth way, is altogether too friendly, too careless, too carefree. Immersed in daydreams, she lacks confidence, pays scant attention to her schoolwork, and her Hebrew is abysmal. Perhaps her private Jewish school, just like the Polish schools, is concentrating too much on unnecessary subjects. And she fidgets so! Sixteen soon in August, plump, yet attractive in her own way, wholesome like the *kasha* (buckwheat) in her nickname: Basia-Kasha. Is she losing her baby fat? Indeed, all of a sudden she is quite tall and curvy – in fact delicious; peach-skin, the uncles call her. Truly, she is becoming a beauty despite that long nose. Danger looming. Rena reviews her method of protection. She'll work on Basia a little more: remind her of the perils of this world, continue instilling caution, warn again of the disgrace of fallen women.

Turning her thoughts to the baby of the family, Rena smiles with pride. Celina is her clever one, so good at schoolwork; only twelve, but she helps Basia with hers. Bookish. Serious. Ah, but it is not good for a woman to be obviously clever. Will she want a different life, perhaps that of a pioneer in far-off Palestine? Plenty of time to worry about Celushina's prospects.

Three girls, fount for emergence of the next generation.

This is what it is to be content. Thank you, God, for this family.

But, in the World Outside, A.H. is Enacting his Vision[14]

Here is some historical context

Since the end of WWI trouble has brewed in the Weimar Republic.

The Treaty of Versailles – a make-the-loser-pay, grab-what-you-can (usual European postwar tit-for-tat practice) – a departure from the 14-point peace plan proposed by the American President Woodrow Wilson, proved to be a recipe for failure which did not settle prewar disputes, and left Germany with reduced territory.

The declared elements of German angst – dishonour, defeat, denunciation (for starting the war), demilitarisation, deprivation, devaluation (financial and world-standing), damages, despair, dread (of socialism, communism and Catholicism)[15] and desire (for more of everything, for revenge) – were a fertile medium for germination of nasty ideas that defy description.

In 1924, Adolf Hitler, from a Bavarian prison – where he served eight months of a five-year sentence for his failed coup – had put to paper his revelation for, and action plan of, a Utopia to restore his view of the natural world; one where the fittest reign supreme uninhibited by any moral code. Word-smithed by Rudolf Hess, *Mein Kampf* (*My Struggle*)[16] was an instant bestseller; clear and arrogant, he'd blamed all Germany's woes on the Jews – especially the loss of WWI – and outlined what he would do: drive eastward for living space, take over the Soviet Union; share world power with the other great powers – England and the US; eliminate lesser beings: unproductive, mentally ill and handicapped, communists, Gypsies, Jews.

Germans had voted vote for him primarily because of his promises: to revive the economy, restore German greatness, overturn the Treaty of Versailles, and to save Germany from communism.[17]

It is all there.
A mission statement with background, rationale, and goals identified.
Comprehensive. Bold. Ruthless. Astute. Seductive. Dynamic. Vile.
A.H. the leader – not mad but bad:[18]
Der Führer, the Leader; A.H. did not act alone.
I call him A.H.[19] *so as not to speak his name.*

On 30 January 1932, Germans had given government to the National Socialist German Workers' Party, the NSDAP, commonly referred to as the Nazi Party. Their slogan: *Ein Reich, ein Volk, ein Führer* – One realm, one people, one leader. Democratically elected, A.H. secured office as

Chancellor with unlimited powers. Aided by the fact that Germany was well organised, he swiftly took over every aspect of German life. The Nazis' 25-point program made sweeping demands and committed all those defined as German citizens to aggression against those deemed non-citizens.[20]

Blaming the communists for the Reichstag fire of 27 February 1933, A.H. used the pretext of national security to marshal sweeping powers that enabled his elimination of opponents, curtailment of the press, and removal of personal freedoms guaranteed in the constitution.[21]

1933 also saw *Mein Kampf* translated into English. Debated, understood; in-favour, against; ignored, discounted. Yes. No.[22] Read by the world's leaders? Seemingly ignored. In any case, National Socialism[23] was seen by many as a bulwark to Soviet communism. The versions made available in English were abridged, and though much of the antisemitic vitriol was left out,[24] it was still an all-out hateful attack blaming every woe, especially the loss of WWI, on this tiny portion of the population.

Calling for fanaticism and intolerance[25] A.H. advocated that 'the nationalization of our masses will succeed only when, aside from all the positive struggle for the soul of our people, their international poisoners are exterminated.'[26]

The population of Germany in 1933 was around 60 million. Some 20 million were Catholic and 40 million Protestant. Less than 1 per cent of the total population was Jewish.[27] Shortly after Pastor Dietrich Bonhoeffer's declaration that the role of the church was to stand up for the Jews,[28] on 10 May 1933, students of 34 university towns burnt 25,000 'un-German books' in the 'Action Against the Un-German Spirit'. Widespread newspaper coverage, radio broadcasts of speeches, songs and ceremonial incantations went live to countless listeners.[29]

Books burnt? Franz Kafka, Bertolt Brecht, Sholem Asch, Sigmund Freud, Ernest Hemingway, H.G. Wells, Lion Feuchtwanger, Jack London, Thomas Mann, and many others. The greatest writers and minds deemed unsuitable.

As far back as 1821, Heinrich Heine warned: 'Where they have burned books, they will in the end burn people.'[30]

Foiling the West on 16 May 1933, just days after the book burning, making a show of accepting Roosevelt's Peace Plan, and promising to destroy armaments.[31]

So the world's newspapers told:[32]

GERMANY ACCEPTS ROOSEVELT'S PEACE PLAN

Passing the Nuremberg Laws[33] in 1935, A.H. stripped the Jews of Germany of citizenship and classified them. Ever gathering control, he had long done away with all democratic parliamentary processes, crushed opposition, killed opponents, introduced conscription, banned trade unions, built on the Hitler Youth (created in 1922). He used the opportunity presented by Germany's hosting of the 1936 Olympic Games to promote an image of a new, strong, united Germany while masking its racist policies and growing militarism, thus allaying Western concerns. Businessmen, within and outside Germany, supported him, threw money at him[34] – fawned over him. Everyone was aroused, with secret proceedings, any dissenting voice silenced, no trial, property confiscated. The Brownshirts or Storm Troopers – the Nazi Party's paramilitary, also known as the SA – burnt homes, shops and synagogues. Thousands were incarcerated in 'holding camps'; hundreds of windows were broken in one night.[35] Gentiles who voiced concerns were thrown into concentration camps.

A most sinister act is unfolding: in October 1939 –
A.H. will sign the notorious T-4 Euthanasia Program.

The consummate liar, A.H. was not alone in favouring elimination of those judged unworthy of life. Indeed, his schemes could appear rational – a logical consequence of ideas on how to bring in a better world. Many Utopian visions – that of H.G. Wells, for one – generated by a genuine concern with imminent overpopulation, racial degeneration and limited availability of resources, sought answers in Social Darwinism's distortion of Darwin's 'survival of the fittest'. It was just a small step to eugenics and notions of racial purity.[36] A.H. took advantage of these rampant notions and applied a dynamic organic force by unifying and inspiring his ideas into being. The German populace, lauded by A.H. as Aryan thus as 'the carrier of human cultural development'[37] believing itself 'overwhelmed in the mixing of races',[38] longing for change and inured by persuasive arguments, would acquiesce: mass sterilisation programs were accepted; a medical workforce was trained; the murder of severely handicapped children was enacted with flow-on to unproductive adults and the elderly – social engineering extraordinaire. An overture to the mass exterminations to come.

And what were Russia and Italy thinking? And the countries of East Europe? All embroiled in a blatant frenzy of land grabbing.

This is a glimpse of the crazy world outside Basia's nice home.
I asked my mother, 'Why didn't you just leave?
You just had to know what was going on.'
She answered:
'Yes we knew, but we never thought it would come to us.'

Pinkus catches his wife's fond smile and divines her thoughts as she surveys the girls. He congratulates himself. Yes, the girls are flourishing in this upbringing, traditional rather than religious; thank goodness the crazy ideas sprouting all over the place have not turned their heads. Replete from the excellent meal, he casts away the longing to light a cigarette. His mind turns to pressing matters: increasing taxes, union trouble – the usual problems. But government actions in nationalising industries and turning them into monopolies are making it increasingly difficult to do business. Will they go as far as Germany? Thank God, the Birenbaum family left there long ago. He sighs.

A concerned look from Rena; a gesture to assure her that all is well. He re-engages in the thrust and parry of the table talk for a bit. The girls are debating the merits of swing music versus classical. His preference is for something he can dance to: a romantic waltz or nippy foxtrot; this swing is a touch risqué. Pinkus slips a slice of lemon into his strong black tea, takes a sip and relaxes. But dark thoughts return.

Only 25 years since the Russians saved Warsaw from German takeover, and again there is talk of war. How has it come to this so soon after the last never to be repeated horror of World War I? Things are terrible for Jews in Germany. The *Sejm*, the Polish parliament, is also emphasising differences, distorting the inclination to fairness and honour in which the Poles take pride. Surely it could not get too bad. Britain and France have promised to back Poland. War? Yes, it seems there will be war …

Rena would love to go to Palestine – build on the land[39] you've bought. But that way is at present closed[40] and why uproot the family to go to such a hostile place? Leaving behind everything in Poland is too dramatic, too drastic. Even if war comes, it will be a blitzkrieg – over in a flash. Life will go on as before. No need to worry Rena. Not on *Shabbat*.

Dear Grandfather Pinkus

I look at the one photo that I have.
You are well-dressed. Your mouth is
well-formed; there is an attractive cleft
to your chin. Your eyes, under furrowed
brows, are thoughtful. Your nose is long.
That's where Mummy got hers from.
Pity she had it bobbed.

I bet that I would have had you twisted
around my little finger until I was a big girl
– say five – and then I'd have sat in your
presence in dutiful attendance.

But later, we would have enjoyed
full-on discussions.
Or would I have held my tongue?
My mother speaks of you with such loving respect.
Indistinguishable from any urbane Pole after 800 years of shared place,
your mind amazed; ideas, figures, solutions zapped in dynamic flashes
such that Rena and the girls teasingly called you computer-head.

To me you would have been Papa or *Zayde.*
Z as in Zion, *ay* as in say, *de* as in delight. *Zayde.*
Imagine all the fun.
Picture all the love.
Birenbaum. Pear tree. Delicious fruit. Pinkus Birenbaum.
Dear unknown Grandfather Pinkus.
I long for your gaze.

Wish I'd known you.

Smile at your sensible wife, Rena. Darling Racele. When dinner is over, light that long-awaited cigarette. Draw in its fragrance, sigh, this time in pleasure. Look how well she keeps you in line, while deferring to you. Everything organised for your comfort and with such a sense of style. Ah, what darlings you have, what a blessing it is to lavish love on them all. Indeed, what is a man if he does not do everything in his power for his family, even take on this crazy world. Anything to keep this good life, here in Warsaw, here in Poland. Here is home.

My mother's home; the one she wept for all through my childhood, the one she talks of every time we speak, that home was the place of her childhood. My home, until I married, was always where she was. And our first home in Australia, until I was eighteen, was in South Yarra.

They say 'home is where the heart is' and I know this is true. It is early spring 1955; I am nearly ten. We live in a rented flat at 5/28 Park Street, South Yarra, near the Botanic Gardens where Mummy sometimes takes us after school.

Our flat is on the first floor of a two-storey building. Our door – one of four – has a protective mezuzah on the side – as do two others.

Off the long corridor are two bedrooms – the first is the one I share with my sister, Janette; she is just four and has eczema. She scratches in the night. When her asthma strikes Mummy sometimes moves Janette to her bed. Our room has two divans each with two drawers, one for bedding and the other for our treasures, and a bookcase Daddy made from a kit – with my help.

The bathroom, cold and bare, with a concrete floor painted red, is small with everything crammed in: a shower over the bath, a toilet tucked into the corner under a small window of diamond-patterned obscure glass that is hard to open, and a small basin with a mirrored cupboard above. Lying in the bath, I inhale the crisp fragrance of Blue Clinic shampoo, and if I half close my eyes, in the patterns on the shiny wall lining, I see continents and faces.

The kitchen is near the entry. A sink sits under a small window with no outlook. Next to it is a stove in a tight alcove and a small cabinet, and on the other side, blocking the back door, is a chrome and Formica-topped table with four matching vinyl chairs. Cramped and dark, here is where we eat and talk – not in the large bright dining room at the other end of the corridor that you walk through to get to our lounge room, which looks out onto the street; here in the kitchen is where we sing along with the hit parade and listen to serials on the radio: Hop Harrigan, Captain Silver, Biggles and, if Mummy lets me stay up, my favourite, Larry Kent.

Out the back door onto a landing, down the rickety timber stairs, into an open concrete yard with rotary clothes hoists. Garages and laundries are tucked under the building; all this space is shared by several blocks of two-storey flats.

There – for two shillings – I help my Daddy wash his Holden.

My mother's washing day is Wednesday. Washing is a big job, and during school holidays, I help. Mummy works hard, scrubbing shirt collars, moving clothes, towels, sheets in and out of the big copper. Sometimes she swears in Polish, using words she tells me not to use, like '*Holera schluck cref*' whatever that means.

Now I know: *Cholera psia krew*, cholera dog's blood – spoken as an oath.

The boiling water emits steam and a not-nice soapy smell. Hot and sweaty, she tells me she never dreamt she would work like this:

her family was well off;
they had a maid, a lovely apartment, a country house.
She'd had a beautiful engagement ring
and a gold wedding band ...

Brushing away tears, she grumbles, especially about our long corridor. I remind her how close we are to my school, gardens, beaches and Luna Park, and how sunny are the bedrooms, and spacious the lounge.
She smiles at me and says, 'Yes we are lucky.'
Taking me in her arms she says,
'You and your sister, you both are my jewels.'
Then she is quiet, her eyes mist again.

I try to see what she sees. I see only her tears.

I want to tell her I know her heart is in another place, but, I only say, 'Mummy, don't be so sad.'

When eventually I did ask,
'Mummy, we are so lucky. Why are you so sad?'
She replied:
'Oh Sarele, I loved the people; all of them, they were good people.'

CHAPTER 2: MUCH TO THINK ABOUT

The Birenbaum family home is a pleasant apartment on the third floor of a three-storey block of flats at 18 Muranowska Street, Warsaw – corner of Pokorna, adjacent to the square Plac Muranowski. The building is U-shaped and backs onto another; together they form a rectangle around a courtyard where over a hundred families live. A concierge guards the only entry through iron gates that he closes at 11 pm; out-of-hours attendance attracts extra pay. If the girls come in beyond the curfew, Rena chastises, 'Aren't you ashamed before the concierge?'

To avoid being found wanting by this guardian-of-the-door, Basia, caught out after a night out with friends – at the pictures or doing homework – gives a soft call to Pola, the servant, not much older than Basia, asleep in the kitchen of Basia's apartment above. 'Polunia, Polunia.'

From the basement, an echo mocks, 'Poo-loonia, Poo-loonia.' Loud is this harsh voice in the still night. Turning her head towards the cracked ground level slit of a window, Basia catches a glimpse of the young, shabby, and none-too-clean girl around her own age.

Disgraced, caught locked out, Basia endeavours to appear nonchalant. Just how many are squeezed into that one subterranean room? A previous maid had lived there and Basia had once seen inside so she knows the dank despair of it and the bitter cold when snow lies thick on the ground. Terrible.

Thinking of that poverty evokes cousin Sara Czosnek, who lives in poverty such that she has to work with her parents; denied schooling she steals bits of time to devour books, never satisfying her hunger for knowledge. Though their life is difficult, there is always food on the table. Not like this wretched lot in the basement. Basia shudders, thinking again of her bright intense older cousin, and she trembles for her. What if Uncle Mayer and Auntie Leyele find out their darling Sara is a communist?[41] That she hides pamphlets under her mattress! If she is caught she could be interrogated, even executed. The whole family is in jeopardy of arrest. She believes the way to fight those who would exclude Jews is to have a society where all are equal and with everything divided according to one's needs. She says things with such passionate conviction: 'Prayer will not bring about a better world'; 'God is dead'; 'Religion is the opium of the people'. Where does she get such ideas?[42]

Thank God! Here at last is loyal, tall, blonde Pola to open the gate; Pola won't tell on her. It is so good to be home; the boxed scroll of the *mezuzah* on the door, offering protection of God from the Angel of Death, enhances the sense of security.

Untouched by accounts of pogroms in the countryside, Basia enjoys boundless love for her city. She takes sustenance and pleasure in the felicity of all manner of outings. A walk along the boulevards, visits to shops, cafés, the Yiddish theatres, crammed in a tram zipping across the city to visit a friend or an excursion to the zoo. Everywhere one mingles with people of many nations and walks of life while immersing one's senses in aromas and colours. Closer to home, it is a delight to park oneself on a sunny park bench in the Jewish sector of the Krasiński Gardens – just a short walk via Nalewki Street – but never to the Ujazdowski Park frequented, so Rena warns, by antisemites.

And Basia loves her home. Light floods into the apartment from the huge double-hung windows and you can stick your head out or sit on one of the three balconies to shout to someone in the street or in the courtyard. As in each preceding year, birds build nests amongst the sweet blossoms, and pale-green spring leaves clothe the solitary tree's welcoming branches.

Warsaw was renowned for its beautiful trees.
Was the courtyard tree perhaps a Linden tree?

The birds' dulcet morning-greeting and evening-farewell songs mingle with busy sounds of the comings-and-goings of tenants and music, courtesy of the radios.

Airy, roomy, bright, this apartment has everything: a spacious dining room, three bedrooms, a separate kitchen; the bathroom boasts both an internal toilet and a full-length bath. It is heaven to luxuriate in water, hot from a coal-fired boiler, whose fire is kept going by wonderful Pola.

In the dining room there are cream-coloured damask curtains, a large Persian rug on the polished timber floorboards, a credenza for crockery and crystal glasses, a small cabinet with glass doors for miniatures, and a solid timber table and chairs which complement the timber panelling and architraves; and presiding over all this is a huge framed photo of the three girls. There is no lounge room, but a study nook with a desk and books. The parents' room – bright, spacious, furnished with cream coloured furniture including cupboard, bed and dressing-table – is off-limits to the girls.

The sisters occupy the second bedroom. Zosia, as the eldest, could have the small third bedroom to herself but chooses instead to share; so, while Pola sleeps on a folding bed in the kitchen, with her few belongings stashed in a small trunk, the third bedroom serves as a storeroom.

The girls spend hours together in their cramped haven. They have much to laugh and talk about: friends, pictures, school. Basia adores her sisters. To her, Zosia, in her secret-from-Mother, hidden-from-Father lipstick and touch of eyelash-lengthening mascara, is Dorothy Lamour incarnate. How would *she* look in lipstick? No, she doesn't dare. Not yet. One day soon. After all, as Rena instructs, a little lipstick is all right, but only prostitutes paint their faces! *Kurva*s! Disgraced, fallen women. Tight, slinky, skimpy clothes – nothing left to the imagination, eyes ringed in black, voices husky from cigarettes and wine, red lips emitting ugly words. Rena warns that such a woman has nothing special to give to a man, therefore, no prospect of a husband and eternal shame before everyone. Basia, well-schooled, mimics: fancy a woman giving away that most precious offering of a husband's pride and honour for money!

However, despite Rena's refrain, 'Knowledge is an open window to the world', Basia is repeating Intermediate Level; a private tutor gives her extra coaching. After the holidays, she'll face final exams. She asks, 'Please God, at least a pass so I will have my *Mała Matura.* For Mamma.'

Basia has another shame, a kept secret: just last week, she caught a tram to see a boy across town. Moreover, he took the liberty to steal a kiss. Yes, she likes him, but is this how it would feel to be in love? How will she know? Her head is so full. The more she learns, the more confused she becomes. Why can nothing stay simple and beautiful like the excitement generated before *Pesach* approaches each March? The apartment spring-cleaned from top to bottom, and every corner searched for each offending crust, biscuit, or hidden packet of barley or rice. These being *chametz* – unfit for Passover – are pounced on with much laughter, disposed of one by one, until everyone is convinced everything's ready.

Now, with *Rosh Hashanah* – Jewish New Year – approaching in September, will she have new clothes? Everyone wears their best when they go to synagogue on these two days marking the New Year. She'll be a year older and her old coat just will not do. A new coat? Yes! Plus new black patent-leather shoes with a small heel – and silk stockings – no more flatties or white socks.

Oh, there is so much to do; she resolves to talk to Mamma.

As my mother told me these things,
I absorbed her longing for Rena.
On a wintry night, 20 June 2009, words spilled out.

Longing for Mamma of my Mummy

Rena, unknown grandmother of mine,
as I type, you look out of the photo frame
as if you see me.
Your soft neck evokes
a womanly plumpness.
A beret of unknown colour merges with
your hair. I do not know you:
I have not felt the touch of your hand.
Nor heard the music of your voice.
You never shushed my cries.
At every opportunity,
Mummy invokes
your thirst for knowledge,
your patience, and kindness.
I know the ordinary details:
homemaker, loving wife, adored mother, benefactress.
Your library grew day by day:
Steinbeck, Victor Hugo, Tolstoy.
Is it from you I get my love of books?
Tears gather …
(My other grandmother, Sara, is present,
made visible in remnant family – here in Australia.)
Of your line, there is only my mother.
Is she like you?
She is not like me.
But tonight, I see a bit of myself in the expression
of the indistinct image of your sad dark eyes,
the heart shape of your face, your widow's peak,
the restrained smile of your painted mouth. Is that a touch of mascara?
Wait! Go back. Sad eyes? Why did I say that?
Why would they be sad?
My life soaks up your absence.

Rena, at 43, knows where the lines separating the various duties and aspects of her life are drawn. Certainly, everything is *beshert*, predestined, but one can still take charge: of self, life, and husband. A well-educated woman married to an uneducated businessman; let people scoff at the match – it works just fine. Apart from watching over the physical and spiritual wellbeing of her daughters, Rena ensures her husband's unconditional place as master in his own home. To shout at the girls is not on. As for any physical disciplinary action, such degradation is unconceivable! A silent look, cool withdrawal, a gentle reprimand: 'Your children will give you back,' is still sufficient to keep the girls' enthusiasms in check. Her tools of admonishment and reminders are administered with skill, to ensure the maturing girls maintain a respectful demeanour towards their father, never bothering him with feminine problems. Indeed, for them to answer back is unthinkable. In this home there is a place for everything with everything in its place, a role for everyone and everyone knows their role; joy guaranteed.

This eulogising of you comes from my mother's memorialising.
But you were more than a woman of love and duty.
The unrest in the countryside and in the Sejm *was surely troubling.*
Family had gone to Colombia due to antisemitism in Poland.
Things had changed: unkempt students barred from university hung
about; religious brethren in the villages and smaller shtetlekh
forecast the Messiah was on his way or already here![43]
Did you worry that the Hassids *with their ecstatic ways*
gave ammunition to those National Democrats
who sought to decry all Jews?[44]
And you were a Zionist. As far back as 1937 you tried
to convince Pinkus to leave Poland and take the family to Palestine.
Whatever was to come, did you believe God would provide?
Seeing Pinkus was determined to stay, and you would not leave without
him, did you challenge God to get more involved?
I imagine you did.

'Don't turn your back on your people because some displease you! Even the *kurwa* does what she does to survive! Ah, don't tell Basia I said that! Oh, these stories from Germany are awful. Are you angry at those that assimilated and forgot their covenant with you? Even here some have converted – such a loss; the death of that person as a

Jew, their parents mourning them – sitting *shiva* – as if the convert is dead.[45] Is that why all this is happening? Can it be punishment?

'Don't forget most of us are good people. Not perfect. But we try. It is not easy to be faithful to our ways; if we are to keep the Sabbath, we trade five days, the Christians trade six.[46] And kosher meat is hard to get and expensive. Are you testing us? Our sages say *Si fueris Romae, Romano vivito more* – When in Rome do as the Romans do. Are we not trying to do as the Poles, while keeping our duty to you? How then do we displease you? Please weave a miracle to make it all right.'

These words and thoughts imagined but did she talk to God?
My mother does. I do. I wonder did Rena believe in God or not?

My mother does not. Neither do I.

But in the way of many Jews who do not believe in God,
like Chaim Bermant quips,
we like to think that God believes in us.[47]

How can we know the unknowable?

My mother's anecdotes, concomitant with recorded Polish-Jewish life,[48]
are of people who had a life; they are an aspect of the real.
I cannot, I will not ever know them.

But oh, Mummy, how I do remember you.

Delight of Life: Melbourne, Summer 1955

I have just turned ten.

My parents work hard all week, rushing home so we can eat by six.

While she is cooking, my Mummy does some funny things. Like, if she spills some salt she gets upset, because apparently, that means a fight, so, she'll sprinkle some sugar, just in case, while telling me with a laugh how it is nonsense to do so. She talks to herself all the time, making a spitting sound 'peu peu' each time she has expressed happiness or praised one of us, so as not to tempt the fates. When breaking eggs, she is delighted if there are double yolks. 'Twins,' she exclaims. But if there is a speck of blood in the yolk, she throws it out.

I ask, 'Is the egg no good?'

'The egg is fertilised, it is the start of life and we don't eat that.' Seeing the look on my face, she adds with a laugh, 'But I am not superstitious.'

It makes no sense, but I know from religious instruction classes, eating blood is forbidden, so that must be it.

The Village Belle in Acland Street, near the beach and Luna Park, is where my Mummy does her shopping. She gets the meat from Mr Redlich, the continental butcher. In the school holidays, I go to help.

Mr Redlich stands, wiping his solid hands on his big white apron. The red colouring of his face contrasts with his very black hair, and is further given a rakish look by his large gappy teeth which are revealed as he breaks into a big smile of welcome when we enter.

He exchanges pleasantries with my mother and as he selects cuts of meat for her, she asks, 'Is it good?'

He loses his smile and seems offended. 'Am I in the meat?' he replies, raising his hands in a gesture of unknowing.

Gathering her courage, for she does not like to complain, she says, 'Last week it was not so good.'

He considers this and, selecting another piece of brisket, says, 'I'm sure this will be good.'

She leaves, reassured, but still a little anxious – if the meat is tough, or not tasty, my father will not be pleased. As we walk, she chuckles,

'He is right; he is not in the meat. I will tell your Daddy. I am not in the meat, either.'

On Friday, Mummy does not go to the factory to work. She stays home to make a Sabbath dinner: chicken soup with noodles, boiled chicken, shpondra and carrots, boiled potatoes, green beans, lettuce and tomato salad with a lemon dressing, and apple compote.

The table in the kitchen is set with a white tablecloth. When all is ready at six o'clock, my mother lights the candles and says the Sabbath prayer.

My father cuts the golden challah, he gives each of us a piece, and I am allowed a small glass of Marsala wine.

Oh, I forgot the *kishke*!

This is a sort of sausage. Earlier I watched as my mother stuffed skin from the neck of the chicken with minced chicken fat, onions, salt and white pepper. She sewed the ends up and put it in the soup to cook. Daddy loves it, and Mummy is so pleased watching him enjoy it, but *kishke* makes my tummy turn; I just can't eat it or any foods with strong fishy smells like sardines and herring. Mummy and Daddy like to say that with my fussiness and the way I glare – Daddy calls this my black-look – it is not possible I am their daughter; they must have brought the wrong baby home. Anyway, we all love chicken. Daddy has the first chicken leg; Janette and I take it in turns to have the second; Mummy laughs at us fighting about whose turn it is; she says the chicken should have three legs. Her favourite piece is the tail (I will learn that is called 'the parson's nose'). Dinner over, while we have a nice cup of tea, I think about how later tonight we will have our usual peanuts. We just love this. Every Friday Daddy brings home a whole lot of roasted unshelled peanuts wrapped in newspaper. After dinner, we will open the parcel and, sitting on the bare wooden floor of the lounge room – not on the bulky red upholstered arm chairs – we will crack open peanuts and eat until our tummies can take no more.

On Saturday afternoon, maybe he and I will go by tram to see a movie in the city – the theatres are huge and very fancy; especially grand is the theatre called 'The Forum' with statues down the sides and stars on the ceiling – I can already see us walking hand-in-hand down Collins Street chatting about what we have seen at the matinee.

Then it will be Sunday! Most Sundays start lazy. Mummy and Daddy like to sleep in on Sunday after playing cards or partying, sometimes dancing away the night until early hours of the morning – mambo, samba, tango.

Though we long to open the shut door to their room, neither my sister nor I would think of doing so.

I have a set of red building bricks that come with white windows and doorframes – the pieces click together with a snap; sometimes I build houses while I wait, or play with my Meccano set, pretending the hinged sections are cranes.

Time seems to stand still.

At last, they call 'Come in'. Sometimes we have to knock a quiet reminder – permission granted, Janette and I rush into the room; leaping in between them, we laugh and cuddle until Mummy gets up. Then we lie, one on either side of Daddy in the big bed. On the wall are photos of the grandparents we never knew. Daddy gives us rides and plays tickling games until our sides hurt from laughing; we pummel him until he says 'Enough'.

We plead for more. He tickles and throws us around and tries to get out of bed; we hang onto his arms forcing him back; on it goes until he manages to escape.

Breakfast is scrambled eggs Polish style, and, while we eat, Daddy is busy on the phone making arrangements.

Every Sunday we go out. Sometimes we visit friends or relatives for afternoon-tea – there is always cake and strong black tea with lemon, sweetened with cubes of sugar.

Or we go to Studley Park in Kew, to watch people flying models, airplanes and kites, or we stroll around the Shrine, a memorial to fallen soldiers – it seems these people had a war too. Or we join the crowd at 'Music for the People' at the Botanic Gardens and maybe feed the ducks, or have a picnic, or go to Luna Park, or to the beach.

One thing is certain, whatever we do, we do it with as many of Mummy and Daddy's friends as can make it.

Sometimes we go for long drives to the country: Ocean Grove, Olinda, Yan Yean Reservoir, Healesville. We have picnic lunches of crusty rye bread and fresh crunchy Kaiser Rolls filled with good things: ham, sausage, sliced tomatoes and cucumbers. We bite into hard-boiled eggs, quench our thirst with soft drinks and hot tea out of thermos flasks and declare everything 'Delicious!' 'Fantastic!' Everyone agrees.

Daddy swings Janette on his shoulders. We set off to some distant scenic destination 'to walk it off', the grown-ups tell each other, all the while cracking jokes they find side-splitting and I don't get.

What do we look like, this happy crowd of picnickers? Most of the ladies have blonde hair, a bouffant style held in place with hairspray and hairpins. They have lightly tanned skin – the only make-up they wear is coral lipstick. Mummy – with her shoulder-length brown hair, rosy cheeks, smooth skin, always a smile or laugh, never a frown or cross word – to me she is the most beautiful.

The men are well-groomed: brilliantine in their hair, faces close shaven.

Mr Rotstein, my godfather, wears a colourful cravat; like my Daddy, he has a trim black moustache. The style of dress is casual: open-collared shirts, shorts or slacks and flat shoes, and cardigans, in case of a change in the weather.

The grown-ups flirt with each other. They have *sympatias* which my mother explains means special, but platonic, friend. Mummy and I like to tease Daddy that his favourite *sympatia* is Mrs Enker; I know Mummy loves Mrs Enker too, so it is all okay. It is clear that several men would like to be Mummy's *sympatia*, but she just laughs and keeps an eye on my Daddy.

Yes, it is perfect – well, nearly. Even though we have all kissed each other on both cheeks to say 'hello' and will do the same when we say 'goodbye', there are always one or two men who are not satisfied with just talking or hand kissing; they like to try for a bit of a cuddle and maybe a kiss on the lips. The women are good at getting free with a laugh or a friendly slap.

I deflect unwelcome hugs by running off to play with the other children, which is a pity, as I do like to hang out with the grown-ups.

Going home, pleasantly exhausted, watching the scrolling scenery, my heart full at evening glory, I vow never to forget the sky, fluffy pink clouds, rolling green hills, neat patchwork fields, trees and windbreaks of dark green pines, animals grazing peacefully, all aglow in the golden light.

My sister, four years old and in kindergarten, gazes out of the window. Spying a flock of lambs, she exclaims in a piping voice, '*Kaczkele, kaczkele*' – duckling, duckling – we correct her gently with 'No, *shepsele, shepsele*' – lamb, lamb.

She gazes at us, nods, repeats, '*Kaczkele, kaczkele*'.

We laugh and laugh. Everything is good with our world.

This Sunday, maybe we will go for a drive in our Holden. This is our second one; Daddy loves everything Australian – especially Holdens and Peters ice cream which we know is the Health Food of a Nation.

We eat lots of ice cream …

Maybe we'll picnic at Maroondah Dam again. And as we walk we'll stomp our feet and we'll be singing 'The Happy Wanderer' – 'Valderi, Valdera …', or mimicking Frank Ifield we'll yodel, 'When I'm calling you oo oo …' and then we'll break into 'How much is that doggy in the window? The one with the waggley tail.' We'll finish off with my favourite – the Bella Bella song: '*Bei mir bist du scheyn*'[49] which I know means 'to me you are beautiful'.

Daddy interrupts my thoughts with an announcement:
our destination for the coming holidays for two weeks,
while 1955 will turn into 1956, is decided. With many of our friends, we will go to a place called Lakes Entrance.

Janette claps her hands,
Daddy and I beam at each other,
Mummy laughs with us.

All of a sudden, Mummy is quiet. Her eyes mist.

She says, as if to herself,

'Ah, what do you know?
Nothing, nothing, can compare, to a holiday in Świder.'

CHAPTER 3: THE LAST SUMMER

Warsaw: 1939

I loved holidays,
sledding down icy slopes of the mountains of Krynica;
or basking in sunshine then cooling off in Lake Sniardwy.
But nothing compared to a holiday in Świder.
Ah, Świder. That was my favourite place.'

The Warsaw spring of 1939 turns to summer. Long days and hazy heat herald the holiday season. Having discussed it among themselves, Rena and Pinkus tell their girls of A.H.'s takeovers, the year before, of the Sudetenland and Austria, and the annexation of Slovakia in March 1939.

After all it was in the newspapers.[50]

> NAZIS ANNEX CZECHO-SLOVAKIA
> Anglo-French Attitude 'Calm But Not Complacent'.

But not a whisper to the girls of Nazi agreements with Romania and Hungary, the pact with Italy, or the disputed territories changing hands as countries, including Poland, sign and break agreements, while grabbing what they can. Some friends have sold up, fled to South America. Overreaction surely. What is the point of frightening their girls by dwelling on news of the marching of jackboots through neighbouring countries? No need to lie; the joint Franco-British declaration of support for Poland and the new nonaggression pact between Germany and the Soviets indicate a stalemate; war will have little impact on them. It will be unpleasant but short. The best thing is to hold tight. There is no need to spoil the holidays.

So, as many times before, the family sets off for their country cabin, one of a group of eight, nestling in the forests of Świder, Otwock, 30 kilometres south-east of Warsaw. This property – on acreage with tennis courts and orchards, named *Begeha,* at 3 Zaciszna[51] – is further evidence to the girls of their father's business acumen; consequent prosperity accepted as a reward for good conduct, hard work, and superior intelligence.

As the train passes quaint villages and folk – any wretchedness blurred in the view bucolic – anticipation grows.

At last the township of Świder! Laughing in excitement, the family transfers to two horse-drawn buggies. Waving to each other, they drink in the summer smells, their eyes feasting on fields of bright wildflower-dotted grasses and deep green pine and beech forests, beyond which the Vistula River continues on to Warsaw.

Once at their delightful cabin, a miniature replica of grander places inhabited by the really rich, they settle in; the young people, freed at last from the constraints of the city, fill the air with joyous noise. The shrieks of laughter continue to bring smiles to the faces of the adults all through the day: while they laze over breakfast, are intent on card games as players or just *kibitzing* – talking, commenting, advising – and continue while they enjoy their evening strolls in the balmy last hours of daylight. The exhilarated youngsters, shaking their heads at their sedate parents, run and play while declaring, in English, that everything is 'too too marvellous'.

Some days, while they play volleyball on courts in the cleared area under large trees, Basia is aware of the caretaker Marchin's handsome blond grandson – he makes a show of not noticing her while placing himself in her line of vision. All her senses are aware of him; any sign of recognition or passing greeting is unthinkable. As marriage is inconceivable, a boy like him can only be interested in one thing from a girl like her.

Did she ever, on finding her thoughts turning to him yet again,
arguing with herself about the impossibility of connection,
go beyond the status aspect, and fear of him as 'the other'
to consider the issue of her god and his?
I asked her. 'No', she said,
'A nice Jewish girl simply did not mix with or marry a gentile. Full stop.'
But as she repeatedly told me of intractable religious issues,
and to convey something of the troubling divide,
I imagine she did.

Her God is one: Eloheinu.[52]

She has been taught that her God, the stern jealous creator of everything and maker of all the rules, had, according to the tradition, made the Jews responsible for bearing witness to his moral law on earth.[53] In effect, God's promise to the Jews – increase in a milk-and-honey land – was given in exchange for obedience.

The blond boy's God is one yet simultaneously three: The Father, The Son, The Holy Ghost. Thus many people, at the time, invoked one as the antithesis of the other.[54]

Moreover, antisemitic Poles' hatred of Jews stemmed from church teachings that the Jews had killed the Christians' Christ and from their superstitious belief that Jews used the blood of Christian babies in religious rituals in the baking of *matzos*.

How could anyone believe such abhorrent libel? Many did.[55]

And they called this son-of-God Christ and Messiah. But the Jewish Messiah was yet to come. Certainly, representations of this Christ and of others in the churches were graven images, forbidden by the Second Commandment.[56]

Perhaps, like cousin Sara liked to say, God was just an idea of man to ease the pain of life and the pain of death. Understandably, poor Jews would joke: 'We are the chosen people – chosen to suffer' or 'Choose someone else.'

Perhaps, as Uncle Mayer often said, though never directly to her (being highly religious he neither would nor could acknowledge the presence of a female) God *was* there in the dirt and misery giving a radiance, to all who believed, through the recurring joy of the Sabbath and the holidays.

But why should the poor be suffering while she is happy and carefree and life is wonderful.

Casting away any such concerns, her thoughts return to Świder. One day part of it will belong to her; she will do her utmost to emulate her mother, she will keep her traditions while also obeying those of her country, and watch over her children, just as Rena is keeping an eye on her, in this her favourite place. Marchin's grandson belongs to a life very different from hers; he has no part in her future.

Yet I remember a time, in 1956,
when I knew my mother to be open-minded and
when all she wanted was to belong.

I am eleven; it is near the end of the school year. When my parents come to meet my teacher, he tells them that, as I am such a good student, if I study hard, I could get to go to high school, the best being MacRobertson Girls' High School.

My father's eyes go round and pop in the way they do when he is impressed. In his broken English he asks,

'What does it cost, this high school? It must be a lot of money!'

My teacher replies: 'If Sara's results are good enough she might get a scholarship and even go on to university.'

With this piece of news my parents smile and beam at me.

Now I know what I want.

I will work hard to make my parents proud.

At last, school is over, no more primary school.

Next year I will wear a uniform and go to Toorak Central School!

Christmas Day, 1956, the sound of singing sends Mummy and me running to open the window that faces onto the street. Outside in the morning grey, a small group of people, wearing black uniforms and hats with maroon trims, sing Christmas songs in joyful harmony: 'Away in a Manger', 'Jingle Bells', 'The Twelve Days of Christmas'.

'Lovely,' we sigh. They come to the door asking for money; we find they are Salvation Army officers who have got up before dawn to spread cheer and collect money for the poor.

Mummy empties out all the change in her purse.

Later she explains to me we should always help people less fortunate than ourselves regardless of colour or religion, and, although Christmas is not our holiday, still we are Australians and, as Australians are mostly Christian, it is all right to enjoy Christmas Day.

She smiles at me, adding: 'When in Rome do as the Romans do.'

I laugh at the way she looks so pleased with herself.

The saying has a ring to it and reminds me of what my Grade Five teacher, Mr Borrack, wrote it into my autograph book last year: 'Whatever you do do do, do do do it well.'

Mr Borrack was an inspirational teacher;
my mother's inspirational teacher was her Latin teacher.
I visualise a day of warmth; into it go things she told me.
A day just before, with the onset of autumn,
the angel of history[57] *blew this nice world away.*

CHAPTER 4: BASIA ON THE THRESHOLD

The late summer of 1939 at Świder speeds past Basia in a delicious haze. Soon she will be back at school. The hot sun has warmed and browned her. Lazing on a grassy knoll, rolling over into a shady patch and gazing at the sparkling specks of sunlight filtered through moving leaves, she hums a resounding Carmen – her favourite opera – how heavenly. Drowsy, she hears the Geography teacher's voice thrumming into her consciousness like the drone of a fat summer fly. Basia's thoughts go to far-off countries, to the relatives in Colombia.

She loves Geography – it is her favourite subject. However, the Geography teacher is not like the Latin teacher! The Latin teacher is divine. Shivering with anticipation, or is it a foretaste of autumn, Basia lifts her eyes from the book she's reading, takes in the breeze rustling the leaves above and smiles. She pictures her favourite professor, citing her favourite quote:

Tempora mutantur, nos et mutamur in illis.

The times (all things) change, and we change with them.[58]

An image of the principal of her previous *gimnazjum*, Stefania Schweiger, intrudes, exhorting her to idealism and altruism. Well, despite the carrying on with '*Thou should*'s, she liked that school called *Yehudia*. But her mother thought Basia was becoming too religious so she moved her to a more liberal school – Landerowa[59] – which is not too bad. Her best subjects are sewing and handwork but mathematics is impossible – thank goodness for darling Miss Smarty, her sister Celina. When she recently told her father she'd love to be a dressmaker, Pinkus had derided such an occupation as unsuitable, so what on earth was she going to be?

Of late, in her imaginings of a future, her longing is to be a wife, a mother. For that, she needs a husband; her parents will want to make a match. Will she learn to love him? What if she finds she cannot? She shudders at the thought. She wants to love and to be a woman in love. Ah, love: *głupia miłośc*. Stupid love; that's what her mother would say.

But love and sacrifice, for husband and children, is what she craves; devotion and duty like *O-Lan*[60] in her favourite book *The Good Earth*, which she has read – translated into Polish of course. Imagine having to twist your tongue around those strange English sounds, particularly that *th* one. Her favourite actors, Robert Taylor and Barbara Stanwyck, make the *the* sound sooo refined; her own attempts are ludicrous. She loves Barbara Stanwyck. Especially in *Stella Dallas*, about a woman who sacrifices everything for her daughter. Will she one day have a daughter to love so much? And how different are her sisters' ambitions to hers …

Zosia, with many to choose from, is pragmatic in her declaration that though of course she would love him, her husband will be someone who could give her a good life. She has wanted to leave Poland and go to America with a girlfriend, but Rena and Pinkus have vetoed that, saying, 'What will people think? Young women all on their own.' Now it is clear she is interested in Adam who comes from a very fine family indeed.

For Celinka a good life means learning; perhaps her man will be a scholar. They laugh at Basia for her romantic notions. But they are both as one with Basia in their confusion over their father's disrespect for things, which, for their other relatives, are sacrosanct. Like the eating of ham. Forbidden in all its forms, ingestion of pork conjures the image of invoking God's wrath. And now Pinkus, with his inclination to modern ways, has this year been caught eating ham here in Świder. Of course, her father can do as he wishes. However, if it is such a sin, why was there no sign from God of his displeasure?

Searching her memories for evidence of God's indifference, she recalls the occasion when Marshall Joseph Piłsudski, president of the *Sanacja* regime, hero of Polish independence, had died in May 1935 when she was eleven; she had knelt and prayed for him. A Jew kneeling! That was for pagans and Christians. Mosaic Law forbade kneeling. So how was it that she had not been punished? Perhaps she had, after all she dare tell no one and the memory of those moments on her knees come back to haunt her and trouble her conscience.

Despite her goodie-goodie exterior, Basia has a few new sins to report. This coming October, just weeks away, when she will fast as usual on *Yom Kippur* and, in the synagogue, confess and atone for her sins, there will be more than usual to declare. For one thing, her thoughts are of late out of her control and the curse *cholera psia krew* has escaped her lips just like the bad blood of cholera escapes its victims, contaminating those around – so, as such language is vile, she has broken a commandment. Worse still, is that kiss she gave away last week here in Świder. Not just a kiss! He, the son of her parents' friends, wanted more! She'd had to use all her strength to get away.

Her resolve crystallises into a resolution: 'I will wait, keeping myself for the man I will love. He will be handsome! To him I will give all. And, God willing, I will have his children and devote myself to him and to them.'

During these days of that last summer of 1939, having just turned sixteen on August 22, Basia has the radiance of a healthy farm girl. Her smooth skin and rosy cheeks bring compliments from young and old. Her dark brown hair, curling and long, is glamorous – indeed a friend of the family has called her 'The poor man's Rita Hayworth'. Another even teasingly called her Bathsheba.

A loud laugh, untempered by her mother's gentle exhortations to tone it down, breaks out at the slightest encouragement. Nor do admonishments, 'Do not talk with your hands', succeed in stilling their butterfly motion.

Her white teeth tear into the hard apples she loves, and her full figure and slender legs complete the picture of promise of the woman-to-be who, though confused by the many taboos, tries to live by Hillel's axiom:

'What is offensive to you, do not do to others.'[61]

No longer a child, not yet a woman;
Basia stands poised in the troubled present:
wanting to stay in her happy past, longing for her unknown future.
Unaware that on 23 August, the day after her birthday,
headlines had broadcast an event that caught the world off guard.

> Nazi-Soviet Pact Stuns World
> Danzig Teeming With Activity.
> Germany expects Peace. Expects Britain to withdraw guarantee to Poland.
> German army ready to move.[62]

Anticipating a good life,
different yet the same as
what she has known,
she has no inkling
that this precious time has ended,
she will have no time of 'normal' youth,
and all her adult life
she will yearn for this time.

This time when the world was nice.

This photo was taken in 1937. From left, back row: Basia's cousin Sara Czosnek; Basia's mother Rena; Basia's sister Zosia, eighteen years old; a cousin, possibly Zvi Najer. Front row: Basia at fourteen; a cousin Renia Czosnek; Basia's sister Celina, ten years old; a cousin, Gucia Birenbaum.

PART THREE

NAMES AND EYES OF THE FATHER

DO NOT TAKE THE NAME IN VAIN

Heniek's Longing: To Be a Free Man

Here he is, outside Gestapo headquarters in Warsaw.
My father Heniek, blinking in the daylight,
willing his heart to still.
A new name: Czesław. Papers: fingerprinted, stamped, authorised.

He, with dark hair and crisp moustache – just twenty years old –
looked them right in the eye; they'd seen only another Pole.
With these documents, he can walk around
as if a free man – even work. This possibility entices.

Meanwhile Basia waits for him in hiding.
Her papers – giving her the name Jadwiga – rejected twice.
She, with non-Aryan looks, dares not present.
He knows she will be counting the seconds until his return.
Love motivates him: she must survive with him.
By tram, he heads back.

Soon he would go with her into the bunker.
To the dark place to lie with her – his wife.
What if he had known it was to be for eighteen months?

Oh, my Papa, to me you were so wonderful.

Immeasurable the delight of your arrivals;
we waited for your returns.
You always came: on time, often with gifts or treats,
always exuding adventure, glamour, and a hint of mystery.
So very handsome, especially in those first memories in 1949.

Evening grey. Grey water. Grey sky. WAIT! Brilliant sunshine. A large square deep pool, a kitten. My daddy holding a kitten. I am three. Daddy is keeping an eye on me in the pool, beaming with his crooked smile. There is a man with a pitchfork – we are on a ship. Evening grey.

We are on a new shore.

Light! A white house on a grassy hill. There are new puppies under the house; with a freckle-faced girl, small like me, I crawl under the boards to see them. The puppies are tiny, soft, white and tan.

I am with other children in a long bright clean room. We are all sick with the mumps. Our beds are all in a neat row. Kind strict ladies bustle about, reminding us to behave ourselves. There are many rules to remember and the milk boils over. The burnt milk smell fills the room.

Sunday. Visitors' Day. Daddy is here! He sits on a chair next to my bed. He is very handsome with his crooked smile. He shows me a letter from my mother far away in a country called Israel. He speaks to me in French.

In my best English, I tell him I will soon be four – I am an Australian now, English is my language. No more French. No more Yiddish.

His pride in me peeps out of his eyes; he says he'll be back in two weeks, and as he leaves, he calls me his *ketsele* – his kitten.

I am nearly eight, tall and boyish. My father does not call me *ketsele* anymore. He calls me 'stick'. Though Mummy calls me 'the-clever-one', I am awkward, clumsy, tongue-tied.

My sister, Janette Pauline, named for grandfathers Jacob and Pinkus, two years old, is so lovely, we dub her, 'The Beautiful One'. When we walk her in the pram, people stop to admire.

A recent photo of her decorates the lounge room: hair black with a touch of wave, hands chubby, smile sweet, eyes hazel and dreamy.

There is also a picture of me at three; wearing a white fur coat, I have a mass of jet-black curls and a shy smile.

On Rosh Hashanah, having eaten our New Year feast in the dining room, not in the kitchen like on ordinary days, with the table cleared, picking at bits of oranges and apples, we are all relaxed and laughing.

I ask: 'Where is a picture of me as a baby?'

Mummy and Daddy glance at each other.

Flushed from the festive meal and wine, Daddy says,
'Basia, we are going to look at photos.'

From the credenza, he takes out a used school case and clears a space.
He places the case on the white cloth and sits again.
For an endless moment, he hesitates.

At last, flipping the catch, he opens the case.

He pauses, then tips the contents onto the table.

Photos – black and white, and sepia – spill out making a small pile.
Picking up a photo of a group of people, he says:
'This is my mother, my father, my sisters. This is me.'

There are also photos of my mother's parents, and one of my mother with a group of people – Mummy points out her two sisters:
the serious younger clever one – 'You, take after her,' she says.

'And the older one?'

'Just like Dorothy Lamour, oh, how the men chased after her!'

And here is a baby photo of me.

Lying on my tummy, my head held like a turtle, my face turned to the camera's flash, naked, I am skinny with a huge belly.

Ah, this is a nice one taken a while ago with Janette.

And another with my Mummy and Daddy.

All of us look handsome. Mummy has tears in her eyes.

Daddy says, 'Enough for today.'

He has a strange look in his hazel eyes.

My head teems with questions that do not make it to my lips.

Here is the photo of me and my baby sister Janette.

It was three years later – autumn 1956 –
that I became aware of my family
not fitting in with the Australian family.
A long table covered in a white cloth brings it back.

The retelling of the Exodus from Egypt told.
The Passover feast eaten; four glasses of wine drunk.
The first to toast life in thanks to God for keeping us alive.
The second to toast freedom. The third glass to redemption.
The fourth glass to thank God for taking us as His.
And a fifth special cup remains undrunk for the prophet Elijah.
My first real Passover – intoned in Hebrew, incomprehensible;
happy to be part of it, if only at the edge.

My mother sits at the *Pesach* table, her cheeks rose-red from the wine,
her smile fixed, her eyes glistening; while the others sing – she makes
not a sound. This she will explain to me later, saying,
'They have not been there when I watched my father
conduct the service; they cannot know and I cannot tell them.'

And my father, so refined, has a stiffness about him. An observer not a partaker; he does not sing, neither do I. Nor does he indicate in any way that I should join in. She, he and I, apart together.

Each year, at the telling of the Exodus story,
disturbing deposits adhered:
the exclusion of the son who does not believe, the smiting of enemies,
the bringing down of plagues, the killing of the first-born.
To me the telling was akin to boxes like Pandora's,
replete with evils that beget trials;
God's love was offered only if one conformed.

In a search for insight,
I had cause to look up The Third Commandment.
Understanding comes in a flash:
(un)welcome, troubling, elating, surprising. My perception of
Thou shalt not take the name of the Lord thy God in vain'
had been the customary one that prohibits swearing,
in particular, swearing that includes 'God' and/or 'Jesus Christ'.
But this search revealed: 'not take the name in vain'
means not swear falsely by the name of God.

Thus: not use the name of God to make a dishonest oath;
not affirm as true something known to be false;
not affirm false something known to be true;
not affirm the truth of something obvious (due to its triviality);
not promise some act known to be impossible
or outside one's abilities.[63]

The Commandments Ten had seemed focused on God's ego,
but the instruction to decent behaviour
concomitant with justice
was there all the time.
Gratitude after all for the wisdom of the giants that have gone before.
And the most honest and honourable person I ever knew – my father –
wanting to conceal, protect, forget –
he held back, as, in 1996, I persisted in asking the questions.

Tales of my father's birth, propitious names, various activities,
and serendipitous near misses, are by now family lore
but details of his family elude.
Since I began, I've asked questions that made my pulse race.

Ordinary words caused this terror. 'Daddy what was your home like …'
He interrupts in an impatient tone, 'What do you want to know this for?'
He clams up. I drop it. I try again. 'What was your mother like?'
No answer. He is somewhere else. I change tack.
Of his father, I tease out a description of sorts.
Of the sisters, he gives me their names.
Of his mother, he eventually tells me she was a housewife …

As I persist, there comes a night when he softens.
'Daddy, was there music?'
'Yes.'
'Servants?'
'Yes.'
'Kosher?'
'And how!' Mummy interjects.
And then I ask,
'Daddy, what did you like best when you were a boy at home?'
Silence.
'Daddy, what do you miss most?'

His eyes focus on me;
heart-breaking absence in that look.
Daddy?

His answer breaks my heart.

All of it. The whole thing.

PART FOUR

THE WHOLE THING

Warsaw 1922–39

REMEMBER THE SABBATH

Celia Heller wrote of the Jewish Jews (Orthodox-traditionalists):

> *Individual life ... was ... as a gently flowing stream ... In childhood ... freedom from anxiety; in maturity, the joys of building a household; in old age ... respect ...*
> *One had to submit to one's father, but every father was also a son ...*[64]

Kant wrote in 1784 of the surge that was to sweep through Europe:

> *Enlightenment is man's release from his self-incurred tutelage. Tutelage is man's inability to make use of his understanding without direction from another. Self-incurred is this tutelage when its cause lies not in lack of reason but in lack of resolution and courage to use it without direction from another.* Sapere aude! *[Dare to know!] Have courage to use your own reason! – that is the motto of enlightenment.* [65]

And Terence[66] in 161BC wrote:

> *Homo sum: humani nil a me alienum puto – I am a human being: I regard nothing of human concern as foreign to my interests.*

In a time when some sought a moral order without religion,
and known ways of living were being challenged,
other willed their way to power without morality.

CHAPTER 5: WHERE GOOD CAN FLOURISH

Chaim (Heniek) Heber is born in Warsaw on 22 October 1922. His mother Sara, from the large far-flung Degenszajn family, was born in a small town where survival meant grasping any opportunity. His father, Jacob Heber, the son of Menachem Mendel – meaning comforter – named in honour of Abraham's grandson, had come from the town of Kalisz, and before that from Germany. A jewellery wholesaler from a line of moderate, devout men, Jacob had secured a niche in the trading of precious stones and created a serene environment to insulate his children from the world; a splintered mad world groaning under medieval conditions while aspiring to be a force in the surrounding modernity.

Heniek's birth is at a time of optimism for Jews in newly independent Poland, where, after a hundred years of occupation by its neighbours – Russia, Germany, and Austria – Poland's minorities look forward to a their place as citizens in the fledgling democracy.

But pogroms in the countryside and the boycott of Jewish shops are an ongoing reality, as is consideration of the Jews as inferior foreigners.

Heniek's *bris,* the circumcision ceremony marking Abraham's covenant with God, is a solemn, memorable and joyful occasion attended by all the rabbis and relatives. His nine-year-old cousin Pesakh (who would soon go to a life in Australia) travels from the village of Skierniewice, bringing geese as his family's contribution. Carried by his young cousin Mania (my 'Auntie' Mania), on the special *bris*-cushion, as the last hope for a surviving male, Heniek is given the name Chaim Alter; Chaim (pronounced 'hime' as in time), that he would live; Alter, that he would get old. The rabbis bless him according to tradition: 'May he be raised for the Torah, the wedding ... the good deed.' They decree that he neither wear new clothes nor his hair be cut for a year to seal the blessing of his name. *Hassidim* in the gathering dance to express their joy; all around him, happiness flows. The only boy and youngest child, he is pampered by a congregation of females: adoring mother, five sisters, from youngest to oldest: Inka (Regina), Dorka (Dorothy), Marisa also known as Mania (Mary), Franka (Frances), Fella (Felicity), and many friends and relatives – happy times. Sara and Jacob, fearful their precious son will sicken and die as had his five brothers, watch his every move, panicking if he so much as gives a cough. Though small and weak as a baby, during his first six years, in the company of these many women and doting father, nurtured by devotion, love, and attention to duty, he grows strong. Secure and protected, he knows nothing of the tensions that have driven his cousin Mania's family to sell up, buy land unseen off a map, and travel with illegal documents to a dangerous life in Palestine, where some settlers enjoy fruits, vegetables, flowers, while others starve.

In this sheltered atmosphere, an assortment of languages abound; the parents speak Yiddish between themselves and a mix of Yiddish and Polish with their children, Hebrew for synagogue, *Shabbat* and religious holidays, and German and Russian for visitors. The sisters also bring French into the home: *chérie*, *l'amour*, *la mer*, and interlace the whole with English expressions: 'tripe', 'cool man', 'we had a ball'. Operas and arias fill the air as one or another of the girls play on the piano or listen to the gramophone. Including young Chaim in their play, they laugh as he conducts while they sing along.

The many family members are accommodated in a spacious three-bedroom apartment, with lounge room and separate dining room, at 17 Graniczna Street in a pleasant, not particularly Jewish part of Warsaw, just near the magnificent Saxon Garden and Palace, *Ogród Saski,* on Marszałkowska Street. Running a household of this size, seeing everything is 'fit' in accordance with dietary law, even with the help of several Polish and Jewish servants, both live-in and part-time, is a major production requiring constant attention; somehow, everyone's needs are met. By the time Chaim is five, in 1927, conscious of his only-son status, nothing pleases him more than the smiles and fond looks cast his way from that most beloved of faces – his mother, Sara – his *Mamunia*.

Longing: of Sara, for Sara

Tell me about your mother, please, Daddy.

He stares past me, eyes blank.

In soft moments, he tells snippets of the form of those days:
relatives come to stay, servants to manage. But of his mother, nothing.
One photo is all I have, to give substance to and sustenance for
the longing of Sara for Sara.

Taken or sent, from Europe to Australia,
before 1939. Sister to sister. An image,
I give thanks for this precious scrap.

What can I tell you of her? Not much.

But I speak to her:
I twirl my hair as they say you did.

I see you in my father, and in his cousins;
you reside in me.

Just when was this photo taken?

Perhaps in 1932 when you were 45?

On this night in 2009, as I gaze at you I see
a new light in your eyes; your face now holds a smile just for me.

Any moment you might give me a fond wink, a rich throaty laugh,
a high chuckle. Were you serious? Did you enjoy a joke?

Oh, though all I have is this Mona Lisa mystery, I can tell them
I carry your name and I would have called you *Bubbe*.
Pronounce it Bubba: *bubb*– as in bull, *a* as in almond. *Bubba*.

Grandmother.

And you would have just loved me to bits.

CHAPTER 6: THE FUTURE BECKONS

In Warsaw, it is 1928 and Sara is surely content; healthy family, duty done, relatives accommodated. Luckily, with a bit of doubling up and the use of folding beds, the apartment can take in so many. Sara's sister Faygalleh, who is still camping with her husband David and several of her children in the Heber household lounge room after returning three years prior from toil in Palestine, shows Sara the letters that come from her daughter Mania in Australia. Mania also writes to Sara's eldest daughter Fella and always asks how Chaim is doing. This voice, calling like a siren, is irksome; an interruption to the flow of a known, ordered way of life.

From Mania herself, the details are history,[67] *and thereby inspired, I imagine my grandmother Sara's thoughts about her adventurous niece.*

'These letters from Mania drip with hardships: she lives in poverty – no gas, no proper bed, just a bunk made out of boards; working as a finisher in a factory. And they also entice: she says there is a small Jewish community, even a beautiful synagogue. Surely Faygalleh and David exaggerate about the tensions here. So, a Polack attacked Mania in the street. She should have known better than to be heard speaking Hebrew in a public place. But is she putting ideas into my Fella's head? What if my eldest darling took it into her head to leave – what could you do?'

So Sara muses on this far-off Australia calling her sister to its shore. It is all very well for Faygalleh to go – David, determined to leave Poland, had sent Mania and some of her brothers to Australia as an advance party. But Sara loves her life here. No! She would not like it at the other end of the world. Heat. Flies. Oh, this talk against the Poles, some people want to hurry things; they worry with little ground, and make things worse rather than better. It will work out.

Did she chastise herself with a reprimand?

'What has got into you today?' Isn't everything is as it should be! What a husband! Handsome, of slim build, medium stature, distinguished with a gentle sense of humour; devoted to his vast family; time and energy for duty to God, for extended family – his and hers.

Surely her whole being sings when his eyes, shining with intelligence, turn to look at her in appreciation when he thinks she is not looking. She loves his voice. When he speaks of his reverence for knowledge and learning, she observes Chaim drinking in his words. In this ambiance of the miracle of filial respect and adoration, her gratitude flows.

'Thanks to my husband I was able to help my poor younger brother Zev and my sister Faygalleh. We were small-town-people: mother Frimit died at such a young age from that awful cholera; father Pesakh followed seven days later. I cannot think of the word *cholera* without shuddering. Relatives were kind; life was so hard one of my cousins went, with the rabbi who came to gather would-be brides, to Palestine, still ruled by Turks, and married a stranger – a Sephardi – a Jew from the Middle East (probably Egypt) by the name of Azulouis.[68]

'What luck for a poor one such as me to be matched to Jacob, an educated Levi.[69] Moreover, every day I give thanks that he should have such *nakhes*, such joy, from our Chaim after so many disappointments. Ah, my grandchild, Sara, my namesake. If only you could see your grandfather at the head of the table. What a comfort to hear him speak the words of wisdom in the Torah. Not that he was fanatical. He would keep his head covered at the table, never eat *trayf*, no forbidden food, never take transport on the Sabbath; however, he did not expect me or our daughters to be pious. I was not obliged to cover my head with a *sheitel*, that unbecoming, uncomfortable wig; a scarf was sufficient, nor did I attend the *mikva* – the ritual bathhouse.

We kept the Sabbath, as is prescribed by the Fourth Commandment,[70] but I was not required to refrain from normal basic duties as in some households. Life was full of unexpected twists and turns; one never knew whether to laugh or cry, but indeed mine was a blessed life of duty and delight. And not that it is important ... but he was so handsome.'

Longing: for Jacob (and for Branko)

'Such a handsome man.' Verified in one
photo. Copied from those treasures,
sent by Sara to her sister Faygalleh
in Australia before the war.

Waiting here in Australian for Heniek,
this photo of my grandfather Jacob,
taken around 1930 when he was 45.

Many girls seek a man like their father.
I fell in love with one who to me from the
first moment my eyes did see him
was beautiful and familiar.

A déjà vu yearning encapsulated.

People would say of him: 'Such a handsome man.'
Banal the words we use to convey beauty without and within.

A drawing of my gentile husband, Branko,[71] pencilled by me in 1965, is to the left of where I am typing in 2009.

With other images of the deceased,
it is under the photo of Jacob.

To my eye the likeness is striking. Each
has high forehead,
well-shaped eyebrows, good nose;
Jacob's aquiline, Branko's turned up.
Both have hair fine and straight,.
Enquiring tilt to the head.
Jacobs's dark eyes thoughtful;
colour unknown. Possibly hazel.
Branko's eyes were green pools of pain.

I defied all opposition to marry this man whom I loved entirely.
I would tease him that he looked like my grandfather.
Handsome. Intelligent. And profoundly sad.
Hidden: the inner torment of betrayal by one's own body.
And both dead in their 58th year.

Jacob, in contemplating his lot, gives thanks for his Sara. He appreciates both her down-to-earthness and restraint; but there is more. On occasion, a certain exotic gipsy style about her slips out – a shawl flung just so, a comb to hold back her thick straight hair – bringing a fleeting glimpse of a legacy of wondrous women through thousands of years. Being a devoted husband to her is no hardship. Moreover, what strength of character she has shown in defying the exhausting illness – the family plague of diabetes – to bear yet another child in their Quest For A Son. And the way she manages the house and servants – a few firm words in a barely raised voice keep everything done to his liking.

Perfect! His life is perfect. He has no difficulty in fulfilling his obligations to God, family and community. He enjoys respect as learned and liberal at the synagogue, has standing among his colleagues at the Jewellers' Club, loves his work with precious metals and stones. His office, located in his bedroom – so convenient – has all he needs to conduct his business contained in two tall cabinets and a roll-top desk; after all, diamonds are so small. Chaim loves getting into the room to peek at the boxes with the sparkling jewels laid out in their beds of soft dark pergamon velvet; perhaps he should scold the boy more. Ah well, it is such a pleasure to show the intricate watch workings, explain the values of precious stones, and see Chaim's fascination.

Yes, he is King in his home: a raised eyebrow, a cool look of displeasure is enough to convey the need for restraint or immediate action. If only it could just stay like this. Observing his grown daughters move from the traditional ways towards Polish mores and values is a concern; now Yiddish is no longer good enough for them, so even he has to speak Polish. The world is changing too fast.

He knows his mildly cheeky daughters are pussycats compared to the tigers in other homes. He has heard dreadful stories and observes with his own eyes the Head-of-the-House treated with disrespect, even contempt; the wife shrieking at her husband like a shrew, the children mocking the ancient ways, leaving, throwing everything away in their rush to become like the Polish gentiles!

But another pressing problem demands attention: what is he to do with young Chaim's education? The boy, soon six, spoilt rotten by the adulation of the company of females, is in truth a little wild. It is not enough to take him each Sabbath and High Holiday to *shul* to read the Torah and pray. It is not enough to read together the pages of the Polish-Jewish Newspaper, *Nasz Przegląd* (*Our Review*) – or to let him fiddle with watches; the house is full of women, and the boy needs to relate to another man. He needs to learn beyond the Talmud teachings if he is to succeed in gaining a profession. However, if Chaim is to leave the house every day to go to school, Sara will worry herself sick. There has to be some solution to keep him safe at home while preparing him to be part of the future. A tutor is the answer. A tutor to prepare him for school. The rest will follow.

Remember, Daddy – remember how you passed on
your tutor's teachings to me.

Late in 1956 we gather at my godparents, Mr and Mrs Rotstein's place, to see a new wonder. Though the small black and white picture is not clear and there are 'ghosts', wavy lines and 'snow', we stare engrossed at the thing called a TeeVee. After she has had it for a while, Mrs Rotstein calls it the 'Idiot Box'. We agree, but love to watch it anyway.

Then, before my eleventh birthday in November, Daddy takes me to a new village in Heidelberg; in the grand sparkling new square, we walk hand-in-hand among the crowd under fluttering flags of many nations. With great excitement, we mingle with people from all over the world. The Olympic Games[72] are on!

Several times, we stand outside the new Olympic Swimming Pool, opposite the Botanic Gardens on the bank of the Yarra River, and watch the diving competition; this is just too, too divine. Standing out here, looking in through the huge walls of glass, I become aware of the unusual construction of this building.[73]

It is a towering Vee shape. At the base is the Olympic swimming pool, and the stepped seating of the auditorium follows the slope on the inside. It looks as if, at any moment, it will tip over one way or the other.

Daddy points to the huge cables and explains that these stretch out tight to keep it all in place. He tells me an engineer designed it.

I suppose it would be hard to do. I ask, 'How does a person get knowledge to build something like this?'

There is awe in his reply: 'University,' he says.

'To get this knowledge you go to university.'

Jacob's inspired compromise results in the appearance on every school day of a young Greek Jewish tutor named Spiro who, charged with the task of preparing Chaim for high school, sets to with enthusiasm and dedication. Chaim responds with delight and attention; a new world unfolds. Spiro, himself inspired by the once forbidden books of the *Haskalah*, the Jewish Enlightenment[74] – which conveys a magic and power of knowledge beyond the confines of rules and rituals in the Talmud – passes on his belief in social integration. He believes the liberation of humanity is achievable only by reason, as had happened in France and Germany.

> In both countries, young minds absorbed Western knowledge; in Germany, whether they held onto their traditions or were converts – more to Protestantism than Catholicism – they felt German. Revolution, such as the French Terror and the upheavals in Russia, destroyed too much, allowed the rise of the strongest and the pushiest, while tending to denigrate and dispatch intelligence, experience and knowledge. The dilemma was how to learn from this and create a bloodless revolution.

Spiro's understanding is that for knowledge to be the Messiah of humanity, this young student, and others like him, will have to forge an alliance with the Poles. How else is Jewish life to progress? Not by running off to Palestine. Would not the problems which frustrated attempts to create a better life here exist or occur wherever one goes?

Thus he encourages Chaim to aim to succeed at high school, for beyond lies a chance to go on to university. Spiro describes the different professions: Medicine, Law, Science, Engineering. Engineering! Chaim's eyes shine. Bridges to span rivers, roads, great aqueducts like the Romans built; as an engineer, he could be among those who take Poland from a land of medievalism and paupers, to a land of modernity and wealth. So Spiro spins his view of what it means to be a Jew, within this time within this community within this city.

One view among many visions; all on a collision course.[75]

In Germany, where an outpouring of design and culture paralleled diminishing resources, the hopes of human beings for a richer lifestyle would have unimaginable and unbelievable consequences.[76]

Oh my Papa – despite all you endured
you conveyed a vision of a glorious future.
I remember a day in summer early 1959 where
everything seemed possible;
you and I were on the same page as we sat in the sun
imagining our Utopia.

Mrs E, with her constant talk of France this and French that, is irritating me. Both of us wear flimsy sandals, and as we walk gingerly over a long stretch of sunbaked, sharp pebbles, Mrs E utters little exclamations.

'You stupid woman,' is what I think.

As I turn to throw her one of my black looks, I stub my toe on a stone.
My eyes go to our feet; a wave of nausea hits me; I stumble.
Oh my God! She has missing toes!

My eyes go to the number on her arm. How did I not see this before?

Her hand steadies me; she says, 'Just a bit further and we are there.'

A blonde curl escapes from her headscarf; she is pretty.
Same age as my mother? Perhaps 35.

She smiles fondly at me.'Wait until you see it! It's worth it!'

This year we are holidaying at Mount Beauty in Victoria's High Country,
224 miles (360 kilometres) from Melbourne.
It is January 1959, and we have come to Bright for the day.

As promised, this spot on the river is special.
Just us and our friends. No one else is in sight.
We spread out on the river bank, making ourselves comfortable
on the smooth multi-coloured pebbles. I slip a few into my beach bag,
relishing this Goldilocks day: not too hot, not too cold.

Daddy and I, leaning back on our elbows, sitting next to each other,
talk of many wonders.
Daddy shows me the headlines on the latest space development:
a space probe 'Luna 1' launched to the moon![77]

To top it off, it seems the cold war has eased – the outlook is great!
Beyond the hot pale blue sky, the heavens call.

Our words are of the imminent possibility of manned space flight and
imaginings of a life of peace and prosperity:
long, thanks to miracle drugs; rich, via education;
and harmonious with freedom, respect and justice for everyone.

As my father and I build our Utopia, my mother, glancing our way,
smiles, showing her delight in us.

A shiver of anticipation, a butterfly in my stomach;
in a few weeks I will start high school.

Gratitude for this memory, gratitude for this day.

CHAPTER 7: *SAPERE AUDE*[78] AND (UN)REASON[79]

Warsaw 1933–36

Chaim studies. By the time he is eleven he speaks with fluency akin to any Polish student, excels at mathematics and physics, and, imbued with *sapere aude* – daring to know great teachings beyond those of the Torah – he is both observant and mindful. Observant, using all his senses to read the world around him, mindful not to neglect his own ability to reason; in combination, resisting unquestioning acceptance of stereotyping and dogma. This causes him some confusion because he is also observant of the rituals of Judaic religious ethics and traditions, attending synagogue with his father every Saturday and all the High Holidays.

Such anticipation in the greeting of each event, with extensive preparation, followed by the sheer joy of togetherness. Which is his favourite holiday? *Rosh Hashanah*? The new year is welcomed by the blowing of the shofar – the ram's horn symbolising God's love and leniency for Abraham because of Abraham's willingness to sacrifice his son Isaac. *Kol Nidre*? Releasing all the vows, the prayer is sung at the evening service of *Yom Kippur*, the Day of Atonement. This beautiful prayer cancels ill-considered vows or vows made under duress. *Yom Kippur* – when one atones, fasts, confesses mistakes, asks for forgiveness from anyone towards whom one has behaved unjustly, resolves to improve, and greets another with: 'May you be inscribed in the book of life'.

Or *Pesach*? What a mix of prescribed ceremony and informal festivity. His father and uncles conduct the Seder – the order of the

Passover – with reverence, taking care to include all the traditional symbols, chants and prayers. Yes, the two days and nights of *Pesach* are his favourite.

Despite his desire to be a good son, as defined by his parents' expectations, the reactionary spirit of the times stirs his heart as he encounters ideas poles apart from images of abundance and restraint described in the pages of the Talmud. The observation of the fast-moving world outside, and the observance of the repetitive and solemn rituals of the sanctuary, do not sit comfortably together.

He begins to keep the two separate. One component is deference to his father and enjoyment of the things they do together. This bonding takes place as if on an island inhabited by just two – in effect, a withdrawal from the world at large. The other is the outstretching openness he bears towards his place in the new world that makes the old ways obsolete; a separation of inside from outside that he takes pains to conceal from his beloved parents.

It is with sadness and excitement that Chaim, strong and ready, farewells Spiro. That last day, Spiro, his eyes a little damp, looks at him for a long moment, reminds him he will have to avoid distractions if he is to achieve his goals, and wishes upon his young student the courage to succeed.

With promise to go even further than his sisters, who are all educated to matriculation, 1934 heralds the beginning of a tremendous time for young Chaim. Though he needs extra tuition in Hebrew, the Jewish high school proves enjoyable beyond his imaginings; here at last he escapes the confines of home and mixes with other boys. Through Jewish sport organisations,[80] he plays hockey, basketball and soccer, games he had previously watched from a distance. All the summers of swimming in the waters of the Vistula pay off as in competition it turns out he's a strong swimmer. Water polo especially brings hours of pleasure; his parents delight in his lightly-muscled lanky frame and enormous appetite. The sisters tease him, calling him a horse for the huge quantities of food he devours while gaining not an inch of fat. Life is full of activity, learning, wondrous holidays at lakes, mountains and the sea with fantastic books for quieter moments.

There is excitement and preparation as Chaim, now mostly called Heniek, is bar mitzvahed on his thirteenth birthday. This entry to manhood, further celebrated by a gathering in his parents' home of the many relatives and friends, means that at last he is a man, responsible for his own actions. Two of his sisters, already married, bring with them their husbands; these men, expounding ideas with conviction, expand Heniek's world; the impossible seems logical, achievable, even commonplace.

Family gatherings include cousins and friends with many views represented. Words flow to express enjoyment or despair at the paradoxes of life. Discussions range over diverse topics. Sometimes voices speak out of belief, other times to provoke the intellect. By unspoken agreement, rousing comments on the political situation, the kind that might invite heated debate and tempt intellectual retaliation, such words remain unvoiced in Jacob's presence.

Oh such frustration at holding one's tongue – then and now.
If they had been able to talk things over
would it have made any difference?

Photo possibly Heniek's bar mitzvah, 22 October 1935.

Sara, increasingly tired and longing for another rest cure, contemplates yet another letter from her sister. It is 1936 and Faygalleh writes that Australia is the land of opportunity, husband David is busy manufacturing milk separators and moulds for radios, the whole family is doing well, and living in a magnificent two-storey house in a suburb called Carlton. Sara, trying to picture life under an unremitting hot sun, wonders why her sister makes no mention of kangaroos hopping down the street.

She sighs. What is she to do with everyone running away all over the place? Now Fella, in a bit of a funk, wants to go to see Mania in the sunny far-off land. Well, that takes a lot of money, not to mention papers and permits. If Fella goes, will she ever see her eldest daughter again? Will the others want to follow? There's no way Jacob would ask favours from his brother-in-law to get permits for all of them. And he would not consider going anywhere anyway, especially not with his dreadful arthritis which is getting worse, making it so hard for him to walk unaided. It seems he'll soon need to resort to a wheelchair.

And the diabetes that runs in her side of the family is bringing her low again. No, they're not well enough to relocate, so please God the children should stay here too. Perhaps she'll go to the spas at Marienbad. It has done her good before. But this health resort in Czechoslovakia is far away, the travel is tiring, the atmosphere at the spa is changed. Last time there had been sideways glances at her from a group of Germans and she heard *die Jüdin* – female Jew – in so derogatory a tone, accompanied by a look so threatening, that fear entered and stuck in the pit of her stomach. No, she'll not go, she'll stay home and manage.

This fear thing, an intrinsic consequence of being a Jew, when did I first
encounter it? Ah, yes, two years before we went to Bright;
I was eleven, in the summer of early 1957,
when I first heard my father say: ***Never Again.***

Sundays we go to the beach at Seaford and stay the whole day. Many of my parents' friends are here. One of the men has taken to my mother. He flirts with her; one Sunday he makes a bold grab at her bosom as we walk along the dirt path to the beach. Mummy moves away, takes my hand and runs ahead. I am shocked. She shushes me, tells me to forget it. It bothers me, this awful behaviour.

Anticipation replaces my indignation, as the walk from the cars parked under the shading tea-trees becomes a narrow track of sand, burning hot, through the dunes … and there it is! A sandy beach stretching forever, powdery sand, whiter than the gritty yellow sand at St Kilda Beach, shallows to muck around in and, beckoning beyond the sand bar, the vast waters of the bay. On the shore, Mummy spreads baby oil or coconut oil all over herself – she gets the best rich golden tan. She, who does not like to swim, calls out to us to be careful and watches as, with my Daddy, I swim out to where the green tangy sea is icy-deep, and we race back; he wins, but watch out, Daddy – I am getting faster!

Me, Daddy, Janette

And someone takes a photo.

With our many friends at the beach, we have a picnic lunch. We compare and share goodies, try to keep the sand off the hard-boiled eggs and pieces of apple; make faces at the crunch of the grit, and eat it all with good appetite. Five-year-old Janette grizzles, the sea salt stings her skin, sand irritates. We tell her to be brave, reminding her the specialist says salt water and sunshine are good for her eczema. I keep her company in the shallows while the other children play with a beach ball.

Sometimes the men forget they are grown-ups and they take over, soccering the ball, showing off. The sun lower in the sky, it is time to make sand castles complete with moats and one last swim with dunkings.

I never want to leave here.

On the way home, with the car swerving to the beach road curves, the sun setting in glorious colours on our left, we sing along with the radio: 'Catch a Falling Star' (Perry Como), 'Tammy' (Debbie Reynolds), 'Day-O' (Harry Belafonte), 'Memories are Made of This' (Dean Martin) and 'Wonderful, Wonderful' (Johnny Mathis). Yes, wonderful.

Mummy usually makes a simple dinner, sometimes of fresh rye bread from Acland Street – made more delicious because the law forbids sale of fresh bread on Sunday – and continental frankfurts, which my mother calls *paruvki*; other times we have chopped Polish sausage scrambled with eggs. Yum.

Summer days merge into a golden haze as the holidays go by.

But there is one Sunday, a scary, puzzling Sunday. With the sun growing larger as it sinks towards the water, Janette and I put finishing touches to our sand castle. I hear a strange sound and,
turning my head, I see my Daddy running towards me.
His face twisted in horror; the sound coming from him
terrified and terrifying – I can't make out the words.
I follow the direction of his eyes.
Coming towards Janette and me is a lanky boy. His crewcut hair nearly white; his skin red from a day out in the sun. Stark against this red,
a white pattern, painted on his chest in zinc-cream:
a cross with hooked pieces on the ends.

Daddy has reached us.
Taking an aggressive pose, his hands go around us as if to protect us.
From what is he protecting us?
As the boy passes, he rolls his pale blue eyes at Daddy.
'Daddy! What's wrong?'
'Nothing!' He shouts it, his face distorted, his eyes bulging.

Mummy has been watching and running.
Now she reaches us, all smiles gone. I see the terror in Mummy's eyes;
she takes us in her arms and holds us close.
She is trembling. Daddy is trembling too.
He says, 'It's all right now – you are safe.'
Turning to Mummy, his eyes wide and glaring,
he fiercely speaks the words as if a curse:
'NEVER AGAIN.'

CHAPTER 8: TOPIAS: U–, EU–, DYS– AND KAKO– [81]

Warsaw 1936–39

'I had much love and respect for my parents. But why remain superstitious when science explained our world in logical terms? In the process of abandoning all I had known, I thought the socialists had the right idea and even considered the communists were on the right track to bring about a better world.' Heniek

Jacob Heber commands absolute respect. Discussions on new ideas rage, but not in his presence. Wise Jacob, not risking quarrelling and possible loss of stature, chooses to neither see nor hear, thus his views are uncontradicted, deference sustained; his symbolic role as King-of-the-house is maintained. However, vigorous discussion surrounds Heniek: ideas on equality, on the right way, on the right goals. At meetings of young members of the pro-Semite Polish Labour Party,[82] with its socialistic ideals, he finds a means of being part of making his world change. It is 1937, he is fourteen. Each day he witnesses the growing tensions in a multitude of situations: the picketing of Jewish shops, mocking of traditional Jews on the street. United with other young men against escalating fascism, he takes a stand by handing out pro-Semitic, anti-Endecja (National Democracy) leaflets.

There is a risk for him in political alliance and action with the socialists for, though the Party is comprised mostly of gentiles, it is illegal, and the punishment, if caught by the authorities, is a *Wilczy -Bilet,* a document called a *wolf ticket,* which prevents the recipient from going to school or university. In street fights against the Endecja, the young men, apart from punches, draw blood with knives and knuckle-dusters.[83] Police watch from a distance: when there are fewer of the Endecja youth, they move in and chase off the young socialists, or brand them with tickets; when there are more of the Endecja they leave the under-dogs to their bruising.

Not even a whisper within the Heber home gives away these deeds. Heniek does not invite his Polish socialist friends home. So no one guesses what their darling Chaim is up to, sparing them shock and fear.

In Heniek's new circle, the debate among the Jewish boys centres on how to combine the duty of esteem to fellow Jews, with loyalty to the vision of a modern Polish homeland. These Jews, acculturated with no desire to convert, Polish in manner, dress and thought, find the old religious ways akin to superstition, but remaining respectful of family traditions, they voice their attitude by saying: 'Why take on a trinity of deities and Catholic iconography? Why exchange one outdated religion for another?'

Heniek's aspiration to get into university to take part as a contributing member of his society is reinforced by the Endecja – these antisemitic National Democrats – name-callers who shout *icek* (kike) or *parszywe Żyd* (lousy Jew) – making out he is less than they. Thus his friends alert him that the prime prerequisite to entry into university – beyond a certificate of matriculation and passing entrance exams – is tenacity.

> Any Jew that succeeded in being accepted within the informal quotas (applied to keep down the numbers of Jews qualifying in the professions), faced exclusion from Fraternities; in addition, as Fraternities ran university dormitories, so stayed in special Jewish dormitories, constructed during the early 1920s. Aggression and hostility towards Jewish students was countered by Jewish determination to excel.[84]

With all this I was still thinking that Poland is my country.

Heniek

To the Heber family circle there enters an outsider.

Heniek's sister Inka, only nineteen with carrot-red hair, having fallen in love with Stefan Tadeusz (born of a Jewish mother and converted-to-Christianity father, Stefan, uncircumcised, considered himself Catholic) her love for Stefan causes consternation. However, this man, resolute in his love of her, her family and her people, takes up Judaism; he and Inka marry. An extraordinary move at any time, made more so at this time when Jews are discarding traditional ways, trying to disappear into the mass. The Heber family accepts him.

In this intelligent, outgoing man, Heniek finds new inspiration.

Stefan gladly conveys his intimate knowledge of the gentile world, expressing his views on the similarities between the guiding principles of his old and new religion thus: 'After all, is one not the mother and the other the son? Do they both not have the Old Testament, the one God and Ten Commandments as their basis? Was not Christ a Jew? Does not the meeting of the gentile world and the Jewish world produce incredible intellectual results as in Germany: Freud, Kafka …?'

Heniek, inspired, embraces the concepts of hope and reason and the vision of a better humanity through the emancipation of all men through Man's ability to reason; words of splendour – portent of a better world.

> Truly a young man of his time. One of many, but intentions and hopes, no matter how noble, exist only within the confines of their place and time. And this was a troubled place and time. Where once a haven[85] was, now swirled conflicting visiontopias. For their 'ism' to bring about their vision of Utopia, some called for rationality and reason, others demanded immediate results. Of those that had premonitions of the horrors to come, some wrote to try to shake men out of their complacency; they understood that one may see/know/want-to do right-good action, but do nothing or do the bad action instead. If reason alone does not cause us to do the right thing, and courage and reason may be the enabler of wrong action, there is something else needed. Then, as now, confounders abounded; and we know right action can lead to unintended (wrong) outcomes.
>
> Meanwhile in *Time* magazine's 1938 'Man Of The Year' article, Hitler was labelled the 'greatest threatening force that the democratic, freedom-loving world faces today'.

It is 1939. Poverty and persecution evident, Sara contemplates the tangible disintegration of her family: her siblings, and Jacob's, have gone to countries far away. The entire Kott branch of the family – Jacob's sister Fella and her children Paulette and Jacques who had been studying in Kalisz until late 1938 – were now in France.

Sara's sister Faygalleh and all her children had long gone to settle in Australia. And with all costs having been met by Jacob, even her brother Zev's boys have left: Norman in 1937 after working as a watchmaker had spent a few nights on her couch before sailing; Pesakh, tiring of making socks on a machine, working in the living room at an uncle's place in Łódź, had spent two nights with her before following in 1938. Pesakh, writing that Australia, though no *Gan Eden*, was good, described work as a labourer on farms in places with strange names: Daylesford, Shepparton. Reading between the lines, she divined that he, for one, had neither found Australia to be the Garden of Eden nor had yet made his fortune.

The girls are curious, keen for adventure, want to go. Jacob, reluctant to leave for France or Palestine, finds nothing commendable in the letters that travel to them from Australia.

Perhaps, as he considers the alternatives, a recognition of the dire situation is stronger in Jacob than he cares to admit. A.H. had remilitarised the Rhineland in 1936, annexed Austria in 1938 and the Allies, giving in further to his demands, handed him the Sudetenland, declaring that well, after all, it *was* German-speaking! Concessions granted to keep the peace. They'd heard directly of the parlous situation from Jacob's brother Yechiel Meir – former resident of Berlin – when he arrived on their doorstep. Known as Hilmier, he told of an astonishing ordeal: he'd been driven out of the Third Reich, interned in 1938 in a camp named Zbąszyń in Poland on the German frontier, made to sleep in stables, suffered degradation, beatings, was forcibly moved to Warsaw … A.H. would come to Poland.

Jacob, at 54, his severe arthritis making walking increasingly difficult, reassures himself. Poland is his home. Here he had been born and worked his whole life conducting and combining with sensitivity and consciousness his duty to Poland and to kin and community.

Here he will stay. Here, when God decrees, he will die.

News from Germany continues to be unbelievable. Jacob's brother Felix, who had lived in Hamburg, was gathered with other German Jews, sent to Dachau, escaped internment, made his way to France; news came that he had got to Argentina.

Against this background of seething and erupting violence, Heniek's family live their lives as if everything will be all right. Hoping that those who are fleeing are unnecessarily pessimistic and alarmist, they make no plans for escape.

In September 1939 Heniek, his *Mała Matura* completed, anticipates the celebration of his seventeenth birthday in October. Like two of his sisters before him, he will soon commence his *Matura.* He knows what is happening around him. About him swirls a world of extremes. Bundist argues with Zionist, they both take issue with communists; on the streets of Warsaw religious Jews in flowing traditional dress of caftans, caps and long beards mingle with the middle class in modern dress and the wealthy in furs.

Some Poles mix with Jews, calling them friends – this qualified, lest there be supposition of equality, by naming them not as 'Pole' but as 'Pole of the Mosaic Faith'; others break the windows of Jewish shops. Broken glass everywhere signals the coming devastation; people ask each other where such wanton, unpunished destruction of property will lead. So while a trickle of Jews finds a way out of Europe, the rest, thwarted by differences, restrictions and poverty, argue fruitlessly among themselves.

Heniek, though not tall, with his tanned olive skin, slim build, thick black wavy hair, slanting hazel eyes, and with a charming crooked smile presents a dashing figure.

In fact, he looks like a cross between 'the king of Hollywood' Clark Gable and 'the great lover' John Gilbert.

In the atmosphere of determination to realise the hope for a shared place in Poland, my father Heniek has matured with one foot planted in the embrace of a warm loving family the other hovering over the concealed abyss of promised revolution.

Heniek sees himself as any man's equal.

In this modern world, are not all men created equal?

Isn't that what the revolution and the civil wars – French, American, Russian, Spanish – were fought for?

And the war to end all wars – World War I – wasn't that fought to ensure good and right ways to live are upheld?

So is not the new world going to be a place where, just like a black man in America, a Jew can stand proud and tall, and, not needing to run or hide, no longer be hindered by an illogical imposed image of inferiority?

Yes. For this ideal, Heniek is prepared to fight.

Despite the many difficulties,
Poland is his country.

He believes that out of this cauldron
of passionate and desperate ideas,

Good will be triumphant,
the talk will translate to action,

and in his lifetime
he will be part of

the continuing evolution
of scientific marvels;

the brilliant genesis
and cleansing revolution
of a good way to live.

Photo taken probably in 1937.

Back row: Heniek's cousin Paulette Kott, Natek Mann, Heniek's sister Inka.

Middle row: Heniek's sister Marisa, Jacob's sister Fella Kott, Heniek's sister Fella, Heniek's sister Franka.

Front row: Heniek, aged fifteen.

PART FIVE

(DIS)HONOUR, (DIS)GRACE, (DIS)BELIEF, DIFFERENCE

HONOUR YOUR FATHER AND MOTHER [86]

All my adult years I resolved to 'behave' and be
respectful to my parents;
however, my words and actions often betrayed my intent.
With my father, I got stuck in the safety of
a how-are-you-I'm-fine exchange.
With my mother, when discussions got 'hot',
she'd signal an end with a mixed adage:
'Nothing changes, it is still all the same; every man for himself',
to which, instead of letting it go –
in devil's advocate mode –
I'd retaliate:
'Oh Mummy, that is not true for everyone. Anyway, we must not give up
wanting and working for a better world, for a good fair life.'
And she, shaking her head at me, consistently replied,
'Ah, Sara, you are so naive.'

On reflection, there was a time of great change when, indeed,
it did seem as if nothing ever changes in the sense of the same but
different repetition of horrors – a time when all I could do was hang on.

As events unforeseen amass, imagination struggles to discover delight.[87] On Thursday, 17 January 1991, my inner world goes into free-fall.

A nameless horror grips my heart and soul;
Still I present with a fixed smile.
Teeming head not under my control;
Still I pretend to work for a while.
Resident butterflies regress to gnawing worms;
Still I talk the talk.
Favourite food to bitter ashes in my mouth turns;
Still I eat and walk.
My work, in piles of neat folders, minutes ago vital,
Now become pointless.
Rushing managers issue orders parochial.
Are they blind or witless?
Dichotomies abound, is my reaction extreme?
I feel alone; perplexed.
Bombs explode on the TV screen and in my dreams.
Is Europe next?

That Gulf War – termed Desert Storm, twenty days in the Middle East, we watched, courtesy of CNN – soon over. 'Scud' a new word, familiar as 'Coke'. Aftermath horrors constant: Red Sea creatures covered in choking grease, black smoke billowing, hiding the sun, men capping flaming oil wells.[88]

In 1992, we watch Yugoslavia tear itself apart and the Soviet Union self-dismantle; buried amongst mundane local news, reports in bits reveal hunger, conflict, pollution. My husband Branko, a blend of Serbian, Croatian and Dalmatian, is distraught. My mother's face shows her dismay. Daddy is withdrawn. What happened to 'Never Again'?

'I am so tired,' is all I can say; over and over; a mantra engulfing. Weeks in bed. Ashamed. After all my parents went through. Do I dishonour them? With no deity, order, or grand design to believe in, falling in nightmares, and, when awake, yet again, just as when I was a child, I cling to a belief in life; life for its own sake.

And I remember the first time in 1953, when I was seven.

My mother runs towards me … she grabs my limp arm; we both
scream; my white cast, covered with signatures; my arm itchy inside.

Dr Farran – he who is so kind to Mummy that she goes often and
confides in him – takes it off, puts a new one on; my arm has not healed.

I miss a lot of school. They remove the metal fence bars that were so
nice to swing on; they make rules about the playground.

My teacher gives me lots of coloured paper to take home.
My mother keeps me company and tells me stories.

Back at school … everything is the same, everything is different.

Every morning at assembly we stand quiet and still to attention,
say the pledge,[89] sing our anthem: 'God Save our Gracious Queen'.
We do sums and spelling, we make things; captains choose sides;
I am the last chosen.
Children run, walk on hands, do cartwheels, bump, push.
I, watching from a safe distance, make necklaces and bracelets
out of yellow daisies in the lawn or pull off their petals:
'He loves me; he loves me not.'

Time goes by slowly.
I find excuses to miss school, to be home, to read books …
I feel old as I walk to school through the park; the watchful eye
follows my every step as I take care not to stand on the cracks.
Unknowable faces – men, women, children – once alive, fill my head.
I know the unspeakable …
THERE IS NO GOD … SHH …

The Jewish Religious Instruction teacher, a kind faced woman, tells us
of a just God who has done many things for us – His chosen people.
Except, I know an awful secret.
No real God would let innocent people die.
No, not even one, and there were six million.
And my Mummy cries: for her mother to guide,
her sisters in whom to confide, her father to mind,
for a friend with whom she can connect.
Sometimes, shaking her head, she says: life is so short,
many people still die in war, many live in awful poverty, babies still die.
Maybe there *is* no God; what is it all for?
This new country, these teachers, talking of Queen and country,

they know nothing of these things. I will tell no one of my thoughts,
I will be my mother's friend. I will listen to her – just like a sister …
Different from everyone around me; alone in my difference.
I think: even if there is a God, He no longer cares for His chosen people,
so why should I honour him? Anyway, Mummy is right;
we live only a short time, then we die and become dust,
and the only purpose, the only point, is life.

Feeling different,
out of step with the Jewish community,
a constant sense of not-belonging that I've kept within.

But in the mid-1990s I had cause for dismay: there were some –
Jews, here in Melbourne and in Israel – who declared,
'You are not bat mitzvahed! You don't keep the rituals!
You are married to a gentile! How are you a Jew?'

Me, not a Jew? How could this be?

Certainly, I – being my father's daughter, identification elusive,
able to merge into the Anglo or Euro milieu –
rather choose always to let on that I'm Jewish, thus,
minimising any unintended poor-taste jokes or comments.
And though nonreligious, not honouring the rules and rituals,
there is in me a sense, which no one can take away.

I absorb and inhale the sights, sounds and scents of God's world
and speak one-on-one to Him,
as if He is there and has a desire to hear me.

My inspiration is the desert and Joseph, who,
famous for his coat-of-many-colours,
kept not his father's rigid rituals and rules, but,
doing in Egypt as the Egyptians, making a space and place –
first for himself, then for his tribe –
used his gifts for the good of all.

Thus, I reassert myself a Jew [90] by fourfold reasons:
First: my maiden name, Heber, is biblical.[91]
Second: I have earned it via borrowed nightmares.
Third: because of A.H. – he named all Jewish women *Sara*.[92]
And the fourth is my father's gift of recognition.

Near his end, late November 1999, when asked testingly by the doctor,
'Who is this woman?' Daddy gazed at me.
It seemed he would not speak.
At last, smiling his charming crooked smile,
in his husky-from-too-many-cigarettes sexy voice, he said,
'The oldest woman in the world.'

The doctor, bemused, turned to me and asked,
'Does this make sense to you?'

'Yes.' I laughed – getting it.

Sara, wife of Abraham, the Bible tells, died at 127. And Daddy, his eyes twinkling, pleased with himself, laughed with me, both of us laughing, enjoying his joke. Oh, my Papa. Named by him for his mother and, like her, named back through the generations to the biblical matriarch, Sara, the quintessential Jewess. I claim that birthright and embrace the consequences.

So, in the setting down of all this, I do, after all,
Honour My Father and My Mother.

PART SIX

WITH(IN) WAR

Warsaw late 1939 to mid-1941

DO NOT MURDER

If the last and worst act … had come immediately
after the first and smallest … But … this isn't the way it happens.
In between come … hundreds of little steps …
each of them preparing you not to be shocked by the next.[93]

The particulars recorded, theorised, endless detail disorienting;
events (in)significant, engraved, grown familiar, even banal in the
outpouring of marks and imagery, become generalised, abstract.

Things that my parents did not speak of, perhaps did not know,
I touch on – a background sketch gleaned from the real
and post time records – just a sketch – not the whole, lest we –
you and I – become submerged in facts and numbers
and the individual human experiences
become lost in the general.

CHAPTER 9: WITH SWIFTNESS – BLITZKRIEG[94]

'I have put my death-head formations in place with the command relentlessly and without compassion to send into death many women and children of Polish origin and language. Only thus we can gain the living space that we need. Who after all is today speaking about the destruction of the Armenians?'[95]

Thus, did A.H., having made himself king, announce his intentions to vast violation of the Sixth Commandment.

1 September 1939: the radio transmits the news:

Germany has invaded Poland from the west without any declaration of war, taking Danzig in the north. Panzer units head for Warsaw. Anglo-French immediate ultimatums have no effect;
Britain, alarmed, still avoiding war.[96]

Poland's army in disarray; her cavalry no match for 60 divisions, her airforce largely destroyed on the ground, having not taken off due to pleas from England and France not to antagonise A.H.

3 September 1939: Declarations of war from Britain, France, then Australia and New Zealand. Polish families huddling around radios, cheer each announcement. Having delayed 53 hours, Chamberlain playing gentlemen's rules, restricts bombing to German warships.

British planes drop their payloads over Germany: propaganda leaflets!

8 September 1939: Warsaw surrounded; Poland's refusal to surrender brings an indiscriminate relentless barrage of shelling, artillery, and incendiary bombs; the whole city on fire! Debris everywhere. People flee via Vistula bridges. Men of military age answer the call-up.

Buildings become hospitals. Nuns tend wounded, corpses pile up.
No water; no electricity; Armageddon.
Family members search: find their living; mourn their dead.

Basia, having just returned from holiday, is home alone in Muranowska Street. Hearing bombs falling, terrified, she runs out onto the streets. In the chaos, searching for Pinkus, she finds him and together they make their way back to Świder to be with Rena, Zosia and Celina.

Heniek reacts to the noise and smoke by dashing out of the apartment into Graniczna Street. A scene of chaos engulfs him; screaming, wailing, moaning voices merge with the penetrating shriek of sirens which rend the air, further jangling already frayed nerves. Choking dust and smoke cause confusion all around, the night is grotesque, the air aflame. All the street is burning, homes destroyed … chunks of deformed steel lie on the ground. What is that inhuman sound? Neighing! The stables have taken a direct hit!

Heniek's Uncle Hilmier, having followed Heniek into the street, takes in the scene, sinks to the ground in the middle of the street and sways on his knees.[97] Heniek, his feelings in flux, is distracted; deep love for this dear relative battles impatience: is the man mad? How can a man have faith such as to ignore the collapse of all around him and pray in acquiescence to his God? Heniek tears himself away and turns his attention to freeing the horses.

The deluge keeps the Heber family in their cellar for sixteen days.

A cellar equates to constant damp, little food or water, much noise, and fear – but my father gave no details.

Meanwhile, the Soviets entered Poland in the undefended east, their pretext: to come to Poland's aid and liberate Poland's Ukrainians[98] and Byelorussians. The Polish government, having declared itself: *Silni, Zwarci, Gotowi* – Strong, United, Ready – quit Poland on 17 September via Romania to reside in France and govern in exile. Warsaw fought on with the water supply destroyed. Ukrainian peasants, deliberately starved by Stalin, killed Polish soldiers – revenge for years of oppression. Brushing aside protests by British parliamentarians, Chamberlain's government declared that German industry in the Ruhr couldn't be bombed because it was private property. So certain of success were the Nazis, that on 21 September, Heydrich, the Chief of the Security Police located in Berlin, issued:

INSTRUCTIONS CONCERNING JEWS IN THE OCCUPIED TERRITORIES

This document set out the initial stages of a plan which will lead to a final aim and reminded 'that the planned total measure (i.e., the final aim – *Endziel*) are to be kept strictly secret.'[99]

There follows a day when bombs fall such that the earth shakes –
23 September 1939: The Jewish Day of Atonement.
What a strategy! Resistance evaporates. Where is the Polish Army?

28 September 1939: after a three-week siege, Warsaw capitulated. Five days later, the last Polish units surrendered. So Poland fell in 32 days. Hans Frank, A.H.'s former personal lawyer, installed as Governor of Warsaw, said: 'The Führer has told me that the leading groups in Polish society already in our hands are to be liquidated, and whoever appears to replace them is to be … exterminated … these times lay upon us the duty to ensure that no further resistance emerges from the Polish people.'[100] In this spirit, crushing all opposition, in an occupied area they called the Generalgouvernement, Germany began the crushing plunder of Poland. An indiscriminate reign of terror descended with starvation rations, rapid inflation, factories and offices under German control. Having destroyed the state, Germany turned Poland into a vast killing ground and took 700,000 of the Polish Army prisoner; the Soviets took 200,000.

CHAPTER 10: WITH SMALL STEPS AND WITH TERROR [101]

Late 1939 – mid-1940

With the beginning of a new day, new directives and restrictions; each step adjusted to as the unacceptable becomes acceptable. Then a new day and new directives.

On 4 October 1939, the Jewish Community Council was disbanded. Adam Czerniakow, who was installed as the leader of Warsaw Jews and ordered to select a further 24 elders to a Council of Elders (the *Judenrat*) to carry out Gestapo orders, believed that by cooperation and holding out, most would survive; when offered a visa to Palestine, he refused and stayed to give leadership.[102]

Imagine Being In Their Shoes: The Invaders

Watch many of the pre-war council flee.
Watch the remainder try to compromise!
They think we are like the Germans they dealt with in the last war.
Encourage fragmentation and sense of abandonment.
Let accusations abound against the new council.
The Judenrat: Spineless. Self-interested.
They will execute our orders. Let these Jews blame their own.
Get them to block bank accounts, limit cash.[103]
Conduct round-ups for forced labour.

Use the Poles to point out Jews, to give away their neighbours.
Treat those that do help or shelter a Jew just as if they are a Jew!
Order Jewish officials to prepare nominal rolls,
transmit new regulations, report births and deaths.
Set up a bank account for the Gestapo.

Keep the Jews in check: Compliant. Fearful. Sycophantic.
Take first the valuables, then the labour.
They assist their new masters – do they hope to be part of our strength?
See how the council cooperates with a promise to provide 'workers'.
Frustrate any council effort to create order
by continuing haphazard round-ups with release of people for payment.
Set one against the other and profit in the game. Keep them unbalanced;
be lenient to one, enact sudden, individual acts of violence to others.
Make sure that no Jew walks on the pavement
reserved for the German soldier. They will learn to kneel.

Impose a curfew. Enforce the curfew with rigour. Close schools.
See how the young sink into a lethargy:
a combination of hunger, lack of activity and terror.
England in the Middle Ages marked Jews with a yellow badge.
Use the example of the past. Mark each Jew;
a white ribbon with a yellow Star of David worn on the right forearm.[104]
Those that condemn the Swastika[105] *as the sign of the anti-Christ –*
even be they Catholic – they too will die as an enemy.
Those deceptively fashioned akin to Aryans, they will be revealed.
Plan to concentrate 359,827 Jews.
We know this figure from the census ordered.
Then bring in another 90,000. If any flee Europe so much the better …
Let the West take them and suffer the consequences!

Meet any sign of rebellion with immediate brutal retaliation.
Take 53 for the killing of a policeman,
make them dig their own graves,
shoot them, and issue a fine of one hundred thousand złoty.[106]
Searches unannounced, an illegal broadcasting station discovered;
one of the 'thirteenth bureau' – this paid informer –
he reveals the culprit.
A young nineteen-year-old named Kazimierz Andrez Kott!
In charge of an Underground! He escapes! Retaliate.
Round up 255 – lock them away with no word.
Drive families to distraction trying to locate them
and effect their release.
Forbid more things: travel, change of residence, private prayer;
Close synagogues. Equate Jews with lice and typhus.[107]

Some with means escaped to the Russian zone. Doors to the West, closed tight since *Kristallnacht* on 9 November 1938, stayed closed. Fear of a flood of Jews thwarted any plan to enable intake – even to the propositions to admit children. In America, a special Children's Rescue Bill – to allow 10,000 children under fourteen entry until they could safely rejoin their parents elsewhere – was defeated in 1939, and again in 1940, by an amalgamation of thirty patriotic isolationist organisations. The 'patriots' articulated their reasons bluntly:

... this is just part of a drive to go back to the conditions when we were flooded with foreigners who tried to run this country on different lines from those laid down by the old stock ... children ... all too soon grow up to be ... ugly adults.[108]

Seeking a solution, A.H. and his men, intent on ridding Europe of Jews, considered schemes such as moving millions of Jews to Madagascar; expulsion the goal.[109] With more countries occupied (Holland, Belgium and Luxembourg) the world continued to close its eyes; turn its back.

As Germans debated, thousands of Poles in Warsaw – blaming Jews for harsh treatment from the Nazi invaders – marched to the Jewish Council to vent their anger. Jewish 'carriers' – attackers of belligerent Poles – were waiting for them. These Poles did not try this again.[110]

Mid-1940, Paris fell without resistance. The Polish government-in-exile moved to London. The *Judenrat*, in a state of shock at proposals for a quarantined area – a ghetto – delayed progress by playing authorities against each other.[111]

Imagine Being In Their Shoes: The Ghetto Occupants

But brick walls and barbed wire enclosing;
'sanitary' blocks degrading.
Gazeta Żydowska, an authorised Polish-language
Jewish newspaper, normalising the changes by reportage
uses words as if they convey truth.[112]
The first prisoners, mainly political,[113] *arrive at the huge,*
newly constructed Auschwitz.
And 'Arbeit Macht Frei' 'Work Liberates' –
the great lie, there for all to see.

THE WARSAW GHETTO

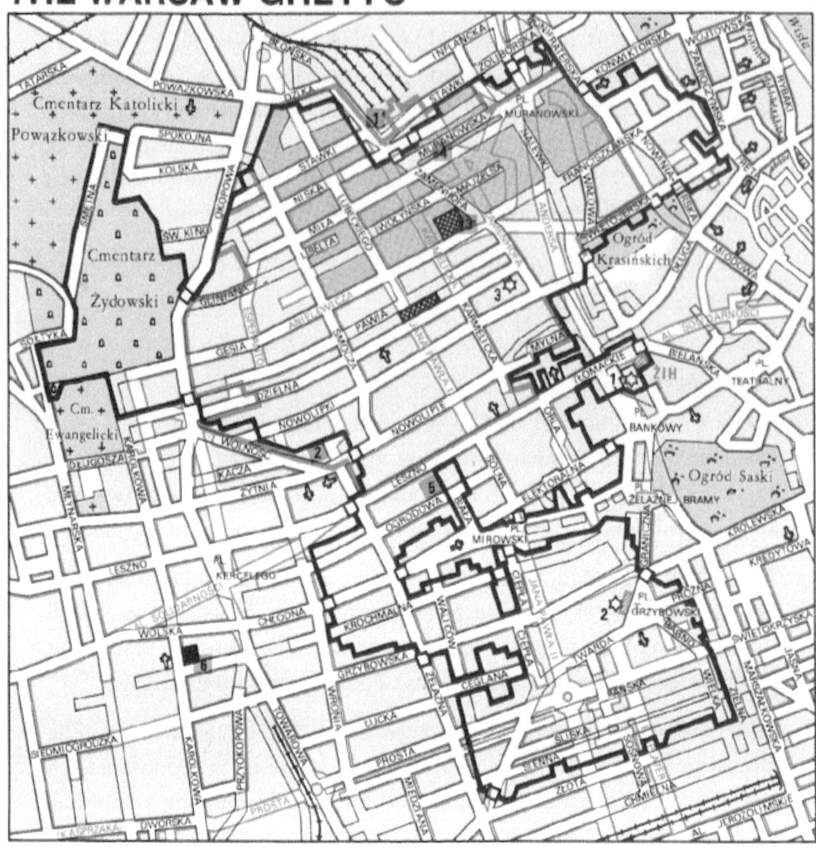

Ghetto walls from November 1940 till October 1941	Contemporary situation:
Ghetto gates	PROSTA Contemporary street network
Ghetto walls since September 1942	Memory sites:
Inhabited ghetto area since September 1942 till April 1943	1 Memorial on the former Umschlagplatz site
CIEPŁA Street network at that time	2 The gestapo building; thousands of Jews were murdered in its cellars in 1943
1 — the Tłomackie Great Synagogue, 2 — the Nożyks' Synagogue 3 — the Moriah Synagogue	3 Memorial to the Ghetto Heroes
Orphanage managed by Janusz Korczak (its site until 1940)	4 A stone slab commemorating the site where the Jewish Combat Organization bunker was hidden
Prisons	5 A memorial plaque on the house where Józef Lewartowski lived
	6 Janusz Korczak Memorial
	T Esther Rachel Kamińska Theatre
	ŻIH Jewish Historical Institute

114

CHAPTER 11: WITHIN WALLS [115]

WARSAW mid-1940

In this ruin, work continues on the construction of a closed ghetto.

The complexity of maintaining important connections for the city outside contributed to delays in planning and execution. Nevertheless, brick-by-brick, piece-by-piece, 3.5 metre-high solid walls topped by shards of glass and barbed wire were erected, thoroughfares closed off, windows and doors blocked. A Jewish quarter, comprising mainly apartment blocks and little open space, was established.

On 16 October 1940, following a decree giving 80,000 Poles in the area two weeks to move out voluntarily, Warsaw's Jews – over 30 per cent of Warsaw's population of 3.1 million (10 per cent of Poland's population of 35 million were Jews) – herded into 5 per cent of Warsaw's area (just over one square mile) – to face dreadful living conditions, with bread rations reduced.[116] Then another 72,000 deportees moved in. Four hundred and forty thousand shocked Jews. Some moved two or three times. Immediate blows or bullets greeted the slightest hesitation.

From Ringelblum's diary entries: 5 October 1940: Christians surreptitiously warning Jews of press-gangs. 16 November 1940: ghetto introduced – realisation that it is to be a closed ghetto came like a thunderbolt. 19 November 1940: Within the ghetto people milled about trying to buy whatever was available; a Christian was killed for throwing a sack of bread over the wall.[117] Jewish shops in 'Aryan' Warsaw were sealed, with twenty-two entry/exits points (reduced to fifteen by the start of 1941); 53,000 persons had crossing permits.[118]

> *'We have entered into a new life ... penned in on all sides ...*
> *segregated and separated from the world ...*
> *driven out of the society of the human race.'* Chaim Kaplan[119]

The Ogród Krasińskich – the Krasiński Gardens – Basia's beloved gardens, once just two blocks from her home, place of park benches, bluebells, lilacs, linden – is now separated from her home by a wall.

The Heber family home at 17 Graniczna Street is a border street[120] to the east of the designated ghetto. Notified by the authorities that they have to move, they take as many precious belongings as they can carry and squeeze into an apartment with one large lounge room and one bedroom. Jacob, his world crumbling, visibly aging, is incapacitated.

Caught in the street by German soldiers, just weeks after occupation, Heniek experiences forced labour for the first time. The cellars of Luftwaffe Headquarters have been flooded, and his work battalion must pump out the water. It is bitterly cold work. Unfed and freezing, but thankfully not beaten, and only for one day, he accepts this indignity.

Then, at the behest of the Jewish authorities – who make lists, notify those on the lists, and require those so called to form in groups outside the *Judenrat* offices – Heniek is sent to work for a German firm breaking up iron machines with a fifteen-kilo hammer. His hands become torn and raw; the work continues. Grimly he bears his pain, hiding it from his family so as not to increase their burden of distress.

Observing the daily movements of groups of workers entering and leaving the ghetto, Heniek sees a way out. Removing his armband, he attaches himself to a group as they leave. Once in the Aryan sector he buys food, including ham and cakes. In the morning, he smuggles himself back in. From that first time, he does this often.

Poles wanting to trade – business-as-usual –
move in and out of the quarter freely.
After the initial shock wears off, during that first ghetto winter,
there are five o'clock teas and dance parties as the young,
their mood dejected, seek to entertain themselves.[121]
And so life goes on. People drink coffee in the coffee lounges;
little groups of 'politicians' gather in courtyards to discuss their theories;
they have 'good' news from 'reliable' sources.

The young fall in love, there are marriages, births and bris.
The sick, old and poor die.
People join one of the distinct political, social or welfare organisations,
each determined to create order and to minimise the hurt.
They give some time, some money, a hand to someone.
There is theatre! Cabaret! Culture alive, flourishing!
Life-enhancing distractions.[122]
Smugglers operate via transit houses, exits, gates, tunnels, low walls.[123]
Family belongings are traded for food.
Cabbages are grown in every spare plot of land.
Rabbis give special dispensation to the eating of smuggled pork.
Coal: scarce, increased twenty-fold in price.
Lice: multiply, harbingers of disease.
Through sewers and basements, unseen hands construct networks
of underground passages giving access to secret meeting places,
clandestine schools, distribution
of Underground papers and contraband food.[124]

How do we know these things?
The written word records,
victims and persecutors recorded,
records survived;
survivors testified.[125]

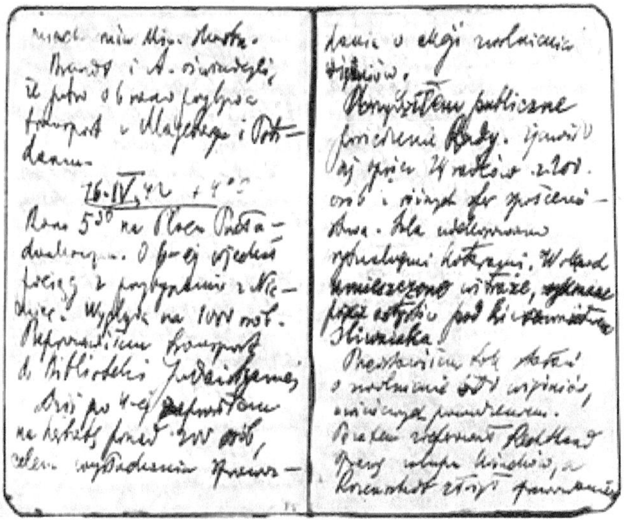

CHAPTER 12: WITH(OUT) COMPASSION AND LOVE [126]

Ghetto late 1940–mid-1941

Jean-Paul Sartre said in 1947:

> *'In whatever circle of hell we live we are free to break it.*
> *And if people do not break it, then they stay there of their own free will.'*

But in what way were these people free?

The poor, rounded up for slave labour, starve and die of disease.
The wealthy sell their jewellery, clothes and possessions,
they buy food, pay tributes.
The assimilated Jews and converts – some volunteer, others forced –
join those they had sought to leave.
The Polish priests try to help the converts, 'their brethren in Christ'.
Some priests speak out to their flock
telling them their duty is to help Jews.
The intellectuals debate the decline in Jewish standards, extol
the spirit of Christian charity and the joy of a God held in the heart,
not outside in the void: Jesus in the heart, YAHWEH in the void.
The Orphanage Director Janusz Korczak – writer, pedagogue, doctor –
despairing, says: 'Life is so hard and death is so easy!'
Once-respected citizens – teachers and writers –
are reduced to the status of paupers; shamed in their circumstances,
they neither ask for, nor are able to offer, assistance.
Polish police brutality is such that Christians are seen wiping their eyes.
The Judenrat have no money to pay council workers.[127]
The Steam Teams stand for hours, wait to be undressed, inspected,
disinfected, released, risk being caught again.
Food packages smuggled in from neutral Europe

> *bring sustenance and bartering.*
> *Youth groups, deflected from their goal of emigration to Palestine,*
> *focus on training for the looming spiritual and physical realities,*
> *and The Oneg Shabbat chroniclers inform:*
> *there are more dead in the street than loaves of bread in the ghetto.*[128]

So, in Warsaw, more than a year passes; over 365 days since bombs fell. Amid apprehension, drudgery, tedium and numbing daily horror there is a midday dance in late 1940 – lively music, laughter of the young, a gay atmosphere. Basia's friend Stella, the girlfriend of Heniek's best friend, introduces Basia to Heniek. Basia is seventeen, Heniek is eighteen, their attraction is immediate, mutual, motivating. The wonder of love-at-first-sight – their voices shy, their hearts aflame, the present endurable, the promise of a future beckons.

Basia is still in her home at 18 Muranowska Street which, being on the corner of Pokorna Street, falls within the north boundary of the area called 'big ghetto'. The small third bedroom, no longer a store, houses a family relocated from Łódź. Their movements, using the kitchen and bathroom, emphasise the lack of privacy, but relative to the general deprivation, this is luxury. And with Pinkus' contacts and initiative they are not hungry.

Heniek's family, now in two rooms in a house at 26 Twarda Street (a continuation of Graniczna southwards), are in an area known as 'Little Ghetto'. The phones don't work, communication is difficult, and travelling from one area to another involves many dangers. But zigzagging a distance of some four kilometres, beating the 7 pm curfew, such things do not impede a young man in love. He comes often to be near his Bashenka,[129] traversing from one end of the ghetto to the other, and each time he stays a bit longer.

For her he is the embodiment of hope.

And for now there is good news. A sign that the world outside sees their predicament comes in the form of life-saving insulin for Sara, sent via the Red Cross by Jacob's sister Fella, from faraway France.

To regulate trade between the ghetto and outside, transactions were supposed to go exclusively via Transferstelle – the German office responsible for the movement of supplies – this with a transfer fee of 10–25 per cent. Officially forbidden, further food was available in the free market at exorbitant prices. Breaking the edicts, both the Polish population and the Germans, bought from Ghetto stocks, further diminishing that available for the inhabitants. Some 4,000 craftsmen and workers worked for Jewish manufacturers filling out orders for the German authorities. Sabotage, such as sewing pockets in upside down, rife and punished. A further 4,000 involved in meeting military needs. Almost 34,000 Jews 'economically active' according to employment statistics. Perhaps 50,000 occupied in illegal trade and, with rations too low to sustain life, Germans turned a blind eye to smuggling because not only did Jewish workers support production, but also, smuggling being the chief form of trade, it offered opportunities galore for the Germans soldiers to profit.[130]

Records confirm that the *Judenrat* officers, including the president Czerniakow, he an engineer, teacher, previous council member and senator, had all suffered arrest and beatings.[131] Dished out for any sign of protest, these assaults were hidden from the Ghetto inhabitants lest this knowledge add to the fears. Czerniakow continued to cooperate, not knowing that the 'Final Solution' (*Endlösung*) had entered a new phase.[132]

To Plac Muranowski somehow wagons bring in vegetables –
the sellers are peasant and farmers; the prices are high.[133]
Those able to provide for themselves decrease.
Relief organisations cooperate, but unable to cope,
they turn people away.
HOUSE COMMITTEES,[134] *set up to organise food to feed the poor*
and sick, become the refuge that the desperate turn to for help;
in the warmth of their kitchens, illegal schools
attempt to continue the teaching of children – For The Future ...
Every problem now connects back to them for resolution:
care of refugees, children's institutions, returnees from camps,
household cleanliness, settle disputes, help needy neighbours;
clandestine meeting place for resistance activities.
While the ghetto appears devoid of compassion, that is the outer layer.
An inner layer, a '... phenomenon ... offering release: compassion
which finds expression in the house-committees ... where
the true Jewish qualities of mercy and charity find realisation.'[135]
And ToPoRol (Towarzystwo Popierania Rolnictwa –
Society for the Support of Agriculture) oversees, during 1941, training

and provision of soil, seeds and cuttings to fill every spare plot, courtyard, balcony, window-box, with vegetables and flowers.[136]

The Birenbaums tackle the needs that present: Pinkus contributes money and uses his connections; the girls help prepare food for the refugees; Rena raises funds. Having employed a tutor for Celina, so she will not fall behind with her studies, Rena sits out of sight surreptitiously taking in the lesson. This is not enough to keep the girls occupied, so, responding to Rena's concerns, Pinkus asks the Muranowska House Committee to allocate additional tasks to his daughters. Basia, given the task of copying out papers, alone, lonely, bored in a cold office, pleads for more useful employment teaching the young refugees crowding into the apartments of the Muranowska courtyard. Request tabled; with her poor school record as evidence, request declined. Disappointed, she accepts the clerical tasks and reads from her mother's extensive library to push away the threatening waves of ennui.

Meanwhile Rena's efforts at fundraising, to give help to the never-ending numbers of displaced people swelling the ghetto population, involves her in the orphanage run by Janusz Korczak[137] with Stefania Wilczynska. Collecting money from friends and neighbours – exhorting them: the orphans must be fed – Rena's respect for this man is boundless.

When Jacob and Sara, early in 1941, receive an offer for Heniek to go to Palestine (at a cost of 10,000 American dollars)[138] the pros and cons are discussed at great length. Why travel with false papers through countries under German rule when you hear of those whose attempts have resulted in incarceration or death? Why take such a risk when the great powers will soon defeat the Germans and sanity will return to the world? The main thing is to stay together. Thus concluding, they discourage Heniek. Some young people do go; he, unwilling to leave his parents, stays on. But staying presents an immediate danger for any young strong man: that of serving time in a labour camp.

A bizarre opportunity is presented to him. He is told that the

Germans have established a technical college as propaganda to show the world, via film, the happy faces of young men in the ghetto; proof of how well they treat the Jews. Heniek sits an entry exam, gains a place.

Here he finds a haven.[139]

> The news of Germany's invasion of Russia in June 1941 raised hopes; the decisions to hold out was vindicated.
>
> Come summer July 1941, despite searing hot days, those in the ghetto felt reassured when German manufacturers' 'shops' appeared. Authorised to operate in the Warsaw area, 'employing' 8,000 workers, they created, via industry, a sense of being needed and safe.[140]

And what of life outside the ghetto?

Those within might have imagined those outside were free,
but no – absolute terror reigned, but not absolutely.
Counter-terror endeavours – acts, small and great, of courage,
persistence, resistance – flourished, albeit surreptitiously.
No poetic justice evident; it was all in the choice
of a moment, good will, good fortune.
Everywhere examples of the best and the worst in Man –
Man supported, Man undermined.
All the shades of the heart. In addition,
Hope, the perennial motivator.
How in all this are we to make sense of the Sixth Commandment?
The one that says, Do Not Murder[141]
and the injunction that says,
Nation Shall Not Lift Up Sword Against Nation.[142]
Yet another dichotomy to confound.
And an oft-heard phrase
whenever one points to the saving help from a Polish gentile is:
'If only there had been more.'
But how to measure how little or much there was?

Gives thanks for that which was.

PART SEVEN

(A)SHAMED

DO NOT COMMIT ADULTERY [143]

An image comes to mind – keys have been thrown into a circle.
My mother's story, told to me in confidence, when I was perhaps fifteen.
Vivid is the memory of her shocked expression at a 'game' being played
by married people she knew: car keys (or was it house keys?)
thrown by each woman
into the centre of a circle and gathered at random by a man.
And a story of a friend who, on discovery of her husband's infidelity,
placed her pretty head in a gas oven.
And a few years later, another taking her departure by way of the
obliging gas. Sad lonely women – survivors of much horror,
courageous in settling in a new country,
and in raising children without families to support
yet unable to withstand the shame of spousal betrayal.

But my concern here is with a shame beyond infidelity.
That of humans being branded, herded, beaten.

Branding brings me an image of my godmother. My Mrs Rotstein.
The picture in my mind is of her on a day I visited her at her city shop,
named Koh-I-Noor after the famous diamond –
a twin shop to the one in Acland Street in St Kilda
which my godfather Mr Rotstein manned.
It was late December 1962, just weeks before I started university.
The day I should have told her,
I Love You Mrs Rotstein.

Her face breaks into a smile as I enter the shop.

'Wake up, Mrs Rotstein, it's six o'clock!' she teases, adding, 'Go wake your muzzer.' And I say, as I had when I was three, 'My Mummy is asleep.'

This memory shared, we embrace. She stands behind the counter as I thank her for her recent card for my seventeenth birthday and we chat about my plans for the summer.

I can see her still. Eyebrows arched, black pencilled Marlene Dietrich thin; brown eyes full of pleasure and affection; lips painted soft red – the red blood-stark against still winter-pale alabaster smooth skin, smile and laugh contagious, her personality enlivening; one could not stay serious in her presence. No sign of ill-effects from long hours in what must be lonely, boring work; a Gracie Allen[144] facsimile incarnate albeit without the hilarious twisted logic. With blonde coiffed hair shining palely, always as if just done by the hairdresser, Anka Rotstein was petite, neatly elegant in a just-below-the-knee straight black skirt, a pleasing contrast to the pastel-pink plain blouse – the blouse's tie held in place with a simple 18 carat gold brooch, the long sleeves buttoned at the wrist.

It was summer. It was a warm day – long sleeves?

Long sleeves to hide the number engraved on her arm.

You do know about this mark – this Nazi outrage. Yes? No?

> In Auschwitz concentration camp 'selection' took on new meaning. Prisoners selected as workers, received a serial number, an indelible tattoo. Prisoners selected to go directly to the gas chambers, did not get a number. The location of the tattoo on the body varied.

My godmother's number, tattooed on her inner left forearm just above her wrist – evident during summer, at the beach or at picnics or out dancing, when among friends she wore short sleeves, bathers, or evening clothes – an obscenity I tried to ignore. In the shop, she kept it hidden.[145]

During the following year, at uni, when I saw *La Strada* for the first time, I gazed at the pale expressive face of Giulietta Masina as Gelsomina. I knew that there, minus the pathos, was my Mrs Rotstein's look-a-like. Endearing Gelsomina arouses sympathy; her demeanour evokes a person mistreated. So alike. So different. The tragedy was there for both but my Godmother's was real and not on show for others.

Whatever Anka Rotstein had lost, like the number on her arm, she kept sadness out of sight. I knew her to sing, dance, work, celebrate, keep a welcoming home, all with gusto and verve; life was to be lived. Childless – any children by her first marriage perished in the Holocaust – she treated me like a treasure. She died in 1983. The love I felt for her was as if I'd had a bit of my grandmother. I wish I had told her. I tell her now:

I love you Mrs Rotstein.

And thinking of Mrs Rotstein begets potent memories of Eli,
and with that glow, in a time when there was so much to love,
a recall of a day when I learnt a 'truth', and past became present.
And Time Lost Meaning.

Easter Holidays already! Passover this year, autumn 1960, is at Mrs Rotstein's home. Fun and merriment. Beautiful table setting, white cloth, silver candelabra and silver chalice for the prophet Eliahu.

A delicious dinner is enjoyed by a small gathering comprising my family of four, Mr and Mrs Rotstein, and Mrs Rotstein's sister and brother-in-law. Mr Rotstein conducts the Seder seriously but not solemnly; it doesn't seem to take as long as at my cousins.

In no time we are singing 'Ehad Mi Yodeah' ('Who Knows One')

and 'Chad Gadya' ('Only One Kid'), finding the affikomen – the piece of matzo hidden for the children to seek – the finder demanding a reward: we let eight-year-old Janette find it, much to her glee! All the while, we laugh so much, and we finish with Mrs Rotstein's favourite,

'What will we do with a drunken sailor?'

Our eyes stream with the hilarity of it.

Just weeks later we are at Hanging Rock, where we have been coming for picnics ever since we stayed at nearby Mount Macedon when I was eight. That first time we surveyed horse races from the plateau at the top. Today after lunch on the grassy slopes, watched by cheeky magpies, who swoop from towering gum trees, we clamber together with many other visitors.

On this glorious day, as we climb, we keep a lookout for koalas.

'There is one!'

'Where?'

'There.'

'Oh, look!'

Every one stops to look and admire.

At last, at the top, we stand near the edge of our private clearing where we can see forever, all the way to 'The Cross'.[146] While the adults perch on rocks to rest and flirt, we children scramble onwards, looking for familiar spots and discovering new ones.

We enter a narrow corridor between high boulders. It leads to an opening with what looks like a giant spider's web etched into the rocks, and beyond that, huge caves, dark and mysterious, tumble. Strange here; despite our exertion, we shiver. Suddenly we've had enough. Back to the group, we are flushed, laughing, happy.

Then to Mrs Rotstein's for a light dinner and Eli is there.

Eli, a recent émigré, being Israeli-born he is a Sabra. He tells me his mother is Mrs Rotstein's cousin. I like him right away. As if we have been friends forever, we lie leaning on our elbows on the floor and rubbish Superman.

TV is no longer a big deal; we've had one for ages. At home we watch it in our lounge room decked out with new Danish deluxe furniture and colourful walls – I love the burnt orange contrast with lime green.

My favourite shows: *Father Knows Best*, *The Hit Parade*, and *The Adventures of Ozzie and Harriet*, starring The Nelsons: Ozzie, Harriet and their sons Dave and Ricky. When Ricky croons, his look from under those long lashes is straight at me; I just know his eyes must be green.[147] This is what Prince Charming will look like. Oh! I nearly forgot – I love *77 Sunset Strip*, with its cool theme and Kookie, played by Edd Burns, always combing his hair while the girls chant: 'Kookie, Kookie, lend me your comb.'

Eli has black hair, cheeky black almond eyes, olive skin. Tall, a year older than me, his American-tinged Israeli accent adds charm to a never-ending stream of hilarious conversation; he makes me laugh until my side hurts with stitch pains.

He tells me he goes to Habonim – a Zionist Youth Movement – says I must come; his group meets on a Friday evening, if I just turn up no one will say anything about my being too young for that group.

To my amazement, Mummy and Daddy say okay. So every Friday night my best friend Slava and I walk in the dark, down Toorak Road to St Kilda Road, tram it to Elsternwick, getting out just a couple of stops before my father's factory, to Habonim, which turns out to be in the same building that was my sister's kindergarten.

The leaders, called *madrichim*, are around eighteen years old. By the time they discover my age, I am part of the group and I convince the *madrich* and the *madricha* to let me stay. The sessions are a lot of talk of Jewish history, of a Theodor Herzl,[148] and someone named Balfour and his declaration,[149] of the history of the formation of Israel, of striving to be Zionists and going to Israel to build a new nation.

My mind wanders; sometimes I feel my eyelids close; I try to keep an interested look on my face. After the history talk, we go into the moonlit concrete yard. Holding hands under the stars we, boys and girls, dance in a circle while singing Israeli songs.[150] We make plans for Saturday night, and of course, there is Eli. So much fun.

All too soon, Slava's father picks us up. All the way home, he hums romantic Polish songs.
So the whole winter passes.

In spring, meetings transferred to Sunday afternoon, we sing,
we dance, in golden sunshine; our voices mingle with birdsong,
our hearts anticipating a magical future.
We are living our parents' rosy dream and we know it.[151]

One sunny afternoon, instead of the mandatory lecture that precedes letting loose, the *madrichim* tell us that we are to
see a film; they warn it might upset us.
Sitting on chairs, we face a small roll-down screen.
Shush. Hushed anticipation.
The projector noise is loud in the room.
The hand-held camera takes us on a slow bewildering tour,
a tour that will shape the rest of our life-journeys.
Peaceful images of long grass give way to paths overgrown with weeds.
Sun-drenched buildings advance and we are inside.
Cubic red brick structures with square metal doors confront.

Before we can frame the question: What is this? …
the film turns into a silent black and white documentary of human
scarecrows and bodies thrown like garbage into a mass grave.

Was there a narrator?
Any words to inform?
What conclusions were drawn?
How long did we sit?

Time loses meaning; it's as if it was yesterday,
not over fourteen years before, that someone filmed these images.[152]

The projector whirrs to a stop; the blinds are opened. We sit speechless.
Eyes to the front – we do not look at each other.
Stunned. Embarrassed. Ashamed.
Blinking in the afternoon sun.
We know we have seen ovens. We know they were constructed and
used to burn Jews. The smoke from the chimneys would have been of
burnt people. We know hell came to earth. We do not know why.
Or how human beings could perpetrate such horror.
Who among us would ask questions? What do the *madrichim* say?
Whatever the words, I do not remember. But I need no one to tell me
that there were people who hated too much, and that Jews,
believing their God would save them, allowed themselves
to be as sheep: herded, branded, slaughtered.

As long as we have Israel, a land of our own,
such a thing cannot happen again and we can walk tall,
safe anywhere in the world.
This is what we know. This is what we believe.

From this day in each breast burns passion for Israel, determination
never to forget, commitment to ensure such a thing never happens
again. Suddenly everyone is reading Leon Uris's book *Exodus*;
for some, a resolve to make *aliyah* – emigration to Israel
to live on a kibbutz, to be part of creating a green paradise
in the desert – forms into more than a wish.

Autumn again – agog we watch as Yuri Gagarin blasts off into space;
Daddy's excitement turns to dismay as the TV shows images
of someone called Adolf Eichmann –

before he switches the channel
I see that there is a trial in Israel of this man.[153]
I sense that Eichmann and the film I saw at Habonim are connected.

In the world, massacres continue;
when I see films or photos of white police striking black people,
something inside shivers.
Why, after all we know, is there is still so much hate?

This question sounds loud in my head, but do not say it aloud.

PART EIGHT
ALL THE PEOPLE

Warsaw Ghetto: late 1941–August 1942

DO NOT STEAL [154]

CONSIDER THE WORD 'ALL'

as in the Anglican Hymn:

All things bright and beautiful,
all creatures great and small,
all things wise and wonderful:
the Lord God made them all.

And in the words of Rudyard Kipling:

All the people like us are we, and everyone else is they.

Now consider the words *all* as in:

'Those ....

Insert: Jews, Germans, Arabs, Poles, Palestinians, Muslim, Politicians, other …

They are all ....'

Insert: drunks, vermin, animals, murderers, parasites, terrorists, crooks, A.H.es …

CHAPTER 13: WHILE LOVE FINDS A WAY … [155]

Days of great joy, with people kissing on the streets in jubilation at good news, followed by despair. Horrifying stories circulate via illegal publications[156] which appear almost openly: the fate of Jews in the Provincial villages – driven from their homes, made to dig their own graves, executed.

In the midst of the shattering of coherence, Basia and Heniek, despite the cramped conditions – due to the extra family in the spare room of the Birenbaum home – find opportunities to steal precious moments to be alone. Basia has little trouble dismissing her conscience's niggling thoughts against intimacy before marriage. She reasons that this is different: the war makes it different – they could die tomorrow. Moreover, he, who can have his pick of many girls, finds Basia lovely, natural and open; the bond between them grows strong and true.

In the evening, sitting in the parlour of Basia's home, Heniek is reluctant to leave. As the sky darkens Basia becomes increasingly agitated for he has far to go – he must cross over Chłodna Street from Big Ghetto to Little Ghetto; with each moment the risk of being caught out after the 7 pm curfew increases.

Chłodna Street is an important thoroughfare; to keep it open Little Ghetto and Big Ghetto are connected by a wooden bridge.[157]

Capture means death: slow in a work camp, instant by bullet or blow.

To stay with Basia in her home is unthinkable as, with the phones inoperable, there is no way to let his parents know he is safe. Basia begs him to leave, pleads with him to give a thought to his anxious mother waiting for his return, and relishes the knowledge that he finds it so difficult to leave her.

When he has left, holding onto her image of him, she shelters in her home, waiting. Minutes tick by; as hours turn to days with no word, her fear drives all other thoughts from her until, at last, she sees him safe again. He is at the centre of any hope for a future.

But in the ghetto and outside, all is incomprehensible.
During October 1941: Little Ghetto is liquidated,[158] *trams abolished,*
boundaries shrunk, number of gateways reduced.[159] *In growing*
numbers beggars covered with newspapers litter the streets.
German soldiers demoralised?[160] *Goebbels' article in 'Das Reich'*
decries as a national crime the feelings of pity aroused in some
Germans at the Jews' miserable state. You have pity for vermin?
Find strength and courage to destroy! So he directs.[161]

The pages of records ring out accusations against fellow Jews
who conspire by action or inaction:
quislings, informers, opportunists, insulated invincible truly rich.
Where else, in your impotence, can you turn?
It seems the world is deaf and blind to your plight.
Wear your new armband:
a black Star of David sewn into a yellow square background.
Know that you are carrier of a loathsome name; despised group.
The 'they' to shun; the 'they' to blame.

Do you censor your words, unable to shame your fellow man?[162]
No wonder, physically and spiritually, you are rent.
Now with winter again, while the converts express disappointment
that Christmas trees have been banned, see children bare-footed in the
snow, see children frozen on the ground.

The people despair at decline in every facet of life and community.
Organised groups[163] *and individual deeds of charity struggle to provide.*
With no agreement on what is right and good, various groups do battle.

THE ONEG SHABBAT: meaning Sabbath Celebrants – convened in October 1939, under the inspired leadership of Dr Emmanuel Ringelblum.[164] The members, of all ages and backgrounds, kept their documentarian activities secret even from each other. Their goal: to maintain morale and convey the whole truth no matter how bitter and dangerous. *Oneg Shabbat* coordinated many illegal activities utilising House Committee kitchens as school, training and information hubs.[165]

THE *JUDENRAT*:[166] This council – installed by the Nazis (most community leaders having fled), advocated that the best policy was to appease and cooperate. Opposing covert activities that compromised relations with the Germans, who they still hoped to manipulate, they deemed attendance at work groups a national duty.

THE GHETTO INHABITANTS: Unaware of the delays, evasions and stratagems, of the *Judenrat*, they had tremendous anger at the council's apparent complicity, which was concomitant with terror of reprisals. With mistrust and dislike internally focused, opposing forces clashed. The general ghetto populace, initially acquiescent, now re-evaluated as returnees from enforced work camps, visibly emaciated and mad from beatings. The returnees found no help had been given to their desperate starving families in their absence; the cooperation policy was revealed as propaganda. Refusing to go, work groups hid.

EDICTS THREATEN: Unmet worker quotas would result in suspension of the food supply; work camps would become penal camps.

THE ORDER POLICE – *Jüdischer Ordnungsdienst*: They enforced round-ups, raiding whole buildings, dragging out the occupants – all done with alacrity.[167]

RESISTANCE GROUPS: Counter to the policy of cooperation was that of resistance. In late 1941, two years since Poland fell, the various youth organisations met to discuss coordinated resistance. While disagreement raged on the form of any concerted effort, the fact that they met generated opposition from those in the community terrified of the wrath of the Germans.

Heniek belongs to the youth club Akiva.[168] His group, like the others, wants to resist but is unsure of how, what, is best.

What if?
Many historians then and now question that perhaps more resistance
and an earlier heroic stance could have translated to lives saved.
The Jews of Poland are variously charged with helping the war effort,
conspiracy in their own extermination, mistreatment of fellow Jews,
mistakenly considering surviving, as they had before,
by sacrifice of some to save the body.[169]

However, each instance is different; only the rule of no rule applies.
One dies by going, another by staying.
One survives by acts of kindness from a gentile; another perishes;
a third survives despite lack of help or betrayal.
The saved report being shot at point blank, injured,
made to dig their own graves; for each saved, thousands are murdered.
Each one's same-different story is individual,
not reducible to archetypal or stereotypical categories.
Until the end of time, many will discuss and debate the what-ifs.

Bear with me. This is the time space place
where thinking of what is to come – then, and with hatreds today –
I become immobilised.

Dream my Way Back

I don't even have to close my eyes to see Grandmother Sara.
She leans over to stroke my hair. Prettier in life than in the photo,
I introduce her to my husband, and my grown children.
Joy sparkles as Sara takes in the jewels …

This image
stays with me, and,
as each fragment makes a contribution,
this recurring waking vision
helps me to continue.

CHAPTER 14: OVERT. COVERT. HURTING.[170]

A glorious poem, recited by many, but not by me,
as, believing it to be of Christian designation, thus forbidden,
I mouthed the words, not wanting to give voice
to a Christian prayer.

Years later I learnt that this prayer was Hebraic in origin.
Such is the blight of ignorance.

Known as the Twenty-third Psalm (of David)
I seek solace in it now.

The Twenty-third Psalm

The Lord is my Shepherd, I shall not want.
He maketh me to lie down in green pastures:
He leadeth me beside still waters, he restoreth my soul:
He leadeth me in the paths of righteousness for his name's sake.
Yea, though I walk through the valley of the shadow of death,
I fear no evil: for thou art with me;
thy rod and thy staff they comfort me.
Thou preparest a table before me in the presence of mine enemies;
thou anointest my head with oil; my cup runneth over.
Surely goodness and mercy shall follow me all the days of my life:
And I shall dwell in the house of the Lord forever.

THAT SECOND GHETTO WINTER OF 1941–42.
The third winter since the invasion – the cold is colder than ever.
Snow lies on the ground; all is quiet.[171]
Long gone are the horse-drawn carriages, cars, trams,
gone are people promenading or bustling about their business.

Any movement in the wide paved streets is of a different nature.
Head down, hurry, make yourself unimportant,
look too poor and too weak to be of interest to anyone. Be as if invisible.
Dive into dark doorways at the sound of marching feet or motor roar.
Trust no stranger, be wary even of friends, motivate yourself,
survive just one more day.

Worn-out clothing? Newspaper will keep out the cold.
Hungry? Find food any way you can. Steal or starve.
And there is no coal.
Are you a worker employed (il)legally?
In a 'shop', or as a smuggler, or a baker?[172]
You who are rich and managed well last winter,
do you now know hunger and cold?
Will you still give from what you have to the desperate and dying,
or hide your shrinking store against coming horrors?
Rich or poor know, you are witness to human evil.
Is some of it yours? Such sin to bring God's wrath?
Even those outside who would be a friend declare:
You must have done something to be hated so!

HOW IS IT YOU STILL MAKE JOKES? Here is one:
Horowitz (A.H.) comes to the Other World. Sees Jesus in Paradise.
'Hey, what's a Jew doing without an arm band?'
'Let him be,' answers Saint Peter. 'He's the boss's son.'[173]

CONDITIONS ARE TERRIBLE
The flow of people from other ghettos is endless;
people are dazed in this strange city;
babies cry as they starve. To such heart-rending cries,
can there be anyone who is inured? The demands too great;
meagre rations insufficient. Obstacles increase, accumulate.

THE FUNDAMENTAL PROBLEM?
HOW DO KNOWN WAYS OF RIGHT CONDUCT APPLY?
Orphans cry in the street and snatch at food.
Dead bodies lie in open view until gathered for mass burial.
The poor lie on the ground covered in newspaper.
Illness due to the overcrowding – fear in hearts.
Even now, people come with cameras: still and movie.
Tourists: Poles, Germans. Observers: Red Cross and Nazis.
Those seeking to do business. Perennial are they.
Thieves bribe their way out of trouble,
the robbed become the guilty party –
revealed as having something to take.
Yet people cling to life; suicides are rare.[174]
Though meetings of any kind are forbidden by decree,
German police act indifferently to noisy discussions which,
after the initial period of secret activity, become increasingly visible.
(Historians will puzzle at the lax enforcement.)
It seems the authorities anticipate no threat from these beings.
It is from the eyes of the Order Police – corrupt by inclination and
opportunity or corrupted by scarcity – that activities must be hidden.

With shame and curses, the dead speak from the records;
they tell of those who, with enthusiasm, invention, and even sadism,
did the bidding of the Germans; thus becoming for all eternity
the Jewish servants of A.H.

So say the ghetto chroniclers, in reflecting the outrage of ghetto residents, directing their rage at the police and not at the Germans.[175]

Heniek, his family forcibly removed from Twarda Street in Little Ghetto to a dreary smaller place at 15 Nowolipie[176] Street is now closer to Basia and no longer runs the gauntlet of the bridge. Apart from contributing to the running of the House Committee kitchen, Jacob and Sara, despite being ill, like many other families, each day share a meal in their home with others; this coordinated through the kitchens which provide succour and a cover for clandestine activities.

Heniek is a 'director' of the Nowolipie 15 kitchen – this is where the business of feeding refugees is discussed.[177] Approached to be a militia man in the Order Police, he considers it. He knows men whose honourable conduct helps deflect the impact of cruel orders on their fellows (and some who let smugglers through without taking any compensation)[178] thereby placing themselves at risk. He knows others to be brutish low-life, with no regard for the consequent suffering of their fellows. They point out the wealthy among Jews to facilitate extortion, satisfying the German's ongoing desire to squeeze every bit of wealth out of the ghetto, one of the odious tasks required of this position. Gathering up people for labour inside and outside the ghetto – to do who-knows-what – is another.

So this is an invitation to be like a *Schmalzovnik*[179] – literally a greaser, a blackmailer or denouncer both of Jews attempting to be incognito, and of Poles providing help or protection. But to be a Jewish *Schmalzovnik*. A Jew-betraying Polack! No, worse than that: a Jew denouncing his own. With the situation getting worse, perhaps he could and should use this post to help his family survive. When he consults friends, they say wait; the dictates of his conscience and his own instinct guide him. No. He would do anything to ensure the safety of those he loved. Anything except this. Not yet.

Many are the signs of collapse: old and young, weakened by hunger and brutality, with their will lost, their strength, their ability to react let alone plan – all essential attributes – diminished. In the midst of this maelstrom, Heniek remains motivated.

From where did he derive the drive?
When I asked him he said, 'We had plenty of vodka.'
But there is so much more.

Heniek was young, healthy, motivated. His family's personal wealth and his tenacity provided food sufficient to maintain vigour. His support network – the links to pre-war socialist comrades in the Polish Underground and companions in his youth club *Akiva,* with their camaraderie and their conviction that they could make a difference,[180] if necessary by their own death – inspired him. He had a beloved family and Basia, his *beshert,* his destined soul mate, to care for. His task, to provide education and cultural programs, combined with a hope that his group and the other youth groups – engaged in constructing bunkers, hiding places and escape routes – would at any moment come together, were future-focused positives that bestowed strength. And Heniek was blessed with an intangible quality: a conviction he could endure and survive to live a good, full, joyful life.

This quality will in the future be called resilience.[181] *And add grit.*

Then there was the huge amount of alcohol smuggled into the ghetto. The Polish Underground, short of arms, unable or unwilling to provide the Jewish Underground with weapons, supplied alcohol instead; bottled spirits energised plans for survival.[182]

In the more than two years since the war began, the time has been spent in adjusting, keeping motivated, surviving and covert cultural and educational activities. Now all youthful energy turns towards escape and resistance. Precious moments with Basia; if only he could tell her how he spent his time – not to brag, but to inspire in her a sense of a possible future. Longing to share, already knowing his Basia well: she would be too apprehensive, fearful of capture, she would nag him to take care, and what would she reveal under duress? He tells her nothing of these things. For her own good. Instead, he reassures her – soon it will be over.

The two young people, just eighteen and nineteen, desperate to marry, see the approaching wedding of Zosia to Adam Poznanski as an ideal opportunity to announce their engagement. Rena discourages them: 'You are too young, there is time for such a step … perhaps after this war.'

Zosia marries her man with a celebration in the family home, the second bedroom, that happy shared retreat of the three girls, now the bedroom of the young couple. Basia and Celina make their bedroom in the lounge-dining room. Hope and happiness and plans.

During all this upheaval Pinkus maintains his links to the outside through his connections to Pan Babicz. This Pan Babicz had been a colleague in the idyllic days before the war; now, as well as being Pinkus' associate, he helps the Birenbaums and their extended family.

He risks much: the German decree of 15 October 1941, exclusive to Poland, concerning anyone caught helping Jews, is summary execution for the person and the person's family. Pan Babicz risks himself, his wife and two sons. Pinkus is not alone in this type of connection.

All shades[183] *of goodness, mercy, cruelty and evil.*

On 7 December 1941, with Pearl Harbour bombed by the Japanese, America entered the war. At last the USA to the rescue! Rumours of the occupation of Vilnius[184] by the Russians on 2 January 1942 further raised spirits; predictions of the impending end of the war took on an aura of credence. But financial support from the American Jewish Joint Distribution Committee ceased, the self-help organisations that had relied on voluntary donations, now desperate for a means to find money, imposed taxes. The house committees imposed a double monthly payment: one for the benefit of self-help, the other for the needs of the apartment house itself. 'A person carrying a bucket went from apartment to apartment, collecting food, goods and clothing from the more fortunate ... To enforce its effectiveness, the house committee's weapon was to shame the selfish, by displaying their family name at the entrance to their apartment building.'[185]

To everyone's surprise, there was an offer from monasteries: refuge for a fee.[186] A token look-good last-minute effort? The Catholic Church and the Pope had thus far played a shameful role. This surprise offer was cause for debate, opportunity and danger: the opportunity of life, the danger of conversion. Some said NO – better to be a martyr. Some said YES – martyrdom is not part of Jewish history[187] – the risk is secondary if some souls are saved for the future. The rule of individual conscience dictated: some children left the ghetto to safety and a Christian life.[188]

A little girl begging in the snow is heard singing:
'Winter is come, winter is here'.[189]
The Zionist organisation Hashomer, in mid-winter January 1942,
begins armed resistance with an armoury of two pistols;
the Socialist Bund independently coordinates with the Polish socialists;
the club Akiva affirms its links to the Polish People's Army.
Boisterous discussions identify two mutually dependent problems: the need for arms, and the need to link to the Polish Underground who, contemptuous of all this infighting, make their condition for aid clear: they will not deal with separate groups.

As pressure builds, the ideologically incompatible resistance groups, with their disparate views, struggle, unable to speak as one voice.

Pan Babicz and Pinkus open an 'office' in January 1942 in the Hotel Britannia which, located at 18 Nowolipie Street, provides excellent cover.[190] In the cellar of this hotel is a nightspot; there one can find revelry and opportunity for loose conduct at high prices.[191] Here Pinkus and Babicz meet 'on business' as 'Directors' and make plans without arousing suspicion. Soon it will be over! Imagine, soon one will be able to walk alone or with friends in a park or cross over the Praga Bridge and visit the zoo. Imagine life back to normal! Thus they make their plans in the context of a rational world with some shred of remnant coherence.

How could Pinkus and Pan Babicz know an unimaginable singularity
that would normalise the unbelievable
occurred around the same time that they set up in the hotel?

THE WANNSEE SINGULARITY – WITH HINDSIGHT

The killing program thus far had varied with demands for labour by the war efforts and enterprises. However, A.H. desired the removal of all Jews from Europe (some 9.5 million to 11 million men, women and children)[192] to somewhere else. This was proving too difficult; the rest of the world would not cooperate! Killing since *Kristallnacht* continued: by car exhaust fumes, bullets, blows, incarceration, ghettos, hard labour, starvation; all methods – too slow, too costly, too obvious. Those who witnessed were terrified; those who were directly involved in these methods of murder – particularly of children – complained that it left a bitter taste in the mouth … thus it hampered the war effort.[193]

The Wannsee Conference, held in Wannsee, Germany, on 20 January 1942, organised by SS Major Adolf Eichmann, under direction of, and chaired by Chief of Security Reinhard Heydrich (Heinrich Himmler's right-hand man in the SS), had exhaustive discussions; there, a group of fifteen high-ranking German officials from various agencies were brought together ostensibly to discuss the 'final solution' of the Jewish question.[194] The answer to that question, whether reached here, or before, or later, or never, is still debated, but regardless, in being effected, it brought an inferno, beyond that of Dante's: killing the innocent – not in hell but on earth. This question was not 'officially' resolved at Wannsee. Proceedings kept secret; documents found, subsequent testimonies given[195] – made clear that politics overrode law and labour needs; cooperation was demanded – all eleven million European Jews were to be 'evacuated'.

Thus with responsibility for killing Jews turned over to bureaucrats, the killing – strategised, resourced, systematic, efficient – took on a life of its own, giving new meaning to 'following orders'. From history we know too many would participate, some with enthusiasm, and profit in grotesque ways through enforcement of human misery, but do not imagine there was universal acceptance of annihilation. Rumblings in Germany were such that the Nazi leadership appealed – to duty, courage, conviction – and warned: beware you who still think to not conform, you will be targeted, incarcerated; cooperate or be eliminated.

Among A.H.'s elite, discussions on ways to hasten fulfilment of their goals, became increasingly daring in scope.

Thus did the Nazis, incredibly clever and cowardly, with conviction and self-awareness – inheritors of Goethe, Rilke, Hegel, Kant and Beethoven – descend to unknown depths of evil.[196]

And over eighteen months after the Wannsee Conference, on 4 October 1943, Himmler addressed the SS generals at Poznan and complained that every German had an A1 Jewish friend.[197]

In spring, 14 April 1942, there is shocking news:
a Łódź Ghetto refugee tells of deaths in Chelmno;
two Lublin refugees tell of the massacre of 70,000 Lublin Jews.
There is disbelief and another layer of hopelessness.
Judenrat leader Czerniakow says General Governor Frank
has assured him the Warsaw Ghetto will not meet the same fate.[198]

ToPoRol continuing its endeavours to grow food, even breeding
rabbits, reports on the jeopardy of successful supply
due to the difficult financial situation.[199]

CHAPTER 15: RESOURCEFULNESS DELAYS, BUT ... [200]

One of the Germans' many 'mistakes'[201] was that in sealing the Warsaw Ghetto, seeking to generate quick disintegration, they had not counted on the efforts of many to help each other. This two-thousand-year-old mutual-aid tradition delayed the Germans from reaching their goals. Despite starvation rations and a reign of tyranny, in spring 1942, a macabre semblance of a social and community order combined at every point with a desperate and indignant disregard for the many edicts. Nor had it occurred to the Nazis that such a well of resourcefulness, skill and courage abided among the Jews. Aided, in no small part, by Jews and gentiles outside.

Such a stubborn lot.
Consider those who blatantly wear the garments and mien of the pious, yet refuse to wear the distinguishing patch; thus by refusing to behave as slaves consciously invite the resultant beatings and sometimes death. Consider those who use subtle ways to be disruptive and disobedient, while others rush to convert, or shave their beards to try to disappear; all can be seen as disobedience and resistance.
Nothing has thus far stopped the defiance: not beatings, not threats, nor edicts, humiliation, degradation, murder.

The Nazis continued with execution of their plan and made adjustments on the go. In today's parlance: lateral thinking, fast tracking, innovative thinking. Without parallel?[202]

Propaganda films to lift the mounting depression among German soldiers, to counter the opposition[203] at home, for use in public relations outside Germany, require film crews to come into the ghetto. With plot-lines nefarious, shoots show the world how German police intervene to save Jewish adults and children
from beatings handed out by Jewish and Polish police.

Excursions to the Jewish graveyard by German tourists are popular. Some, viewing the daily heap of near-skeletons scheduled for mass burial, voice loud approval of this evidence of the Führer dealing with 'The Jewish Question'. Others mutter: 'German culture!' with evident distress. Further entry of Germans is forbidden on health grounds.

New edicts and stratagems: Industrialists and manufacturers are encouraged – with factories, in and near the ghetto – to take advantage of slave labour, to produce goods for the war effort. Under instruction, placards entice: Double Bread Rations! to convince would-be-workers by this ploy to volunteer for this work, for the pass given, for the promise declaring it gives exemption from work battalions and work camps. The lies are believed!

Some 95,000 are registered and many have invested their wealth
for the right to 'work'.[204] *But some question these workshops.*
Are they a haven or a trap? This work. What is it for?
A sense of security? A bowl of watery soup? An extra piece of bread?
As time passes, more and more people come ...
and the work is not really work. What does it all mean?

Many move from their houses to live in flats allocated to the factories,
treasuring the papers identifying the holder as a 'worker'.
Papers that will protect! Against what can these pieces of paper protect?
Perhaps they are something tangible in which to believe.
Proof that I am more than a slave sentenced to death ...

Oh, God surely I do not displease you too much.
Surely I will survive. Surely, oh my God?

With the British RAF carpet air-raid on Germany in late March 1942,
hopes rise, spirits lift, hearts beat. Come soon;
an in-vain plea to a hoped-for saviour – any saviour will do.

In March 1942 construction began on turning the penal camp of Treblinka into a death camp; Jewish labour built this instrument of extermination. Before Treblinka, the population in the ghetto – 350,000 previous citizens plus 150,000 refugees, minus all the deaths – now stood at 400,000. On the night of 17 April 1942, unseen hands dragged 52 people from their homes and murdered them on the street. News filtered through: in other ghettos on this night there were similar raids.

During the day, rumours circulate that 'workers' are promised immunity.
Each night another raid. The foretaste of the new terror.
Many die monstrous deaths at the hands of the imaginative Nazis.
5,000 die of disease in May 1942. Twenty die per day of forced labour.
Many others die the cruel death of slow starvation. Children,
sent out by emaciated starving parents, steal and beg,
all semblance of the essence of childhood gone; desperation –
a symbol of the inability of the community to stem the rising tide of need.
An indelible mark of guilt and shame on a community
that prided itself on looking after the needy,
but cannot curb the ways of death. The worst epidemic is confusion.[205]

The punishment for leaving the ghetto and for smuggling, since November 1941, was death. The Polish police executed women and children along with men. Still, smuggling continued. Smugglers paid off four parties: Polish, Jewish, German police, and also civilian agents. Killings on the street and executions in the prisons took an ironic turn; different branches of the Gestapo destroyed their own know-too-much agents, fearful of discovery by Gestapo rivals.

The Gestapo increases street executions
On 12 May 1942: Four resistance leaders are shot in one night.
On 30 May 1942: More British RAF air raids, this time on Cologne.
On the streets, a better class of well-dressed beggar appears. They
silently present, or politely inform passers-by: not a bite has been
eaten today. But see how shabby are their clothes, how pale their faces.
All worldly goods gone. Furniture become firewood.
The last silver candlesticks sold or traded. Destitute. Choirs of children
and musicians, play in the street. Everyone prays for a cold winter,
to bring a Bonaparte-style defeat to the Germans in Russia.
Another winter before the end of the war? Too long!
On Friday, 26 June 1942: A transmission on English radio BBC
reporting all the facts of events smuggled out by Oneg Shabbat
through the Polish resistance. Realised is a sense of historic mission;
at last the world, which has been as if deaf and dumb,
is proven no longer ignorant of the slaughter.

And a new joke circulates: Two Jews are being led to the gallows ...
The first remarks: 'Anyway, I can see it is turning out for the better ...'
'Silly, going to be hanged and you say it is turning out better?'
'Stupid, can't you see that if the Germans could spare the bullet,
he would not be taking us to the gallows?'[206]

But for most Warsaw Jews, it was too late.
On 19 July 1942 Himmler issued the order for the completion of the 'Final Solution' in the General Government.[207]

ON TUESDAY 20 JULY: HOSTAGES TAKEN –
including Judenrat members and people shot in the street.[208]

ON WEDNESDAY 22 JULY 1942: A DEPORTATION NOTICE[209]
This declares all, except those in jobs for the Germans or the
Judenrat, are to be resettled. The stunned population splits:
those who still believe the lies; those prepared to die resisting.
The first of the selections thus launched;
the Nazis call them Gross Aktion*s.*

THE FOLLOWING DAY: THURSDAY 23 JULY 1942,
THE PRESIDENT OF THE JUDENRAT TAKES CYANIDE.
Adam Czerniakow, the man in charge, refusing to sign the deportation
order, with his attempts to steer, save, stall, all having failed, he
suicides. (His diary, published much later, reveals he truly believed
he could save most of the people in the ghetto.) His final note:
'They want me to kill the children of my people ... I am powerless,
my heart trembles in sorrow and compassion,
I can no longer bear all this ... '

ON TUESDAY 28 JULY 1942:
THE KERNEL OF THE ŻOB IS FORMED.[210]
Hashomer Hatzair, Dror (Habonim), Akiva, these three Zionist
pioneering youth movements put aside their differences.
With Poalei Zion (Workers of Zion), a Marxist workers group,
and the non-Zionistic Socialist Bund,
they call themselves ZOB – Zed Oh Beh:
Żydowska Organizacja Bojowa. The Jewish Fighting Group.
Formed as an extension of the youth organisations, with most
members having been young socialists before the war, now tenuously
linked to the Polish Underground – the left-wing Polish People's Army
– with no weapons, its purpose is to continue to:
prepare forged documents called 'Passierchein' (passes),
to disseminate information within the ghetto and to the outside,
construct escape routes over rooftops and through the sewers,
circulate Underground newspapers,
build and equip cellars and bunkers as hiding places,
acquire uniforms of the Waffen SS, and generally disrupt and sabotage.
The largest bunker at 18 Mila Street,
the ZOB headquarters, holds 300 people.

Mila Street is one street from Basia's home,
18 Muranowska Street – where there is also a bunker with 28 people.
At 7 Muranowska – which will be the headquarters of
the ZZW (the Jewish Military League)
there is a cellar with access to the Aryan side.[211]

ON WEDNESDAY 29 JULY 1942: POSTERS GO UP
offering 3 kg bread plus 1 kg jam
for voluntary reporting to the Umschlagplatz –
meaning holding area or transferral point.

ZOB warn: the lures of food to volunteers
for resettlement to 'work' camps are a trap. Resist.

Each shop or factory organises its own combat unit.
The Order Police, feared and blamed by the population
for their enthusiasm in doing the Gestapo's work,
bring people in for increasingly intensified transportations.
Many realise the German-fed rumours, of requiring only a small
portion of Jews, to be deliberate deception, and not even the children
will be saved.

Most people, with the hopelessness of the circumstances revealed,
still refusing to believe, minds confused by deprivation,
cannot make sense of the unbelievable.
Stories of the deaths of masses of people in work camps and gassings.
Unreal. Such Things Just Cannot Be.
The inferno is (not) fantasy. The news coming out of Treblinka
from the escapee Zygmunt[212] *has to be wild imaginings!*

Many inhabitants are refugees; Warsaw is not their home.
Bewildered, having been moved several times and, so far, survived,
they choose to believe this is just one more resettlement;
surely, had the Germans wanted to, they would have killed them by now.

So hungry, many no longer care; they come voluntarily to selections,
just in hope of the promised bread.
Some cursing, some fearful, some passive – in God's hands;

ALL IN THIS TOGETHER.

The found writings of the *Oneg Shabbat* tell of these final days. Nineteen-year-old David Graber was one of three men who buried the archive, on 3 August 1942, fourteen days after the trans-settlements began. This extract, part of his Will and Testament, is an example of the outpourings:

We would be the fathers, the teachers and the educators of the future.
We would be the grandfathers of the bards who tell to the grandsons,
to the young the stories of defeats, of keeping alive and perishing ...
We shall certainly never live to see it ... therefore do I write
my last will. May it fall into good hands. May it last into better times,
may it alarm and alert the world to what ...
was played out in the twentieth century.[213]

David Graber, 3 pm, Monday 3 August 1942

CHAPTER 16: ALL THE FAMILY STILL ALIVE

5–9 August 1942

Especially do not feign affection. Neither be cynical about love,
for in the face of all aridity and disenchantment it is perennial as the
grass. … Beyond a wholesome discipline, be gentle with yourself.
You are a child of the universe no less than the trees and the stars;
you have a right to be here.[214]

Max Ehrmann

In this place that once boasted a stimulating cosmopolitan life:
purposeful bustling people enjoying cafes, trams, beautiful parks
with flowers and courtyards with their shade trees filled with birdsong,
on the hot summer day of 5 August 1942, the orphanage director
goes to his death with his children. This highly respected and
dedicated doctor, pedagogue, humanitarian – the man who'd said:
'Every man wants to contribute one more thing' –
marches with his 200 orphans. Joshua Perle, an eyewitness, tells:
'Two hundred pure souls, condemned to death, did not weep.
Not one of them ran away. None tried to hide. ...
The very stones of the street wept at the sight of the procession.'[215]
The director, known as Janusz Korczak, born into an assimilated
family, could have chosen safety in Palestine or sanctuary
offered by Zegota, the Polish Council to Aid Jews.[216]
This day it is not he that has been 'collected', but the children.
Such is the esteem in which Poles and Germans hold him, that at
Umschlagplatz comes another saving effort from one of the SS officers,
acting on his own or under instruction.
But Korczak will not abandon his charges.
In silent orderly protest he and the children
enter the already jammed waiting death train.[217]

Yet another escapee[218] *from Treblinka, 50 kilometres away,*
returning to Warsaw, tells of the ovens and beseeches:
'Don't go! Fight! Die on the spot!'

The Order Police, aiming to soothe the populace, still declare:
'The selections are for trans-settlement!'
When they took on this unpaid work,[219]
these men believed they could thus survive.
The dead and living mourn them and curse them for their complicity.

From the ghetto Underground come heroic instructions:
Fight! Do not allow yourself to be taken. It is a trap – hark our motto:
To Live with Honour and Die with Honour.
Resist! Die with dignity! Rise up, our people, fight with your lives.

And hear those souls who cry out to their leaders: are you blind?
Haven't you learnt anything from Lublin? We too will all die!
But in our dying may we at least alert the Poles,
who must know they are next.

Hassids still cite scriptures: at last to meet the Messiah!

The hungry, so long subjected to disorder – confused,
compassion dulled, having lost themselves – still volunteer!
Meek, they fill the quotas by offering themselves
to feed the waiting trains.

Soldiers proclaim: The Jew is verflucht*! Accursed.*
Daily quotas grow: 6,000 ... 10,000 ... 15,000 ...

Jewish police! Don't you want any more to meet your portion of quotas?
That's okay, your family will do.
Too late, the Order Police watch their families taken away.

And a cry goes up: pray for redemption for all who suffer!
Pray for the whole world.
Save the young that they emerge calm and steeled.
Ready them for a better world.[220]

Four days later on 9 August 1942, Rena and Celina are gathered and taken to the Umschlagplatz. That night finds all the members of the two families assembled at the Hotel Britannia, where for some time the Birenbaum family has been living. Rena and Celina are there too, their release effected through frenzied activity on the part of Pinkus – this involving many exorbitant bribes.

The depth of the nightmare irrefutable. A cataclysm is upon them.

Sensing the next day will be worse rather than better than this dying day, there is unanimous agreement: Basia and Heniek must marry immediately, while they are all still together.[221]

Everything has been made ready. No time for proper preparation; no wedding dress or invited guests to mark this celebration. But this is not an occasion for lamentation.

In the midst of their beloved family, under a hurried *chupah* (canopy) and with the breaking of the glass, the young couple: Basia nearly nineteen, Heniek nearly twenty, are married by Heniek's Uncle Hilmier, President of the Berlin synagogue.

On this important date, 9 August 1942, from Jacob comes a surprise gift of a beautiful engagement ring, promise of eternal beauty and goodness.

And to join them in long life as man and wife, the blessings are sealed with a plain gold band, the *mazeltovs* resound, toasts are drunk: to life, to health, to happiness.

The young couple cling to each other, happy in their love.

Alive in the present.

The whole family.

Still alive.

I write the words. I treasure this moment. No more for now.
I return to the present lest in such remembrance I lose myself.

PART NINE

LONGING FOR THE (IM)POSSIBLE

DO NOT BEAR FALSE WITNESS

Nietzsche said:

> *Words are but symbols for the relations of things to one another and to us; nowhere do they touch upon absolute truth.*

Carolyn Forché, unveiling of the manifold ambiguity of truth, said:

> *Figures dead and alive whispering not truth but a need for truth when one word is many things.*[222]

Lion Feuchtwanger said:

> *But many motives combine to produce an action … of every action base and noble reasons are inextricably mingled. There is no truth which does not consist of many truths.*[223]

The Commandments Ten
do not include tell the truth *as a categorical imperative;*
it is the Ninth Commandment – 'Thou shalt not bear false witness' –
taken to mean not lie – that implies the telling of 'the truth'.
Its intention is to prevent slander and perversion of justice.[224]

Andy Andrews asks: *How do you kill 11 million people?*
He answers: *Lie to them.*[225]

And A.H. – the great liar was also a truth-teller
in that he said what he would do and then did it;

speaking not of himself but the Jews
he identified the concept of the big lie.[226]
His words are commonly simplified as:

'Make the lie big, make it simple, keep saying it,
and eventually they will believe it.'[227]

Though truth hides in the shadows,[228]
all these words are true, and knowing the truth will set us free.
This we are told; is that what we believe?
The black and white tsunami of words and images on our pages and
screens, an endless inadequate assault of the record that –
no matter how true – conveys but the outer reality.
Facts are facts: ships sail on water,
the sun 'rose' this morning, the ovens were,
but, in the light of such knowledge, who knows truth?
And is it okay sometimes to lie?
There was a Sunday morning in July 1995 when
Auntie Mania told the truth;
I wish she had not.

My sister Janette and I sat, restless after being regaled for over two hours with a sparkling account of Auntie Mania's life. Daddy's cousin, Mania, beloved keeper of the stories of long ago, in all the talk in her accented English, had not, alas, revealed anything new. As Janette and I made eye contact over her head, voicelessly confirming our mutual dismay, Mania divulged that she had corresponded with her cousins in Poland, particularly with Fella, Daddy's eldest sister, just two years older than Mania; their letters revealed their desire to come out to Australia. We hadn't known that!

And then …

'In 1936, Faygalleh – my mother – brought out her brother's children Pesakh and Norman Degenszajn …'

Mania stumbled.

'Mother wanted to bring her sister, and all the family, out of Poland.'

Janette and I, we sit: silent, immobilised.

'Father was a hard man. He said to mother, "Those girls don't even know how to make a cup of tea; how would they manage here?"'

Mania paused … I suppressed a rising scream.

'We did not know what was happening in Poland.' Glancing at me, seeing I did not protest, she continued: 'A few years after the War, Dr Atlas came to my father's house in Bay Street and told us Heniek was alive in France! Oy, we were so happy!

'When Heniek came after the war we were all still struggling … Your parents found it hard to adjust. My father wasn't easy. Your father started manufacturing. You were a beautiful little girl, only three, but so clever. Your mother was so beautiful – whenever we walked together, everyone turnt around.' She sighed. 'Your father …' Her eyes conveyed the young man Heniek was. 'Your mother – she gives in.'

Our smiles firmly fixed, we awkwardly nodded our agreement. Abruptly Mania brought out a box. A box of photos. Most we had seen before, but a few were new to us. Giving in to our pleas, she let us take them to copy.

Once we were in the car, Janette expressed her rage. I soothed her, saying at least Mania had told us the truth. Exhausted and despondent, envying Janette her energy, I just wished I could see those faces beyond the two dimensions. Janette took possession of the photos.

The following Friday at Mummy and Daddy's she set the originals and the copies on the table. More disappointment: the lovely faces we had taken to be different sisters, each one was of the eldest, Fella.

That night, gazing at this face, sadness engulfed and a flood of words spilt out onto the page. Over the years, more adhered. This angst ode to the inexpressible – beyond my understanding of symbolic or real – an opaque cry to bear witness – I called *A Face in the Sepia.* And have put it away for another time.[229]

Truth – knowing it – telling it.
Kant declared one must truth-tell
even if it causes the death of another,[230]
But way back, Socrates, via Plato, taught:
'Is it true; is it kind, or is it necessary?'
Is the converse of telling the truth necessarily false witness?
Our words fail.

What if, to prevent hurt, to soften reality, to survive, to save a life, to answer an inner truth – you needed to tell an outright lie?

Consider Sister Simplice in Victor Hugo's *Les Miserables*. This nun, renowned for telling the truth, lied twice: first with a 'yes', then with a 'no', in answer to Police Inspector Javert's questions. She did so offering her soul in exchange for Jean Valjean's freedom. Could you, in discernment of right from wrong, tell such a lie and risk damnation? To save a friend? Yes? Good. Bless Sister Simplice, her example. What if, in order to survive, you must break the law of the land? Would you? Yes? No? Anything to survive? Anything? What if, to help another, say someone you don't like, even dislike, could you, would you, defy edicts – edicts that lay claim to being the law (and thus to encompassing what is true), edicts punishable by death? Yes? No?

You don't know. I don't know either.

Some say that truth can only be experienced
and changes in each moment.
Our courts purport to discover/uncover truth but don't always get it right.
Language betrays yet the individual is a witness
and via words and images can convey what is true.
Can we find the space between?
The space between your truth and mine, between rules and anarchy,
the space wherein resides common sense, humanity.
Choice – choice can be our ultimate freedom – and the right thing to do.
Over time I find many have tried: to define, refine, transcend.
Some say only God can know the Yes-No of a situation –
where Yes–No denotes one who knows
when to say Yes, when to say No;
Yes No is conversely a contemporary cliché conveying ambiguity.
Both apply.
Within the Warsaw Ghetto all concepts of (un)truth,
(in)decency and (im)morality were tested;
the inhabitants that had adapted had hung on this far.
What unfolded in the prelude to the finale to the ghetto purgatory
still eludes our understanding.
My mother would ask: 'How did all this happen?'
And then answering her own question, she'd say:
'I think it is all beshert.*'*

PART TEN

BESHERT?

Warsaw: 12 August 1942 – early 1945

DO NOT COVET

(Re)Defining Beshert

The Yiddish word *Beshert* is about things meant to be.

Definers variously say it is:

fate,

destiny,

given,

inevitability,

synchronicity

finding a soul mate.

But doesn't beshert *only apply if you are still here*
to reflect on your good and/or bad fortune?
In which circumstance
Omar Khayyám's immortal verse pertains:

'The moving finger writes; and, having writ,
Moves on: nor all your Piety nor Wit
Shall lure it back to cancel half a Line,
Nor all your Tears wash out a Word of it.'[231]

CHAPTER 17: I WILL NOT WANT?

Warsaw Ghetto: summer, 12–26 August 1942
The year 5702 of the Hebrew calendar

In the year believed by some to be 5702 years after the Creation by the Almighty (blessed be He?), Basia, Heniek, Pinkus, Rena and Celina, are at work in at a German saddlery, *Kurt Roehrich,* at 80 Nowolipie Street, at the corner of Żelazna, right on the ghetto boundary adjacent to a gate.[232]

Five hundred people are employed to manufacture leather goods.

Zosia and her husband Adam are at a different factory.

The soldiers come into the factory, in their execution of a routine selection.

The Gatherers:
They are huge, tailor-uniformed.
They carry awesome weapons.
They shout '*Raus*! *Raus*!'
Such a racket they make.
As if they are many.

Everyone running. Everyone queuing.
Family members separated,
with promises of resettlement.
These terrifiers gather a portion of furnace fodder,
from the factory floor.

The Gathered:
Basia is rounded up with Rena and Celina.
As they stand together,
Rena pushes Basia to the front of the line.

In the counting off – left-right –
Basia is separated from her mother;
is sent back to the work group.

Horrified, Pinkus looks on helplessly;
Rena and Celina are in the pack,
herded with shouts and threats,
to what the terrified call the modern Morlock,
to *Umschlagplatz* go the gathered.

The quotas must be met. No one is safe.
No way to rescue. All attempts fail.

This time Rena and Celina, morphed
into the morass of non-human humanity,
are not destined to be released.

The Countess

Heniek finds a place in the knitwear factory, Felix*;* a Countess, it is rumoured, runs this factory. The 'workers' stand at machines, but in this factory there is no real work. The place, located adjacent to Kurt Roehrich, is in fact a dummy, a surreal haven where, while time passes in endured seconds, numb terrified 'workers' pretend to be busy at machines and tasks; gates are locked against the conduct of selections by the influence of the unseen Countess.

Hear the amazing rumours: this German aristocrat, having had Jewish friends, uses her influence to protect her Jews. People whisper, she is a princess of some kind. The factory is in two parts – one inside the ghetto and one outside – and with 200 people coming and going, this factory acts as a transit point between the outside '*Arysh*' world and the ghetto. The factory's starvation rations are supplemented by purchases from Poles and a restaurant not far away.

Heniek has sheltered here for two weeks. Several times Countess Felix has stopped the soldiers from coming in.

Unknown unsung Countess, bless you.
I long to know about you. I name you 'my Righteous Gentile'.[233]

Whosoever saves a single life, saves an entire universe.[234]

But Where Are You, *God?*
Absent? Weak? Indifferent? A trickster?
Are you, after all, begun as a blank page, not omniscient,
being written by, and thus, learning with us?

Yehuda Bauer[235] *poses: God, if absent, then callous,*
responsible and no longer relevant. To rescue the Jewish God of
Justice and Compassion, Bauer invokes the medieval hypothesis that
God is become weak, not all-powerful
and is thus in need of Man's help. And Psalm 115:16 says:
'The earth is given to mankind', implying responsibility.
A foundation for the future: whether one believes in a just God or not,
giving God a helping hand – taking responsibility –
is surely the way to go. Yes.

Regardless, there is no intervention
on the hot morning of 25 August 1942.
The Lord Is My Shepherd I Lay Me Down …
Forever I shall weep when I read these words.

Junaks – Latvian and Ukrainian units.
Do the Jews know this means 'the heroes'?
Curse them![236] *Curse this name.*
These horrifically special commandos – Angels of Death
under the direction of the Einsatz Reinhard[237] *– they come for all,*
not only the first-born son.

Junaks close off the streets. Armed with carbines, Schmeissers (sub-machine guns) and pistols, screaming and howling, they pound on doors, enter each building.

'*Alle Juden raus!! Alle Juden runter!*' All Jews out. All Jews down.

Everyone knows this is it.
They've seen and heard, since 22 July 1942, of the people rounded up
being driven under threats to Umschlagplatz, where
sadistic Schmerling – the Jewish Order Policeman in charge – waits.
Meaning simply transferral point, this square –
adjacent to the goods station which is now
for the deportation of humans
to Treblinka to suffering and death; not to trans-settlement.
Worn, demoralised, confused, near starvation;
beaten by nearly three years of terror,
by incomprehension of knowing themselves as abandoned,
They walk like sheep. No resistance.
They will be blamed for clinging to hope:
That the lies are not lies. That they will live.

Basia and Heniek, having moved in with his parents Jacob and Sara, are in a dilapidated small two-bedroom factory flat in Smocza Street. Known as 'Smocza', the flat belonged to the factory Felix.

When the noise starts, Basia comes in from the balcony. Jacob says, 'Go, the Germans are here. My life is over.'

They hastily construct a hiding place for him, to conceal the door to his room with a cupboard. Back to the landing to see what is happening; caught in the evacuating flood of people … Heniek, for the first time confused, wants to turn back; back for his parents.

Back for Jacob, 57 years old. Crippled with arthritis; unable to move without a wheelchair.

And back for Sara, 55 years old, who almost left but turned back to be with Jacob, who cannot walk.

But this human deluge has Basia and Heniek caught in its motion.

Heniek, realising that this is it, takes Basia's hand and runs past the armed German at the entry.

In the as yet empty courtyard is just one Jewish Militiaman;[238] he points the way shouting, '*Gai*! *Gai!*' Go! Go!

They run, fall into a trench, lie there, quiet, as if dead.

Immeasurable time – minutes? Hours?

Day was, now is night.

All noise, all movement ceased.

Look around. All clear … leaving that trench-of-life, inconspicuously attach themselves to a departing work group.

Back to the flat, climb the stairs – an outrage confronts. 'Mamunia!'

Sara, shot on the stairs landing, her hand stretched out – a pointer.

Enter the room. Take in the scene.

The cupboard shoved aside. In his bed – oh my papa;
thus they lie sprawled as they have fallen.

Both shot. Both dead. Jacob with dum-dum, that bullet which, expanding on impact, creates a larger wound.

Screaming in his head at the horror before him, Heniek seems not to grasp the situation.

Everything goes blank …

Oh, why no tears! No sound!

Alarmed by his stare, Basia calls his name, shakes him, pleads for him to return to the here, the now.

Pain. You. Must. You must. Return. She needs you.

Regains control … Placing his mother next to his father, he stands head bowed. The consuming hollow sensation threatens to engulf him again.

And in his mind Heniek knows it is his duty to recite Kaddish, the traditional mourner's prayer for a close relative, but he is silent.

Oh, where are you now?

In the morning, trusting strangers, he makes arrangements for separate burials in a proper grave, not in the communal grave.

Rest in peace.

Heniek will never know whether those he paid to bury his beloved parents honoured their promise.

On that day, 26 August 1942, Heniek finds all the rest of his family, except for his sister Marisa, have been shot or taken.

Horror follows horror.

No sign of Pinkus. Vanished. Never to be found.

News of Zosia and Adam. Taken.

During. Yet. Another. Selection.

All gone. No more. Blank.
Never to see me hear me know me.
And I never to know them.
And an unanswerable question:

'Why one and not the other?'

My mother's question.

CHAPTER 18: MURDER. SUICIDE. EXECUTION. DEPARTURE.

Selections continue. Basia and Heniek flee; their way out is through the factory Felix, situated on the ghetto boundary near the Lezno Street Gate. In the western *Arysh* sector, they shelter for a couple of days in a place arranged by Director Babicz then hide out in another factory outside the ghetto.

> The final act of the mass deportation took place on the Day of Atonement, 21 September 1942; its victims were the Jewish policemen and their families. The number of Order Service police were reduced to 380. In some 61 summer days from 22 July 1942 to 21 September 1942 the ghetto population had been decimated; of the remnant 50,000 – 60,000 nearly half were 'wild' in that they were not registered. How many had been murdered within the ghetto or taken away to Treblinka? Figures vary.[239] Say 275,000.

275,000. Two hundred and seventy-five thousand.
Try counting it. One. Two. Three …
Give each person his or her name, imagine their face,
acknowledge family members. Spend one minute on each person.
Continue each day. Twelve hours a day every day of the week.
Take over a year to do the saying.

> In the ghetto, the official zone was of two strips either side of a wild zone where the 'wild' hid. Witnessing the roundup of Jews and hearing of the killings at Treblinka, gentiles living around the ghetto fled to the countryside. To stem any sympathy from the Polish population the Nazis broadcast their policy: Death for anyone assisting a Jew.[240]

An announcement by the Chief of SS and Police to the Polish population made on 5/09/1942, and the population reminded days later via both German and Polish posters:

> ANNOUNCEMENT
>
> Concerning the Sheltering of Escaping Jews
>
> A reminder – in accordance with paragraph 3 of the decree of October 15, 1941, on the Limitation of Residence in General Government (page 595 of the GG Register) Jews leaving the Jewish Quarter without permission will incur the death penalty. ...
>
> According to this decree, those knowingly helping these Jews by providing shelter, supplying food, or selling them foodstuffs are also subject to the death penalty.
>
> This is a categorical warning to the non-Jewish population against:
>
> 1) Providing shelter to Jews.
>
> 2) Supplying them with food.
>
> 3) Selling them foodstuffs. Dr Franke ... 9/24/42 [241]

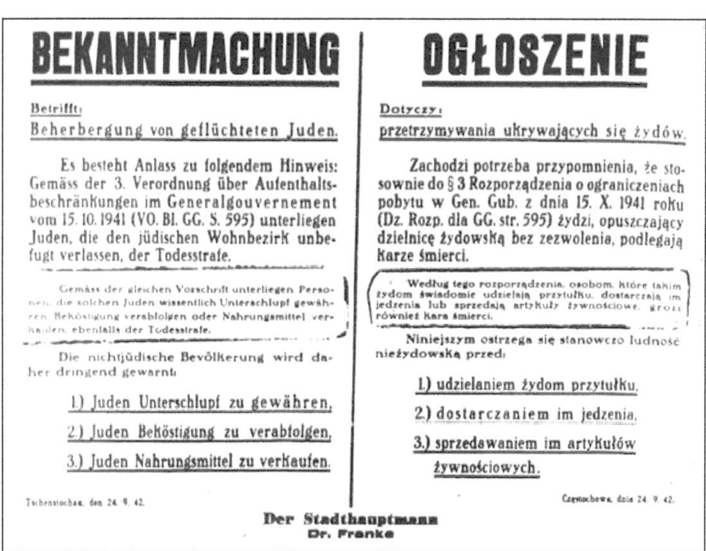

BEKANNTMACHUNG

Betrifft:
Beherbergung von geflüchteten Juden.

Es besteht Anlass zu folgendem Hinweis: Gemäss der 3. Verordnung über Aufenthaltsbeschränkungen im Generalgouvernement vom 15. 10. 1941 (VO. Bl. GG. S. 595) unterliegen Juden, die den jüdischen Wohnbezirk unbefugt verlassen, der Todesstrafe.

Gemäss der gleichen Vorschrift unterliegen Personen, die solchen Juden wissentlich Unterschlupf gewähren, Beköstigung verabfolgen oder Nahrungsmittel verkaufen, ebenfalls der Todesstrafe.

Die nichtjüdische Bevölkerung wird daher dringend gewarnt:

1.) Juden Unterschlupf zu gewähren,

2.) Juden Beköstigung zu verabfolgen,

3.) Juden Nahrungsmittel zu verkaufen.

Tschenstochau, den 24. 9. 42.

OGŁOSZENIE

Dotyczy:
przetrzymywania ukrywających się żydów.

Zachodzi potrzeba przypomnienia, że stosownie do § 3 Rozporządzenia o ograniczeniach pobytu w Gen. Gub. z dnia 15. X. 1941 roku (Dz. Rozp. dla GG. str. 595) żydzi, opuszczający dzielnicę żydowską bez zezwolenia, podlegają karze śmierci.

Według tego rozporządzenia, osobom, które takim żydom świadomie udzielają przytułku, dostarczają im jedzenia lub sprzedają artykuły żywnościowe, grozi również kara śmierci.

Niniejszym ostrzega się stanowczo ludność nieżydowską przed:

1.) udzielaniem żydom przytułku,

2.) dostarczaniem im jedzenia,

3.) sprzedawaniem im artykułów żywnościowych.

Częstochowa, dnia 24. 9. 42.

Der Stadthauptmann
Dr. Franke

Unable to move without papers, money, or things to barter, Basia and Heniek, bewildered about what to do, vacillate. To go back into the ghetto is madness; to stay outside without provisions is suicide.

After a time Basia wants to see what is happening in the ghetto; perhaps it is not true that most of the family is gone.

It is impossible that they are so alone ... Besides they somehow need to get fresh clothes. Heniek, also restless and curious, agrees, and so, at a German checkpoint, where people waited with their papers to enter the ghetto, Heniek and Basia break through. Thirty or 40 people run with them into a German factory, pursued by soldiers shooting point blank so that it destroys the factory; miraculously Basia and Heniek manage to cross into the ghetto unharmed.

There they find a strange lull and, from a high-ranking officer of the Jewish police, comes surprising news of a bag of diamonds. Sara's jewels. Heniek asks him to get the jewels to his sister Marisa. News comes back: Marisa was shot; the jewels have vanished. With her goes the last trace of their families. No one left, not one ... bewilderment.

> A recognition that it had taken a mere fifty Germans in command of 400 Junaks – assisted by two thousand Jewish police to gather and dispatch over 300,000 people with efficient ease, created a sense of numbness. How could this be? Swamping shame at not having resisted did battle with enduring fear of retribution for acts of resistance. This was accompanied by dismay at the ignominious role of the unarmed 2,000 Jewish police! Without them the Germans would have had to tie up their scarce resources to bring about the desired aims.[242]
>
> Furthermore, the efforts of the slave labour, desperately doing anything to stay alive, had inadvertently served the Nazis towards attainment of their goal; thus contributed to prolonging and aiding the war.
>
> The first shipment of guns and ammunition (five pistols and eight hand grenades) had come in August 1942 from the Polish Communist Underground. During September as ZOB rallied to form a desperate gesture of resistance, several ZOB leaders were killed and arm caches destroyed. In October 1942 this kernel of ZOB came together with all the youth groups and with political leadership from ZKN – the Jewish National Council. This secret union of hitherto clashing Zionists and socialists by November 1942 was some 500 strong, and part of the Polish Home Army, AK – Armia Krajowa, who provided weapons and training.[243]
>
> The deportations had stopped; the ghetto and 'shops' were now a labour camp enclosed by a wall of barbed wire under the authority of the SS, with Polish police guarding the wall.

Jan Karski – Polish soldier and spy – delivered his report on the horrors of the ghetto to British Foreign Minister Anthony Eden.[244]

A press release detailing in full the creation, life, management, and emptying of the ghetto was published on Tuesday 1 December 1942.[245]

POLISH FORTNIGHTLY REVIEW

'The Warsaw Ghetto'

POLISH MINISTRY OF INFORMATION

PRINTED AS A PRESS BULLETIN

London – Tuesday 1st December 1942 – No 57

POLISH FORTNIGHTLY REVIEW

EXTERMINATION OF THE POLISH JEWRY

WHAT HAPPENED IN THE WARSAW GHETTO

In mid-December 1942 London MPs Stood In Silence. This was reported in the Press.[246]

> 'The House of Commons, moved by a great emotion, abandoned its routine today to stand silently in abhorrence of Germany's cold-blooded extermination of the Jews.'

While some hide in concealed spaces in false walls, cellars and attics – often with no food or water, Basia and Heniek work again in a German factory.[247] Basia mends and Heniek irons huge piles of uniforms caked with mud and blood, presumably of dead soldiers. Agonising minute by minute days stretch in infinite tedium. The work is not hard, in fact they do little. Even somewhat cheered, they speculate on the significance of the uniforms and the nature of the war raging beyond the walls.

Pan Babicz comes to Heniek with a strange story of hope:

'I have good news for you. You can to go to Hotel Polski[248] and for $US100,000,[249] you will be sent overseas.'

Heniek has heard of Hotel Polski – a place where Germans resided in luxury. Babicz affirms those that took up this offer also lived in luxury.

'No ...' Heniek reasons aloud. 'How can the Germans be so stupid as to permit witnesses out of Europe?'

'You're right; stay where you are,' Babicz agrees.

Then Basia finds that she is pregnant. Jewish babies are anathema. To show defiance of the edict forbidding conception of a Jewish child means death from a bullet. To remain undetected then give birth would result in witnessing remorseless Nazi soldiers smash the baby's head. No good choice! Heniek makes arrangements: over the rooftops out of the ghetto (via the secret paths he'd helped to construct) to the gynaecologist, kind and gentle, a Jew who, having managed to remain undetected, conducts the abortion with no medication. While Basia recovers, he tells of babies killed by their mothers at birth.

Dazed, with nowhere else to go, they walk back into the ghetto via a factory; back to the factory Felix where they do little work. Routine selections do not find them; they have their hiding place on the first floor. Removable bookcase, a trapdoor and, concealed by these shelves, they are overlooked each time.

Heniek is able to leave his post and, with his comrades, continues to construct bunkers and connections between the attics of flats. Selections are no longer placid or orderly proceedings; belatedly, people fight on the spot, actively resisting; accepting a bullet or a smashed skull rather than transport. There are no longer flats allocated to workers and it is too risky at night to hide in the factory.

With no safe place to even lie, Basia and Heniek spend the nights balancing precariously, while trying to catch small patches of sleep out in the open, on the sloping rooftops. Startling at each sound. Hungry.

They steel themselves for what is to come.

> *'We knew ... we had no chance ... We fought simply not to allow the Germans alone to pick the time and place of our deaths. We knew we were going to die. Just like all ... who were sent to Treblinka ... their death was far more heroic. We didn't know when we would take a bullet. They had to deal with certain death, stripped naked in a gas chamber or standing at the edge of a mass grave waiting for a bullet in the back of the head ... It was easier to die fighting than in a gas chamber.'*
>
> *Marek Edelman*[250]

The January Aktion: The plan to destroy the ghetto follows Himmler's inspection of it on 9 January 1943. But on 18 January 1943 when the Nazis commence the second wave of selections and deportations, just six months after the mass deportations, they met with a surprise – resistance that became known as The January Aktion.[251]

The Youth Movements' Response: 'Marian', Mordecai Anielewicz, the 24-year-old Commander of the ZOB, is described as young, plain, modest, inspirational, terrifying. He – as well as the other youth movement leaders: Yitzhak Zuckerman, Yosef Kaplan, Zivia Lubetkin – escaped German-occupied Poland to safety; he, and they, came back to guide, inspire and give succour to the ghetto youth during this time of trial. They killed a handful of Germans, with ten pistols and explosive charges purchased from the Armia Krojowa.[252]

The SS Retaliated: with full battle array: tanks, field guns; 1,200 shot (including *Judenrat* members), and 6,000 deported. The Nazi detachment – initially surprised at the resistance by these inferior beings – used their might, then withdrew.

The ZOB posted notices indicting accomplices: officers and functionaries of the Jewish Order Service Directing Board and the Jewish Council,[253] Shop Directors and Administrative Managers, factory and workshop guards, and more. Executions: by bullet of Jewish traitors – the fifth column[254] – followed swiftly; their deaths announced through notices.

Many charged with complicity by aiding the Nazis, suicided, thus saving the Underground the trouble and the cost of a bullet.

Huge sums of money, forced out of war profiteers, went into the purchase of more weapons. In effect, the ZOB with the ZKK (Żydowski Komitet Koordynacyjne) – the Jewish Coordinating Committee incorporating Ringelblum's Archival Commission and the Bund – now governed the ghetto.

The ZOB slogan: 'Let everyone be ready to die like a man.'[255]

The Jewish Military League: A second Jewish resistance organisation (formed of Betar members) called the ZZW (*Żydowski Związek Wojskowy*), Polish for the Jewish Military League, operating side by side with ZOB, were equally instrumental in the Jewish armed struggle.[256]

The ZOB leaders: Commander Mordecai Anielewicz (Hashomer Hatzair), Marek Edelman (Bund), Hirsch Berlinski (Poalei Zion), Yitzhak (Antek) Zuckerman (Hechalutz), Michael Rozenfeld (Polish Workers' Party), Jochanan Mogenstern, and Zivia Lubetkin.[257]

The ZZW leaders: Commander Dawid Moryc Apfelbaum (Lieutenant, Polish Army, 1939), Commander Pawel Frenkel, Commander Leon Rodal.

'Każdy powinien być gotów umrzeć jak człowiek'

'***Everybody should be prepared to die like a human being***', is the resistance slogan, exhorting the remaining populace not to believe the continuing German and Jewish propaganda of resettlement but to accept the fact of death camps and offer resistance. Together the youth groups prepare for armed conflict and direct their people, 'Save yourself if you can or be prepared to die fighting.'[258]

In this atmosphere, Heniek has been finalising plans for quitting the ghetto. He has prepared well: wool, cotton and gold watches smuggled out to Pan Babicz; false papers ready (this through Heniek's connections in the junior Polish socialists); Basia's hair now blonde, dyed by Babicz's wife who came into the ghetto with a permit.

The warning from ZOB leaders confirms this is it; decision made, he and Basia will go, they will make a final move to the Arysh[259] side.

Where, when, how, decided, Basia is to be a maid to the Babicz family, Heniek is to join the Polish partisans. But when Heniek goes to his Polish socialist contact Wydrych to collect their papers, he is in for a shock. Wydrych warns him against joining the Polish partisans, saying, 'I like you too much to let you get a bullet in your back.'

Heniek expresses his disbelief; 'What are you saying? Me – a Jewish socialist – to expect death by way of a partisan bullet?'

An embarrassed Wydrych spells it out. Many young Jews having escaped to fight alongside the socialists of the Polish Underground have met their immediate death from a bullet in the back. Heniek is astonished. The ZOB resistance has generated respect; Poles now reportedly laugh at the German soldiers. But it seems this is not enough for the partisans to accept a Jew as an equal. Bitter at this betrayal, he takes in the advice. Meanwhile Basia, desolate at the imminent separation, is terrified at the thought of being unprotected in a strange house without Heniek. That settles it; they decide to stay together no matter what. Everything they own they have given to Babicz, who makes the arrangements.

They leave in early April 1943.

So simple to rush now with the telling, to get through hurdles to find the happy end. Reflect for just a moment. Basia and Heniek left just days before the 'Uprising', a liquidation few survived. Those who took part knew the symbolic importance of this act of defiance and these fighters would become the exalted symbol of the Jew in Israel. Heroes, or just choosing the manner of their death, as Marek Edelman insists? Why either–or? Some of them – especially those who could pass as Polish – could have escaped, as did my father, but instead chose to stay. Each one who died, each one who survived, they are all my heroes. God's will be done?

Escaping by attaching themselves to a work group, they leave the ghetto and go directly to the first place; this has tombstones. The owner of this business, a woman with two small children, hides five other people. Guided by a Polish policeman (arranged by Pan Babicz) they move from place to place, danger at each, the risk of death for them and their hosts. They have lucky escapes each time as their leaving is just days before that place is discovered.

Papers are essential for their survival: Babicz arranges for the submission of their false papers through a Polish policeman. Heniek, confident of his ability to pass himself off as a Pole, collects them from Gestapo Headquarters. There fingerprinted, he maintains his cover. Basia's non-Aryan appearance and lack of composure put her in danger of being pointed out by a *Schmalzovnik* – without whose participation many more Jews would have been able to hide themselves in the Polish sector. The policeman suggests she had better not go. His advice proves to be sound. Basia's photo, even with her bleached hair to emulate a Polish Catholic, does not pass; the papers are rejected; new papers prepared, resubmitted; again rejected. Success the third time, but never authenticated with her fingerprints.

It is from Babicz they hear news of The Ghetto Destruction.[260] Everything is levelled. Nothing and no one left.

> In the months of February, March and April 1943, 20,000 people had left the ghetto using their connections to take their chances on the *Arysh* side. Some were hidden; others passed themselves off as Poles.

> Henryk Wolinski, as head of the Jewish affairs section in the Polish Home Army, had liaised with ZOB and had helped gain arms for the uprising; now he begged his commanders to help rescue Jews. Many Jews were linked to the cell of the Polish Underground named Zegota, The Council to Aid Jews. Nearly every Jew who survived was helped by one non-Jew or many.[261]

A blessing upon the Righteous Poles of Żegota, and all those who, in ways big and small, risked their lives to help a stranger. What would you do? What would I?

Heniek's lifeline is Pan Babicz. Babicz's latest idea gives him food for thought. It seems that, as their Polish papers belong to people killed during fighting outside the ghetto, Basia and Heniek could undergo a church wedding to better authenticate themselves as a Christian couple. Heniek debates with himself: on the one hand, it would be great to move about; on the other hand, there is a deep, emotional consideration that he must think through. Before the war – eons ago, though he had held respect for religious observance in his relatives, the Jewish tradition had been for him something self-enclosed, not a part of the new ideas or the multiple possibilities of the modern world, so not the way for a modern Pole like himself.

Now layers of experience: the brutal murders of his parents and sisters, the events of the ghetto, the loss of a way of life – these cement in him a defiance. How can he sully his hard-won Jewish identity by taking part in a ceremony in a church dedicated to a Son-of-God he believes to be venerated by the Nazis? So his decision is formed. No.

Even if it means his death, he will not enter into a sham wedding, in a Christian church, with his beloved; his *beshert*.

He says nothing of this to Basia.

He steels himself for what is to come.

CHAPTER 19: GOD'S LITTLE MICE

He who has a why to live can bear almost any how.
Nietzsche

We were lying there in the dark. Me and your daddy.
Unable to move. Eighteen months in a hole in the ground,
I thought I would go mad,
but I saw a white tablecloth.

Basia and Heniek cling together, dependent on strangers. They are in a hiding place. Blackmailed by *Schmalzovniks* – these denouncers demanding payment – Director Babicz pays, utilising Heniek's goods that he holds in safekeeping. Eventually he finds Basia and Heniek a more permanent set-up: the home of an old retired policeman, Karol Smolarczyk, where Karol lives with his niece Lodzia, in an outer suburb of Warsaw.

For a short time, Karol hides them behind some steps, an ingenious space he fits under a higher floor level with sitting space only. Afraid of possible denouncement by neighbours, in his workroom (which is in the backyard away from prying eyes) Karol constructs a bunker; this he digs out under a large heavy machine that is used to saw timber. Food brought to them once a day is invariably potato soup and occasional scraps of meat. A can, which had once contained tinned cucumbers, now serves as their toilet; Lodzia takes this away daily. Once a week she brings a bowl of water for them to wash their face and hands. The bunker is so small: one-metre-wide by one-metre-high by two-metres-long. Unable to stand, they sit, or lie, in the dark, separated from the dirt floor by a thin matting, with just a threadbare blanket, thus enduring the long days and nights.

Heniek, inventive in helping pass the time, recites poems and school lessons, and makes a draft board and checkers out of bits of card and paper. They read by the light of ends of candles. When they realise this takes their air, Karol rigs up a pipe to the outside; they read for as long as the candle lasts.

Once a month or so Babicz comes: with money to pay Karol, with news of the outside world, with the Underground papers. Basia and Heniek come out of their hole while Babicz, perched on a step, tells of the progress of the war, of the broadcasts on American and English radios, and of direct pleas from Władysław Sikorski, the leader of the Polish government-in-exile, urging the Polish people to hide and help the Jews.

Living in such proximity to their host Karol, they learn of his ways and thoughts: love for Poland, despair at the martyrdom of the Polish people by waves of invaders seeking territory and people to subjugate, deep hatred of the Nazis for the rape and dehumanisation of his country. He gladly shelters these two Jews in defiance of Nazi decree. And, they cannot help but realise that Lodzia warms his bed as, on occasion, does her sister. They also surmise that Lodzia, a woman in her thirties, is jealous of her sister, loves Karol, and both sisters hope to inherit his cottage. Karol, full of hate and love in his concern for his two charges, tenderly beseeches them:

'*Myszki, ne miejcie małe myszeki.*'

'Little mice, please don't make little baby mice …'

In this way,
in the dark, filth, loneliness,
they lived for eighteen months.

ONE AND A HALF YEARS!! 78 WEEKS.
Try to count the over 540 days.
78 Mondays … 1 2 3 4 …
78 Tuesdays …
78 …

Entombed with no knowledge of what the future will bring.
How does one measure such time?
It takes less than two seconds to say eighteen months.
However, it is as if enduring many lifetimes to live
these days and nights.
The time between the repetition of the few minor activities –
food to be brought, snatches of reading, the imaginary games –
are as if weeks have passed.
The time between weekly ablutions stretch out as if months,
the less frequent visits by Babicz are like years.
How to occupy the mind in that cramped space?
Contemplate all that has occurred,
imagine what is happening in the world outside.
No way to know whether or when it will end.

And they wonder, what kind of world will they find if they survive the bunker? Heniek at times believes that Basia will not keep her sanity – indeed, that she has lost it. He is sustained by a conviction that he can fulfil his destiny of long life. This quality is best explained by Primo Levi's description of a friend Leonardo:

> Besides good fortune, he also possessed another virtue … an unlimited capacity for endurance, a silent courage, not innate, not religious, not transcendent, but deliberate and willed hour by hour, a virile patience, which sustained … miraculously to the very edge of collapse.[262]

Basia, in a state of repulsion for the filth in which they lie, consumed by fear, sometimes talking to herself, her mind falling apart, wanders dazed through the twisting corridors of confused thoughts, trying to grasp that her God could have permitted this destruction of His good people. Caught between memory and nightmare, she withstands collapse due to two distinct sources.

One centres on her love for Heniek, and the hope that his strength makes possible. The other comprises a fantastic conjuration: in her wandering thoughts, Basia is often home with her mother, with all the family present. That brings too much grief, so she creates a magical vision: a table set for *Shabbos*. She builds this picture in her mind, imagining with all her heart and soul that in some distant future, somehow, somewhere, all her family will be reunited.

When reality intrudes and it is too painful
to contemplate the faces and fates of her loved ones
she just longs for a time in the future
where she can have at least the tablecloth.
Yes. A white tablecloth on a table
welcoming all in joyful symbolism of the Sabbath
and on that cloth she sets a candelabra with lit candles,
plates, cutlery and glasses, a fragrant golden fresh *challah*.
She embraces the vision of these familiar vanished items
all beautifully displayed on that gleaming white cloth.

And now at last we come to vignettes with magic headings:

KAROL CAME BACK

In September 1944 as the Russians approached, the Germans intensified their searches and raids. Harbouring Jews meant death.

Fearful of discovery, Karol takes them into the garden where he has constructed a dugout area under a tree. There concealed, cramped in an awkward sitting position, they stay for three days – without food, water, or movement – before receiving the all clear and returning to their bunker under the sawing machine.

The battlefront comes closer and orders come from the Germans to clear the district. All the inhabitants flee.

Apologetically, Karol came to tell them he has to leave. He gives them what food he has been able to find: scraps of bread, onion rings and a bucket of water; then he and his niece leave.

The whole earth shakes with the force of battle raging above …
Three days? … Five days? … More?
Basia and Heniek fight over the crusts:
Heniek for her to eat a bit more,
Basia for him to eat a bit more …
Karol and his niece come back. Back to check on his charges …
Back with food and water …
Back to see if they are still alive … at great risk.

THE LUCKY SHOT

Days pass. It is November 1944.
They no longer hide in the bunker.
There is little food and no news;
it seems the Germans have abandoned this part of Warsaw.
Karol hesitates, afraid to go out.
Though weak, Heniek leaves the house
to see if anyone else he knows is alive.
He checks several hiding places – he finds no one.
Dressed in blue overalls, he looks like a German pilot.
He enters the underground shelter from which Karol,
afraid of his neighbours' sharp eyes, is to collect him.
An alarm sounds; someone has seen Heniek enter the shelter.
Someone bellows at him to come out.
Heniek, not knowing who is shouting, does not answer.
Bullets whizz past Heniek's head, and then a grenade.

Chance, good fortune, fate, good design – take your pick – decrees that the effect of grenade blast is restricted to the shelter's zigzag entry.

Heniek shouts: '*Yevreh*!' (Jew)
and, barely able to walk,
comes out into the open.

THE RUSSIAN SOLDIER'S DELIGHT

A Russian soldier, hardly more than a boy, taking in the sight before him exclaims: 'Oh my God! I could have killed you!'

Overcome with emotion he embraces, kisses and makes a fuss of Heniek.

He introduces himself: Jasha Smirnov.

They go to collect Basia. Jasha Smirnov makes a fuss of her.

Taking them both by the hand to the Russian headquarters, he presents them and all the personnel make a fuss of them.

THE BITS OF TOBACCO

Russian carriages pass by with Russian soldiers.

In one, a soldier is smoking; he leans out and in a gesture of generosity gives Heniek some bits of tobacco rolled in newspaper …

Oh, that is forever delicious …

THE POLISH SOLDIER

Both are incredibly pale: Basia, bloated like a balloon, is barely able to walk; Heniek, emaciated, barely stands.

A passing Polish soldier comments to his companion:

'*Z niego nic nie będzie.*'

That one is finished; there will be nothing of him.

But the war is not over yet.

The Russians had been advancing on Warsaw since August 1944; in September, they had taken the Warsaw suburb of Praga. Having liberated eastern Warsaw, they remained camped on the east bank of the Vistula River while the Germans still held the west bank. In the German-occupied zone the Polish Underground, under instruction from the government-in-exile in London, though mindful and fearful of imminent socialist takeover, prepared for a 'Rising' in anticipation of Russian help; this was to be 'the revolt of a fly against two giants.'[263]

While the Russians make no move, biding their time, Basia and Heniek camp with them; clinging desperately to life, they contemplate the evil, and the kindness, they have experienced, and wonder: What lies ahead?

CHAPTER 20: WASTELAND: ALL GONE [264]

Warsaw early 1945

In all of Poland, in January 1945, out of over three million, only three hundred thousand Jews remained.[265]

Basia and Heniek are treated well at the Russian camp on the east banks of the Vistula River. Despite Spartan supplies and accommodation, they think, soon this war must be over. Good will have won. Men will be free.

But as events unfold, freedom remains out of reach. And good too. The Russian Commander calls Heniek to meet in private. Asking many questions which Heniek tries to answer, to Heniek's amazement the Commander, himself a Jew, accuses Heniek of being a spy. Leaving this man, Heniek, terrified at what might eventuate, waits for subsequent denouncement or action; none comes. Heniek ponders this mystery. A spy for whom?

On 12 January 1945, the Russian final offensive on eastern Warsaw coincided with the Allies advance from the west. They both entered a Warsaw reduced to rubble. The Soviets, having tricked the Poles into believing that they had entered Poland to rescue them from the Germans, grabbed territory. The Polish 'Rising' that had sought to greet Stalin as an independent Poland, was crushed (western Warsaw had surrendered to A.H. on 2 October 1944). Resistance leaders, those heroes of the Polish Underground organisations, were found guilty by the Russians for collaboration with the Germans; this nefarious lie was a means to an end. The heroes were eliminated; the legitimate government was afraid to return; the way was now cleared for a new regime. The new provisional Polish government, formed in and active from Lublin, took the opportunity while the pre-war government continued to stay in London.[266]

In early April 1945, with Warsaw 'liberated' and in ruins, Basia and Heniek roam through the destruction seeking family members but find none. They search for Karol – their saviour – but do not succeed even with help from the Red Cross. Director Babicz, the key to their future, to whom they had entrusted all the wealth of their families, they find safe and well. First, he expresses surprise: 'What, you are after all alive!'

Second, delight: 'It is good you have made it.'

Then, the blow: 'All gone. All gone …'

Heniek takes in these words, turns them over in his mind and shakes his head to clear the red fog. Trembling from head to foot, he exclaims: 'Impossible!'

Nevertheless, Babicz stands with empty hands, and where gratitude had flourished for him as a saviour, there is now an odious black emptiness, too awful when combined with everything else; deep burial of this rage is the only way forward. In their minds, Babicz has robbed them with evil avarice. Without money, how will they get food, clothes, and the means for some kind of life elsewhere?

They tell each other, 'He only helped us so he could steal our possessions.'

Was it possible all men were so perfidious? Stunned and hurt at what had to be betrayal, they seek out Heniek's home.

All of the ghetto area has been levelled.[267]

They find only unrecognisable ruins.

Though the government has authorised the return of property, Poles who had been witnesses to the ghetto shame, themselves survivors, throw stones, shout obscenities: *'Parszywe Żyd'* – 'Dirty Jew' – 'Get out! Go to Palestine!'

So, Basia and Heniek find no welcome from their neighbours.

Many, helped themselves to accommodation,
jewels, gold and other goods.
Thus do they deny themselves Eudaimonia – well-being?[268]
Violating their Lord's instruction to be as the good Samaritan,
and, having 'acquired' their neighbours' property,
they break the Tenth Commandment – do not covet[269] *–*
and the Eighth Commandment, as well – do not steal –
forever tying themselves to hating those they stole from.

There were other reasons why returning Jews found no welcome.

The most significant was a belief that the Nazis had been so hard on the Poles as punishment for the acceptance of Jews as equals. Secondary but significant was the use, by the Nazis, of Jews to compile lists of Polish Catholics for deportation; at this, even the most tolerant of Poles were enraged such that Jews fighting with the partisans during the war had hidden their identity to escape summary execution. Add to that stories of Jews helping the Soviets (indeed Jews did become leading officials in the post-war communist regime) such that Poles that had helped Jews during the war, fearful of the continuing hatred, kept mute and exhibited little sign of sympathy or regret.

Survivors repeated harsh words to each other as evidence of hatred: 'The Poles say, "The one bad thing about Hitler ... he didn't kill all the Jews."'[270]

In my family circle,
this circulated as evidence of Polish loathing of the Semite.

Despite the new government's attempts to house and succour returning Jews, spontaneous rejection manifested. Poland lay in ruins. The toll: four million Poles murdered in the area of the General Government; about a million Poles who'd been forced to work as serfs in Germany were trying to return home. People took what they could. There was solidarity of being among one's own. Poles greeted their previous neighbours at best with antipathy, negating 'love thy neighbour',[271] rationalising that the Nazis' murderous regime had been solely responsible for all that had eventuated, consigning the past to the past and looking to a new world free of these others. The ancient bias of the Catholic Church against Jews as sinful and evil had laid the foundation. Nazi propaganda built another layer; greed for 'found' or allocated property played a part, as did the apparent meekness with which the Jews had submitted to and been used by the Germans. Now among these returning Jews were some who, playing the system, behaved in regrettable ways, grabbing

> what they could and using the good intentions of the government for their own profit. This became justification for hostility; proof the Jews enduringly equated to vermin. Vermin are to be squashed.[272] It was twelve long years since the election of A.H. and the start of the One Thousand Year Third Reich. Jews, returning home, were murdered by Poles. Though poets' words – notably those of Czesław Miłosz – had wept, there was no welcome, no home anywhere for the Jews.[273]

Heniek has the hatred spat out in his face: 'You are like rats, we keep killing you but you keep coming back.'

Thus, did Warsaw welcome its returning Jews.

And with this knowledge
when I finally made the trip to Europe,
in May 2000, one night in Warsaw was all I allowed.
Wish it had been more. Shoulda Coulda Been My Town.

Late May 2000, just two months after my husband Branko died, forces conspired.

First, an unexpected gift of money from a dear friend, conditional that I spend it on a holiday; second, pleas from my daughter Jessica, working in London, to come and see her. Third, recent contact with my husband's cousins in Croatia – cousins he'd never known – bringing an invitation to come and stay, coinciding with my wish that my children know where their father had come from. Fourth, the French connection: contact with Dad's cousin, Jacques Kott in Paris, who also extends an invitation.

Poring over the map of Europe, Poland called, especially Warsaw (Warszawa) and Gdańsk: the former as the place of my family's history, the latter as the birthplace of 'Solidarity' and as the symbol of Polish-German tensions. Yes, Poland was a must do. But No. How would I, still in a daze after the loss of my Dad last December and my husband just two months ago, in March, cope with Warsaw?
I choked thinking of it.

In an epiphany, just days before, I had resolved to say Yes. Yes to whatever life brought me. So, didn't I have to say, 'Yes' to this? Yes.

But I couldn't risk more than one night in Warsaw.

In June 2000, my son Jade and I, both students at Melbourne University – he final year Architecture, I several History and Philosophy subjects – take advantage of the three-week semester break, turning it to five by stealing a week at each end, and arrange to meet Jessica in Zagreb.

A whirlwind time with my husband's Croatian family and a glimpse of that part of the former Yugoslavia: Zagreb, Nova Gradiška, Split and island Hvar brings insights into Branko's longing for the Adriatic, indelible memories: the countryside, the excellent coffee and cafés out in the open; hospitality and connection; Diocletian's Palace, great ice-cream, boats, beaches, nude bathers; and now …

Day nine, Tuesday 27 June 2000: destination Warsaw. Luxurious flight Zagreb to Munich; I'm okay with hearing German spoken but find myself fighting a desire to sob at the first sounds of Polish overheard at Munich airport; back on the plane, my eyes begin leaking. Why?
Arrival 4:30 pm. Overcast. Cool.

An English-speaking Polish cabbie touting at the airport sweeps us up and carries us through peak-hour traffic. In a charming accent, spinning a web of silky words undoubtedly in the hope of engagement for touring on the morrow, he knows all the places for such as us to go.

Maybe Treblinka. Maybe Auschwitz.

We shake our heads. No. Just one night, we explain.
Our eyes connect behind his back: he has spotted us as Jews; it seems others have come before.

Bags dumped at the Hotel Ibis, armed with a map, we set out; it is 5:30 pm. Amy, my travel agent niece, had chosen well. The hotel is adjacent to the area where the ghetto had been. Walking. Walking. Jade asking questions, Jess listening to what she already knows – both hushing me, as my voice gets higher; telling the story of their grandparents. A recent connection between us as adults having germinated in our sojourn with Branko's last trial in the palliative care hospital, taken leaf in Split, budding in Hvar, it now blossoms on these streets that have known desolation.

Tears unashamedly in our hearts and our eyes, we walk joined in grief.

Where once were charming courtyards, apartments and shops, now stand rows of bland medium-density five-storey housing, testament to the drab housing 'solutions' worldwide. Landmarks are few. *Umschlagplatz* is reduced to a wall inscribed with words, and in a park a huge memorial, but we find nothing of what had been my parents' homes.

Back at our hotel. 8 pm. Let's have dinner out!

This enthusiastic exclamation from Jade who, having consulted his guide, takes charge yet again. Taxi to *Stare Miasto* – Old Town.

A restaurant of charming reconstruction: timber panelling, booths, patterned carpet. A wondrous feast: garlic mushrooms, chicken livers, duck and apple, borsht and dumplings, wine, and for me a whisky. Listening to Polish. Enjoying it all. Laughter and connection. Laughter?

The next morning, rising early, we feast on a smorgasbord breakfast, then set out for the Jewish cemetery in Okopowa Street two blocks away. A place of great beauty and history. Spending a long time at the mass grave grotto, we walk through old sections, find monuments to Korczak, to the child smugglers,[274] but nothing we can connect to family. We walk eastward towards Targówek, the suburb of Warsaw on the other side of the Vistula River, where my parents had found sanctuary. We are not near. Jade is flying to Berlin later that morning, Jess and I are to train it to Gdańsk. We head instead in the direction of our hotel and find ourselves in a steep, broad city street.

'I like this place,' says Jade.

'So do I.' Tears spurt. 'This could have been my place.'

My Mother's Town. My Father's Town.

All The Lost Family's Town.

Shoulda Coulda Been My Town?

The return of the Jews coincided with that of the Red Soviets. Indeed, among Russians with prominent positions in the government who now sought to take over Poland, some were of Jewish descent. Other Jews openly supported the Reds in their aims. Chaos, the continuum. The Home Guard, still taking orders from the Polish government-in-exile in London, were suppressed by the new regime; civil war was breaking out; the whole of Poland was on the move with Poles, displaced from the East by the Russians, evicting Germans who had lived there.

Bitter and confused by the enmity from their Polish neighbours, Basia and Heniek return to the Russians who, busy rebuilding and establishing Soviet territory, send them together with other displaced Jews to Praga; then they walk the 170 kilometres to Lublin where accommodation for survivors is in a converted two-storey mansion called *Peretz Heim*.[275]

> The committee running this Peretz House had learnt little from recent history; factions argued about everything. Funding and competitiveness bedevilled all relief efforts. Agencies fought for funding for supplies; some sources say money came from Russia, others that Russia diverted money – regardless, some got through.

Shelter for Basia and Heniek within this miserable place is a room with no facilities, shared with five other people. Here Heniek stops walking.

> Of food, there is little. Exhausted, emaciated, afflicted; people died, waiting for their fate to be decided, while the war continued. With millions of dazed refugees – Cossacks, Frenchmen, Serbs, Belgians, Silesians, Ukrainians, Croatians, Germans, White Russians, Albanians, Slovenians, Slovaks, Italians, Romanians and Jews – on the move, most making their way home, others fleeing home, everywhere in camps, persecuted and persecutors were thrown together in inadequate conditions. The distressed invading armies of the Allies, confronted by piles of hair, eyeglasses and shoes, mass graves and huge mounds of emaciated bodies, testified to the depth of a denying nation's complicity and debauchment.
>
> Meanwhile A.H., showing his contempt for the German people, ordered executions of 'deserters' – many of these mere schoolboys – and ordered all installations to be destroyed, thus leaving a wasteland. His decision: the German people will go with him into oblivion.

A Jewish doctor, diagnosing both Basia and Heniek with severe anaemia, instructs that the best medicine is food, food, food; but they have no money. Heniek finds a way. At home, he loved to tinker with the watches that his father repaired; now, fixing watches for passing Russian soldiers, with every bit of money he buys whatever food is on offer: bacon, fat and more fat. He begins to walk.

Inspiration leads to gathering of bits of flint to sell at the market, adding to their meagre hoard; gradually their health improves.

Hunger sated, the next consuming need of these adult orphans is to search for family members.

Clues come in the form of notices on boards and messages
through people sending out their whispering
pleas for connection to a loved one.

But for Basia and Heniek,
  there comes no welcome
  snippet of information, no answer.
  And, with the American soldiers
  uncovering and reporting
  to the world, the horror
  of the concentration camps,
  there is no end, no new beginning
  in sight.

PART ELEVEN

AMOR FATI?

CHOOSE LIFE

My formula for human greatness is amor fati*: that one wants to have nothing different, not forward, not backward, not in all eternity. Not merely to bear the necessary, still less to conceal it ... but to* **love** *it.*[276]

So said life, beauty, and freedom-affirming Nietzsche.
His amor fati *– love your life / love your fate –*
part of his concept of 'eternal-return',
aligns with the Hindi tradition of dharma,[277]
which is not the same as karma,[278]
nor the pre-destiny my mother calls beshert and some call kismet;
and I do try to love my fate.

Whereas beshert, *as a form of determinism,*[279]
can be a licence to not be responsible, amor fati *is more;*
it embraces a concept of a tragic soul –
'... containing and affirming good and evil ...'[280]
Love it or not – choose life.

This thought reminds me of Clara Sternberg. Clara is one of Oscar Schindler's chosen people. Taken to Auschwitz with a group of Schindler's women, terrified, unaware of his efforts towards their release, she has just survived another selection. Her reserves of hope gone, Clara seeks out an electric fence. Unable to find one, she asks an acquaintance: 'Where's the electric fence?'

The acquaintance answers, as if the question makes sense:
'Don't kill yourself on the fence, Clara …
If you do that, you'll never know what happened to you.'[281]

Clara heeds this insight. She turns around; that afternoon an instruction reaches the Schindler women to prepare for departure from Auschwitz – departure to life.

All else in the book has become hazy, but this exchange is stuck in my memory; the wanting-to-know how-it-turns-out message has helped to save me too. More than once.

Not long after these musings,
one day in December 1996,
Mummy declared her life worth living.

Watching him restless at my questions and knowing the sun was calling, I scribble away, trying to capture every word until, excusing himself, Daddy leaves for the local pool to bask on this Saturday afternoon.

Just me and Mummy, comfortable on the couch, we continue teasing out her memories. Today, I get carried away, telling her of the plight of the Poles in being caught between ruthless powers and considered by Germans as inferior Slavs, next only to Jews and Gypsies, and in line for enslavement and obliteration.

Agitated, she interrupts my rhetorical flow.

'But Sara, those Poles were so antisemitic. When we were hiding in one house the lady had two little children – You know the house with the cemetery stones – and those children adored us. The little girl was always hugging me. One day the little girl came into our room, as usual, took my hands, and while kissing them all over said, with real excitement and pleasure: "I just saw a Jew being killed." She was so happy. I could not believe it. Why? How could she love me, and speak like that?'

'You never told me about that before.'

'Well … but how could she! I was so mad I wanted to choke her!'

'Yes, hate the group, love the individual. Mummy, we all do it.'

She accepts the barb without protest.

I pause, wondering what kind of Australia is unfolding?

'Look at us. We consider ourselves tolerant; are we? Admit it: we are conservative, fearful, mourn the loss of everything – even before it happens. We all just want a coherent life, in a world we can understand.'

We are silent for a moment, side by side on the couch, digesting … In unison, she and I, emit a long sigh, look at each other's serious face, crack it – laughing, tears running down our faces.

She puts her hand on my head and with her long slender fingers, lightly strokes it as she did when I was a little girl, and says, 'Sara your tiredness … is it because you were born from the war?'

I reply, 'Maybe.'[282]

'But you had a good life? It's my fault. Daddy didn't want children but I … I should have waited a few years …'

'Then it wouldn't be me! My life has been worth living. And still is!'

'Mine too,' she says.

We laugh together – easy; grateful in each other's presence.

Oh Mummy that was the first time I'd heard you say
your life has been worth living.
Know this – your courage has helped me live mine.

PART TWELVE

(UN)WELCOME

Europe early 1945 – late 1948

At the End of the World: 1949

MAKE THE STRANGER WELCOME

As things stand now, we appear to be treating the Jews as the Nazis treated them, except that we do not exterminate them.

Earl G. Harrison, Aug 1945[283]

The Holocaust[284] *... blew down the walls of home, making us ... naked and free ... [opening] new horizons ...*

Rimvydas Silbajoris[285]

Welcome the stranger into your home, for you were a stranger.
You shall also love the stranger,
for you were strangers in the land of Egypt.[286]

Unwelcome. Welcome.
Imprisoned. Free.
Hostility. Hospitality.
They. We.
The Neighbour. The Stranger.

CHAPTER 21: (DIS)PLACE. (DIS)TRUST. (DIS)COURAGE(D).

In Poland in the spring of 1945 displaced people of all nationalities sought assistance to find family, or make their way home. The authorities of all nations, in ignorance or indifference, treating the Jews as if they were like others displaced by war, directed them to return to their places of origin. Those, like Basia and Heniek, who'd already returned to their homelands, had found only hostility. News of shocking murders circulated. Survivors, terrified to go back to their villages and towns, wondered – anyway, where was back, where was home? More and more layers building: layers of mistrust and cynicism towards the Gentile world – towards the goyim – layers of longing for one's own.

Basia and Heniek, still seeking some family link and desperate to get out of Poland, go to Łódź to look for Irka (Irene Poznanski) – the sister-in-law of Basia's sister Zosia; they find her there, but she does not have the means to help them to get out of Europe. Where would they go anyway? So they stay with her.[287] Trying to grasp colliding events.

Organisational responsibility. While individuals in the numerous relief organisations[288] dealt with the difficulty of finding a way through the vast war bureaucracy, an internecine power-struggle erupted; charged with the transfer of urgently needed food and supplies, the organisations expended precious time and energy on who would be the agency to get the credit for bringing relief. The complexities and difficulties were considerable. The conquering nations, the Allies, divided responsibility between themselves according to who-got-where first. There were Soviet, US, British and French Zones. It was a vast mess. Those who had been targets for annihilation mixed in among millions of other DPs.[289] These others, not targets but tools, had also suffered, under Soviet or other oppression, then Nazism – twice invaded – and now faced threatening communism.[290] They were all trying to survive; most had little affection for Jews.[291]

Who were these other DPs?[292]

Direct partners or tools of A.H.: Millions of accomplices of all nationalities: quislings, guards, police, Nazis, soldiers, and even Junaks – the Latvian and Ukrainian SS who terrorised Jews in the ghetto.

Foreign workers? Millions of people who had been integral to A.H.'s vision: men, women, old people, children as young as ten. Initially willingly or coerced. Exploited as slave labour, they had found themselves treated as inferior beings as *Untermenschen* – the sub-humans. Now they all sought to get back to their homes. They had endured a nightmare of deprivation and cruelty working in factories, which had churned out the essentials for the war effort, including the I.G. Farben synthetic gasoline plant at Auschwitz. I.G. Farben, the producer of Zyklon B gas (a hydrogen cyanide insecticide which was cheaper than carbon dioxide and which killed millions of Jews, Gypsies and other people) was the ultimate example of any system that allows profit as its highest good.[293]

Language desires to define,
but each word conjuring its opposite is exposed as contaminated.
Hero to one, villainous murderer to another.
The guilty, indistinguishable, mere (wo)men,
now passed themselves off as victims.
How was one to know whether this person who now played friend,
was just before a deadly foe?
Moreover, even those who have come to bring aid,
cannot tell them apart
or understand their needs.

Number of people displaced? Estimates vary; all agree the figure is big. A simmering miasma where people of differing experience and beliefs jostled; some just trying to survive, others holding grander plans.[294]

The Jewish refugee component? Uncertain the number. How do you count a people who look like everyone else? Perhaps 250,000[295] – perhaps more: this remnant waited, while the authorities dithered about what to do with them.

The Avengers and Nazi Hunters: Not typical, seldom recorded, yet nevertheless they did exist. In his autobiography, Samuel Pisar[296] tells of his experience as a sixteen-year-old survivor of Auschwitz: rescued by US soldiers, running wild with two friends in Germany, foraging, looting, committing reprisals, revenge, requisitioning, murdering, black marketeering – a brief climate of abuse and violence, with Germans cowed and submissive!!

The Zionists: Their advocacy of moving all European Jews to Palestine, calling on divine right, was hindered by news of strife in Palestine.

The Communists: They made and took the opportunity presented by a vacuum of leadership; members enrolled, communal works commenced – preparation for a takeover.

The Jewish DPs: Emotionless, practical, callous, amoral. Thus history books stereotype. They tell of the zombie-like condition of that surviving remnant who cling to life, speaking the minimum of words. Unable to voice what they have seen, they cleave to any person from the same town as if they were a close blood relative excluding all others, seeing any slight or incident – accidental or intentional – as evidence of further antisemitism. They exaggerate, dwelling in minute detail on real and imagined past events and incidents of racial hatred, defiantly declaring no non-Jews will tell them what to do. A contained fury. Muttering about small incidents that made little sense, screaming in their sleep, they behave as flotsam. No privacy. Men and women: single, having lost their partners, or not yet found their spouses, unhallowed by the bond of marriage, nevertheless they indulge openly in sex. 'Human Dust', the Zionists in Palestine will call them, before transforming them into icons of human survival.[297]

Primo Levi spent a year in Auschwitz. He explains: an attack of moral fatigue accompanies the joy of liberation … having lived at an animal level, without emotions, abject, their moral yardstick altered by filth, nudity, destitution, they steal.[298] Suicides are rare – too busy dying to think about death; penance for sin constant. Guilt abounds: for failing to oppose or resist, or failing to help others; for surviving by putting oneself first.

Heniek is ashamed of being alongside the broken humans that seem to be everywhere. Where are the intelligent, educated, civilised people he'd known? He longs for a fellowship of survivors giving each other a helping hand, a kind word. He does not empathise with what he sees of these people, or their way of resorting to the old traditions to express their bond. How can they hustle and cheat, while fussing about empty rituals and rules? Why pray to a bloodthirsty super-being who does not exist, indeed cannot exist?

As for the nefarious Russians, he had thought them to be the embodiment of socialist ideals made real, but he is witness to their brutal methods to enact their plans; how awkwardly their takeover actions sit with the rhetoric of a just equality. The cause of socialism is tainted further by his Polish socialist comrades' rejection of him in his time of desperate need. A bitter lesson learnt.

Admiration become repugnance: whom can he trust? He longs for the counsel of family and colleagues. In him grows a separateness.

He makes an island comprising of himself and Basia.

> While Europe entered a new phase of political turmoil, the Western Allies welcomed back their heroes, mourned their one million dead and, facing a bright future, firmly closed the doors, refusing all Jewish migration.
>
> How many perished? Estimates vary. In all of Europe and Asia Pacific, between forty-eight million and fifty-eight million five hundred thousand civilians, plus between twenty-one million and twenty-five million five hundred thousand military; in round numbers a total of between seventy million and eighty-five million souls destroyed in five years. Read the numbers again. 48,000,000 – 58,500,000 civilians. 21,000,000 – 25,500,000 military. Total: 69,000,000 – 84,000,000 souls.[299]
>
> The British, worrying about the impact of Zionism, put pressure on the other Western countries to not identify Jews as such, to not list them separately from other displaced persons. Many Jews remained placed with their former tormentors. Others 'liberated' from the concentration camps were still housed in these camps under appalling conditions, every day a tangible reminder of what they had suffered.
>
> No country, not one, on this whole planet, came forward.

Heniek, identifying himself as a Jew but not as a Zionist, his home turned into a Jewish graveyard, denied a new home anywhere in the world, like many others seeking a solution, finds only one. Surely, this present pathetic situation is a temporary aftermath. Perhaps – dare he hope that in that land of biblical promise, a miracle can occur, something good, something new – a homeland reinvented? Yes, the only destination out of malevolent, miserable Europe is to heed the prayer at the end of the Seder: 'Next year in Jerusalem'.

Then Basia finds that she is pregnant. Irene,
with whom they are still staying, also pregnant, says,
'How can you think to bring a child into this world?'
Irene has her unborn aborted; she tells Basia to do the same.
Resisting this advice, Basia prays for a healthy child.

Unbeknown to Basia, the heroes, known as the Jewish Brigade, who will be among her rescuers, had reached the Italian front. From the pages of Jewish history[300] we have the date: 27 February 1945.

'The Jewish Brigade reaches the Italian front in Northern Italy ...'

CHAPTER 22: (UN)LIBERATED WITH A PLAN

'We were ready to go to the end of earth only not to return to our previous home.' Heniek

It is back in Lublin, in February 1945, that a stranger approaches Heniek and in Hebrew declares, 'You are Henry Heber of the Akiva group sending people out of Warsaw.'

Heniek, wondering how this stranger knows his name and that of his youth group, replies, 'No.'

The stranger insists: 'Yes! You are a fighter from the Akiva Group of ZOB. A hero!'

'No! Never!'

'Yes you are!'

'No.'

Again, the stranger asserts. Again, Heniek vehemently denies.

The stranger stands his ground. Confidence emanates from him, reassuring. It is clear he will persist until he gets the answer he wants.

Heniek changes tack. 'What do you want?'

'I am going to send you out of here and, as a representative of Akiva, you will lead a group to Palestine.'

Out of here? To Palestine? After so much waiting. Could it be? What does he have to lose?

Where there had been confusion blooms motivation. Realising this man wanted to depict survivors as heroes, Heniek acquiesces. 'All right. Yes, I am Heber from the Akiva group!'

The stranger, at last satisfied, goes on his way.

> In time, Heniek finds this man belonged to the illegal *Brichah*, meaning flight. *Brichah* is comprised of Polish Jews – partisans and Zionists – led by Abba Kovner (Polish ex-partisans) and Yitzhak Zuckerman (ZOB), not emissaries from Palestine.[301]

Weeks pass. Basia and Heniek wait at Peretz Heim. Contact from another stranger. The plan is revealed. Heniek is to lead fifteen people across the borders and they will make their way into Palestine. The next day the contact gives instructions and warnings: the leaving must be secret; people are willing to pay for information about this illegal activity; others will fight for the opportunity to make this journey.[302]

Then, a message: 'Be ready, you are going tomorrow at five am.'

When my father told us of this serendipitous event,
even though Mummy sat affirming with nods, smiles and interruptions,
it sounded just too fantastic to be true.
Confirmation of this ruse, known as 'The Greek Bluff',[303]
astounded and motivated me.

With money – twenty dollars and twenty roubles[304] – a password and fake Red Cross documents establishing them as Greek Jews going back to Salonika as camp survivors, they travel wearing clothes of death-camp stripes. With them are twelve Polish Jews, passing themselves off as Greeks, and three high-ranking deserters from the Russian Army, disguised as Yugoslavs. Thus, incognito, this small group journeys to Rzeszów (in south-east Poland) where, for three days using only a few Greek words, they wait for document authentication by the Russian Commander. Eventually the authorities allow the sham-Greeks through on their *Bumatchos,* bits of paper, but not the sham-Yugoslavs with no proper passports. Moving on through the Russian zone, rejoined by the pretend Yugoslavs, who managed to get away, they are smuggled across the border into Slovakia in open train wagons returning empty from the front; trains to death transformed to transporters to life.

Meanwhile in Italy: 4 April 1945, the Jewish Brigade set up a camp.

> 'The blue and white Jewish national flag is officially hoisted in the Jewish Brigade headquarters in Italy.'[305]

Everything is arranged and guided by invisible hands and minds. In villages, a small crowd of people – the women in headscarves – greet them with joy, kindness, and offerings of bread. At Hummené they receive a new password, then to Debrecen in Hungary and onto Bucharest in Romania to the headquarters of ZOB. Happily, reunited with Tuvia Cohen and Antek (Yitzhak Zuckerman), Heniek's old friends from Warsaw; here the group stay for six weeks. The plan was for them to go onto Constanța in Romania, from where they were to go by to Palestine; but they learn the Russians have confiscated the ship, so they travel back into Hungary to Debrecen.

In mid-May 1945, they hear the war has been over since 8 May.

Relief is followed by numbness as information about the extent of the death camps catches up with them in their flight. It seems death camps were everywhere!

> How many were liberated but still captive in this prison named Europe? Figures vary. If one does a simple estimate based on the population of Jews in Europe being near nine million before the war, six million dead, this gives three million survivors. But there are many confounders that make this an unquantifiable unknown. Did the number of nine million before the war include converts to Christianity? The Nazis' estimate was eleven million. After the war, Jews converted, intermarried, melded into the population. Some Jews, who had called themselves Christian, now declared themselves as Jews. And there were Nazis who stole another's identity; some even called themselves Jews.[306]

Their next stop is Kibbutz Weihal, a *hachshara* (vocational training farm) in Romania; here they wait several months with little to do. The plan now is to go to Palestine via Italy. Orders at last! Back to Budapest in Hungary. With Basia growing big with child, the group, grown to around six hundred people, smuggle themselves over many borders and mountains; danger is the only constant.

> Jews without satisfactory papers were being arrested and put back into DP camps. Everywhere illegal groups, paralleling legal ones, smoothed the difficult journey. On foot and on large trucks, this endeavour of the *Brichah*, having formed a route from Poland to Romania and then to Austria via Hungary, acted in concert with an unheralded force known as the Jewish Brigade. This special force – formed by Churchill in late

1944 as a unit within the British Army, comprised 5,000 soldiers. Based in Egypt, they had sailed for Italy in November 1944 and fought with the British against the Germans. Now under its own guidance, the Jewish Brigade sought to meet up with these 'Greeks' who were gathered and directed by *Brichah*, achieving an exodus of Jewish refugees across closed borders from inside Europe to the coast; destination Palestine.

Sickened by the revealed concentration camps, the American troops turned a blind eye to this illegal activity even, at times, giving a helping hand, and the American Jewish Joint Distribution Committee responsible for Jewish American aid in Europe, aided this exodus out of Europe, raising and distributing vast sums of money and supplies. The deeply shocked American soldiers – writing home telling of what they had seen, filming inmates still kept behind barbed wire – in effect became emissaries for the Jewish cause of a return of the Jews to the Promised Land.

For Basia and Heniek – journeying through Europe in 1945 – the higher ideal was hope for a new life in a new land.

CHAPTER 23: WANDERING. INTERNMENT. RESCUE. BORN-ON-THE-WAY. SOJOURN.

mid-1945 – early 1949

WANDERING MID-1945

This portion of the surviving remnant now moves through Europe dressed in army order overalls. Basia's obvious bump attracts comments; persuading an end to the life she carries, they say it is selfish to bring a child to suffer into this world; how does she expect to provide with no family for support, with no money? But Basia, wanting this child more than anything, ignores this counsel.

Next, their journey takes them to Graz in Austria where, allocated modern accommodation in the form of a first-class hotel room run by UNRRA – the United Nations Relief and Rehabilitation Agency – they find a wonderful sight: a beautiful bed with pillows and clean sheets. In delight, they lie on the bed, luxuriating in the heavenly sensation, but sleep eludes them. Eventually, lying on the hard floor, they fall asleep.

INTERNMENT

Heading into Hungary, the group tries to break through the border blockades. Stopped by the British at the border, they are taken back to Graz to a disused barracks and held there under British guns. Hours and days pass, not locked up but not treated well. Surely it is impossible that the months of travelling can end here and their baby be born in a prison? And why do these British show no empathy towards them?

> There were several reasons why. Indeed, the British regarded Jews as corrupted, a thorn, and an embarrassment.
>
> ***Corrupted***: In the camps, Displaced Persons operated shady endeavours and found willing customers – Americans and locals.
>
> ***A thorn***: Following WWI the British as administrators of Palestine, were tasked by the League of Nations with establishing a Jewish homeland in Palestine (The British Mandate of Palestine 1921–48) but, submitting to Arab pressure, they had not done so. The result was conflict. The *Haganah*, meaning defence (a Jewish paramilitary organisation), bedevilled the British. The Israel Freedom Fighters, known as the Stern Gang, used terrorist tactics to draw attention to their demands which included the right to bring in European refugees; unmoved, the British refused. Meanwhile *Brichah*,[307] (working covertly with the Jewish Brigade) stole from British supplies, helping themselves to tyres and gasoline.
>
> ***An embarrassment***: The whole world watching developments in Palestine felt horror, anger and guilt due to the revelations filmed by the liberating forces in Europe, now being shown in local cinema theatres the world over. The spectre of 20th century genocide beyond human comprehension, proven and logically irrefutable, caused everyone to have an opinion on Palestine. Ernest Bevin, the British Foreign Secretary, said that as the Jews had waited 2,000 years for a homeland a bit more should not matter. Elsewhere – though few wanted the Jews as neighbours – sympathy for the partition of Palestine gained momentum. And a view that the British motivation had less to do with humane concerns for the Arabs and more to do with interest in Arab oil, increased antipathy towards the British interests. On 2 May 1945 – just five days before VE-Day – the press reported American Senator Robert F. Wagner's criticism of the British; he'd said: 'British policies in Palestine are the tragic survival of the disease of appeasement.'[308]

To Basia and Heniek, hurt and bewildered as the British soldiers laugh sarcastically in their faces, it seems hatred is rooted in their psyche. Can it be that they have travelled so far only to land in this new horror?

On the third day, strangers in unknown uniforms walk coolly into the camp and ask the British officers for the release of the 200 internees; the British officers refuse. It is whispered among the internees that somehow these men are Jewish soldiers. The next day a man dressed as a civilian comes into the camp. Moving from group to group of internees, under the noses, eyes, and ears of the British, he gives instructions: 'You will walk into the woods. Leave everything behind.'

The internees, afraid, nevertheless, at the given time, walk.

Heniek holds Basia's hand, ignoring the British orders to halt or be shot.

No shot is fired.

RESCUE

The 200 people walk out of the camp. In the woods men, placed every hundred metres, half hidden by the trees, direct this confused and exhilarated lot for several kilometres to a clearing in the wood. From this spot, the escapees see fourteen parked trucks. Though instructed to remain in the woods until signalled, many run to the trucks; the Jewish soldiers fire shots over their heads in an attempt to create some order.

In the confusion, Heniek hesitates then runs starts to run, holding Basia's hand. He leaps onto a slowly moving truck; Basia tries to but slips. He grabs her, holds on while the truck speeds away; bit by bit he pulls her on. Shaken and bruised, Basia holds back tears and fears for her unborn child.

With all the trucks loaded and moving, Jewish soldiers block the highway, in front and behind, to stop the British, who follow but do not shoot. The Italian border guards do not attempt to stop them.[309]

A bumpy trip, about 100 kilometres across the border to Tarvisio, where they arrive at three in the morning in late July 1945. There they find another world.

A defiantly gay scene greets the eyes of these people so used to grey misery. From large tents emerge the *shlichim*, emissaries; the whole place springs to life: bustling, under a multitude of lights, a crowd with joyous smiling faces greets this battered group.

In front of the camp, there is a huge banner of brilliant white with a *Mogen David,* the six-pointed Star of David, of unbelievable blue, and even the tanks are each painted with blue stars – marvellous, indeed a miracle!

Joy at the sight of these blue stars, music, Hebrew songs;
for the first time in all these years of horror, thrilled with
the possibility of a bright future, tears well and they weep.[310]
Tears turn to smiles as these remnants, described by
earlier emissaries from Palestine as …
human dust, a psychologically-scarred rabble,
bereft of families, lacking in morals,
unmotivated, untrained, not pioneering oriented,
with no redeeming qualities …
they are issued ready-made clothes, while sewing machines hum
to make shifts for the pregnant women,
and food is there in abundance
for these humans, starved for so long.

And they shall dwell on the land that I have given to My servant,
to Jacob, wherein your forefathers lived; and they shall dwell upon it,
they and their children and their children's children, forever;
and My servant David shall be their prince forever.[311]

BORN ON THE WAY: Italy 1945–46

While General Dwight Eisenhower forced Town Burghers, the German equivalent of Town Mayors, and their wives, to be conducted on 'sightseeing' tours of the camps, and, to consider the horrors their inaction and self-interest had permitted,[312] American soldiers took home the shocking images that are now commonplace and thematised. Allied countries, with one million dead, welcomed their heroes, mourned their dead and, facing a bright future, keeping their doors closed to immigration, set to rebuilding their lives and economies. The happy/sad, cute/intriguing films would pour out to an enraptured audience in celebration of heroic victory and a wonderful new future.

But Basia and Heniek's journey is not over. After four days of resting in this bustling camp of hope and promise, enduring the non-segregated latrines and communal showers, which Basia finds embarrassing, they

are interviewed to determine their next destination. With Basia now clothed in a flowing tunic with pockets trimmed in lace and a crisp white blouse, it is time to leave.

Their next move is to Florence. There, pregnant women, regardless of their term or condition, are put into the hospital, two or three per room. They have only porridge to eat and there is no peace with one of the women crying for her husband. Meanwhile the men shelter in the synagogue; there are no facilities, so they sleep on the floor.

After standing in line for hours to see a doctor, Basia's turn comes. The Italian doctor encourages her, saying she is carrying an intelligent child but being anaemic she must eat raw liver to have milk for her unborn. And so she eats raw liver.

By order of an arbitrary local decision, the men are not allowed to visit their wives; Heniek finds ways to be with Basia, if only for a few moments. In this atmosphere, they wait eagerly for their baby to be born and for instructions.

The organisers set out the plan: Basia will go to Palestine with the legal immigration – *Aliyah Aleph* – as soon as the British give in to President Harry Truman's pleas to allow 13,000 Jews into Palestine. But Heniek is to go immediately with *Ha'apalah*, also called the *Mossad le'Aliyah Bet* (a branch of the *Haganah,* the agency for illegal Jewish immigration to Palestine).

> Le'Aliyah Bet, also known as Organisation for 'B' Immigration, comprised illegal immigration in ships attempting to break through the British blockade around Palestine. Places in the legal immigration were too precious to permit them both to go legally, and the need for fighting men was urgent and immediate.

Terrified at the prospect of separation, Basia pleads with Heniek, 'Wait until we can go together.' He longs to go. Just 23 years old, primed for adventure, the idea of participating in the fight for Palestine is intoxicating. But he knows his Basia. He has been beside her during her fears; he knows her wellbeing, and indeed survival, still depend on him. So he says, 'Yes,' agreeing to stay in Italy waiting for the baby to be born, hoping time will yet bring a chance for them to go together to Palestine.

Italy is miraculously free of the hatred of Jews that permeated much of Europe. In Rome Heniek receives an English uniform, papers, and access to a motorbike. Thus equipped he makes several two- to three-day sightseeing trips through the beautiful countryside. At each return, he sneaks in to see Basia who, bored and lonely with this interminable wait in the hospital, frets until the next time she sees him.

And so 4 November 1945 … Sarena is born.
Born on the way …
On the way to Palestine …
Named for her grandmothers, Sara and Rena,
Sarena is born a twin … born first …
Her twin, Hannah, is born dead.

Just weeks before giving birth, Basia, told she was carrying two, was dismayed. It was hard enough to contemplate how they would manage with one baby, let alone two. But she grieves the loss of Hannah.

Home for this new family unit is a refugee camp located in an old castle outside Florence. Many people share the castle; families set up home in different corners of each room. With no cooking facilities, a roster system allows access to prepare food in large tin conserve cans. Basia, given a few nappies, washes these in a bucket, hangs them to dry on the roof, and stands guard over them as they dry. At first Basia doesn't have enough milk to feed her baby so the wife of one of the doctors sometimes feeds Sarena; at other times it is Heniek's job to collect extra milk with a small pump. This chore causing much mirth.

Here, in Florence, Heniek knows wondrous liberty. But the hoped-for blossoming and bonding remain elusive. Some of the survivors exhibit a cunning that had either helped them to survive or evolved in the process; arguments break out over every scrap, every cent. Loyalties are parochial in that survivors from a town or region band together. Though joined under the one roof, every man is for himself and his family only.

Yet Florence is so beautiful and inspiring in its imagery, Apollonian to Dionysian. In particular, Michelangelo's David, soaring larger than life, is magnificent. Under the indifferent gaze of this immortal ideal, Heniek recalls the impossible story: David had defeated Goliath! So perhaps it is possible that a new breed of free men can evolve if in their own land. And perhaps the time is now. Yes, life would be good.

And so months pass.

> Meanwhile, in Nuremberg, the Allies prosecuted Nazis leaders for war crimes. Twenty-three of the 24 Nazis accused in the first of several trials were declared of above average intelligence.[313] Not until Hannah Arendt's book *Eichmann in Jerusalem* in 1963 did the concept of the banality of evil come into public discussion. Some say her concept destroyed interest in Eichmann and other Nazis.[314] However, the moral dimensions of the 'just following orders' defence remains an enduring dilemma.

Time passes. One day a man from France comes to the camp. Heniek asks about his relatives – the family Kott. As if the fates have decided to smile, this man knows the Kotts. The whole family had been outside the occupied zone and have survived intact. Thus, with rising excitement, Heniek makes contact with his family in France.

Eager to bring Basia and Heniek to France, the Kotts reciprocate by sending gold coins, but the French authorities refuse this illegal entry. Heniek has come so far. He longs for family. He travels to Rome and there obtains documentation from the Polish Consulate adequate to gain eventual approval. The prospect that he will soon see his Uncle Sucher, and his cousin Jacques, exhilarates. There being no present opportunity for them both to go to Palestine, Basia agrees: they will go to France.

A family portrait in best clothes: Mummy in a black dress with lace collar.[315] *Daddy handsome and slim; me cute and pinchable. No hint of where they had been, what they had seen.*
Firmly in place,
a happy face to greet the world.

This photo taken in mid-1947 from France tells it all.

SOJOURN: France 1946–late 1948

It is said:
'A man travels the world over in search of what he needs
and returns home to find it.'[316]
But what if you can never go home again?

The journey to Roanne in Loire in mid-winter of 1946 is by bus. While the beautiful scenery flashes past, seven-month-old Sarena sucks and Basia vomits. At last Ventimiglia, Italy! Then across the border to Menton, France, where Heniek's cousin Jacques waits to take them by train to Roanne.

The family in France: Heniek's father's sister, his Auntie Fella married to Sucher Kott, and their children, the stunningly beautiful Paulette, Jacques with his lovely wife Aline, and their baby son Jean Ricard – affectionately known as Mimi. They take Basia, Heniek and Sarena into their hearts. Strengthened by the protective love of this family, putting the past behind them, the young couple make plans for a bright future.

Uncle Sucher arranges a job for Heniek. The work – making fabric for the family ladies' underwear business – neither inspiring Heniek's mind nor slaking his energy, allows time to daydream. Two desires dominate: hedonistic diversions of travel and enjoyment, and an idealistic passion to find a way to Palestine. But, as no way to Palestine presents, he indulges in the diversions.

No one will look after Sarena; she refuses to eat. When someone slips food into her mouth, she sprays it around the walls. Always inventive, Heniek finds kittens to distract her; she swallows a little, but just for him.

Cousin Jacques had been a student in the town of Kalisz until matriculating and leaving in 1938. A partisan during the war; now a businessman, he is also member of the Council for the Roanne-Saint Étienne district; Uncle Sucher Kott is a fervent Zionist. In Poland Sucher Kott had irritated the Polish authorities, making false papers before the war. He had fabricated passports and documents for illegal travel to Palestine. Caught in 1936, transported for trial to the town of Poznan, which had a reputation for being particularly antisemitic, he had faced a long term in jail. Jacob bribed the prosecutor and the judge. The primed prosecutor's case to the jury was inventive: 'What has the accused Kott done that is bad for us Poles? Has he not sent Jews out of Poland to Palestine? Rid our great land of inferior perfidious scum! Is this not what we want? I say, to jail such as he would be a miscarriage of justice. It is my contention that he should be rewarded! Indeed, he should be given a medal!' Sucher received a five-year suspended sentence, but realising his days were numbered, he made his escape to France while his wife Fella (Jacob's sister) and their young daughter Paulette stayed with the Heber family until 1938.

Friday night discussions in that household are lively and heated, with Auntie Fella trying to make peace, pleading with her men to make the Sabbath nice. Months pass. Heniek works, travels around France by motorbike, goes to Paris; meanwhile Basia, resentful and fearful when he is out of her sight, is obliged to stay behind with Sarena who grows into a toddler amid a loving family.

These safe days of life lull them. Perhaps if no sign had come, they would have made a home in this valley. But, in mid-1947, Heniek and Basia receive the news they had been waiting for: an offer of the privilege of going in *Aliyah Dalet* – the illegal immigration of

European Jews from France to Palestine by boats.[317]

Deciding yes, tearfully they leave their relatives. The first leg is to a base in the port of Marseilles; there high-ranking Jewish officers from all the allied armies – English, Russian, American – are in charge of this military-like camp with artillery, communication equipment, intelligence; a training ground for migrants in preparation for war in Palestine.

Living in barracks, impatiently waiting for news of a boat, they hear disturbing stories of boats sunk with many people drowned and news of the old boat, the *Exodus*, ordered back to Germany![318] There would be no more boats for a while. Disappointed, fearful, confused, their hopes shattered, they return to Roanne.

> On 29 November 1947 there was news of the United Nations' decision to create a Jewish state. Hope for peace; news of riots. Arab and Jewish communities of Palestine fighting.

In early 1948 came another chance. Eagerly they journey again to Marseilles. Excitement turns to disappointment. As they wait to board their boat, Sarena becomes feverish and is covered with a ghastly rash. Measles! A sick child cannot undertake such a journey; the organisers will in any case not expose other passengers to the risk of contagion; to leave her behind is unthinkable. The boat leaves. Sarena gets better. They wait hopefully in the camp … days … weeks … more disappointment. The British blockade of Palestine translates to no more boats leaving Marseilles. Dismayed, they return to Roanne.

Europe, old and decadent, a graveyard harbouring ghosts and horrors, is intolerable; somewhere, in the form of far-off shores, there is freedom from all this history. Visions tantalise: freedom to work, to walk the streets, to make a new life, as a no one, truly unnoticeable. But where to go with the way to Palestine from France closed? Basia's relatives in Colombia? Is that a good place to go?

Impossible imaginings …

CHAPTER 24: (NOT) AT HOME

In the end all of us are boat people.

Dr Magnus Clarke

Heniek, certain his Australian relatives are doing well, imagines that perhaps he could raise money from them to go to the newly declared Israel.[319] In 1948, he makes contact.

The relatives, having recently heard from a mutual family friend that Heniek is alive, unhesitatingly nominate their only surviving family member of the European family; Basia and Heniek receive visas to travel to Australia.

On 12 January on a ship named *Continental*,[320] they leave from Genoa, travelling from one end of the world to the other via the Panama Canal. Men and women's cabins are segregated; three-year-old Sarena is with her mother. Heniek spends time with his wife and daughter on the ship's deck, particularly around the pool which is a source of many delights. At the crossing of the equator, unforgettably, King Neptune, crowned with a golden crown and in his hand a huge trident, rises from the waters of the pool. Sarena spends hours

hanging onto the ladder, kicking her feet in the cool water while Heniek watches over her. And to further entertain her he searches out the ship's kittens for her to stroke. Six weeks: delicious anticipation mingles with a tinge of fear.

> The Passenger List, of Incoming Passengers to the Port of Melbourne from Genoa via Panama and Sydney, lists:
>
> HEBER Chaim – Mechanic,
>
> HEBER Bella – Housewife,
>
> HEBER Sara R.[321]

Their arrival in Melbourne, Australia, is on a grey late summer evening. Anticipating warmth and sunshine, instead a grey mugginess envelops them as a frenzy of activity flows: greeted by cousins, bundled into a car, taken to Heniek's aunt, Faygalleh, the sister of his mother. Her imposing two-storey house in Bay Street, Brighton, stands alone in a huge garden. Everything is different from the charming family and congenial town they had known in Roanne, France.

My cousin Norma's[322] email in early 2015 says so much:

'When the Hebers walked into my grandparents' house in Bay Street when they first arrived, I was a little girl and when I clapped eyes on them, I thought I was in Hollywood; they were such a beautiful couple.'

Basia finds Auntie to be a plain, firm woman. Uncle, a stern religious man, makes clear to his wife's relatives that there is no money to advance their quest. Intimidated in this strange new land, Heniek hides his disappointment. It seems to him his uncle is well-off but lacking in the generosity to give that which Heniek believes is his due. After all, his aunt and uncle, and many of their children, had enjoyed the hospitality of his parents' home for several years before they came to Australia; now they offer him one miserable room, treat his wife as a servant, and refuse to help him in his aspirations.

Several other survivors of the war rent single rooms in this house. Of these, Mr and Mrs Rotstein – Mietek (Moses) and Anka (Anna) – become a special part of their lives. An instant bond; de facto family crystallising; loving friendship and acceptance of the honour to be godparents to Sara (this being what Sarena is now known as, since Basia was advised that Sarena sounds a bit 'funny').

Basia cooks in the dark gloomy kitchen while Heniek finds work in a knitwear factory – five days a week from six in the morning to six at night for a salary of eight pounds and ten shillings. With hard work and careful saving, in no time there is money to send Basia accompanied by one of the cousins – Mania's brother Ben Rosenblatt – as an advance party of one to Israel, Basia, in the hope of reclaiming her father's land; Heniek and Sara to follow.

In the meantime, with no one to look after Sara, Heniek takes her to a children's home in the picturesque mountain township of Olinda. The drive there is lovely and a bit scary. The steep road winds through forests bedecked with giant ferns in gullies, towering gums, sheer drops; at each turn glorious views. The children's home, a neat rectangular building of timber boards and gable roof, is clean and staffed with ladies dressed in uniform like nurses.

Heniek visits once a fortnight on Sunday. After a couple of months, Sara surprises him by telling him she wants to speak only in English. Bemused, he finds tuition from a mechanic at his work so he can converse with his little daughter. Weeks pass, then one Sunday he is dismayed to see she is in bed – all the children have been sick with mumps. He can see the worst is over, as she chats about puppies. Falling back on French, he sings her a lullaby: '*Frère Jacques, Frère Jacques …*'

She pleads for the 'Sara' song; he laughingly complies:

Ah-ah-ah, kotki dwa, szarobure obydwa,

nic nie będą robiły, tylko Sare bawiły …

Oh, oh, kittens two, gray and beige both, nothing will they do, just with Sara play …

Reluctantly he gets up to leave. She clings to him and cries. She is still a baby. He has saved a bit more – soon they will leave and join Basia.

But. But … impossible though it seems after having had one goal for so long, he is now unsure. He's had enough of war. Everyone knows there will be more war in Israel, and his new job at a knitwear factory, called *Wheel of Fashion*, pays £37 gross, £30 clear; indeed a good wage. No one cares about his background. His workmates – Poles, Slavs, Italians, like him, uncomplaining hard workers – are all newcomers. The winter has been mild, spring approaches and as the days lengthen, his new friends assure him the summers are warm and sunny. The beaches, open spaces, huge arc of blue sky, exhilarate; he writes to Basia to come back. Mr Roth, an old friend of Basia's father Pinkus, having come to Australia before the war, has established himself, and indeed having found Heniek the job, will sponsor them.[323] Together they'll build a new life in this free land with its just laws; this land at the opposite end of the world to Europe.

Meanwhile Basia's endeavours to claim her father's property have failed; the authorities decree that the land is not hers due to unpaid land taxes and complications with it being in another's name. Heniek's letter to her finds her on a kibbutz as the guest of a handsome unattached cousin. She loves the pioneering spirit on the kibbutz where everyone speaks Hebrew without fear, and every step is a dance, every word a song. This is being 'at home'. This is being free. Not like the loathsome confines of Auntie's home. And as for her attractive cousin – he wants her to stay.

But Heniek, in his letter has further enticed her with: 'If you come back, we'll have another child.' Having spent just a few months there – she comes back.

Later this would be a treasured family story, retold at every opportunity,
to remember, she came back from the place of inspiration,
to be a stranger in a strange land,
and she'd say it was because her child Sara was there – in Australia.
And we would laugh at this telling because we knew,
of course, she could not leave Heniek, no matter what.

Heniek puts all that had been his history far behind him. He relegates the things he has seen to silence – banished even from his own thoughts – and with total allegiance in his heart for the new land so green and gold and blue, he tells himself he is no longer a wandering Jew; he has found a home.

But for Basia Australia is not home. Everything is a lack – a reminder of how home was and is now not.

Longing for an end to her suffering,
she expressed it to me with her own special logic:
'In my misery and loneliness I longed to die.
But how could I take my own life,
when I had been spared,
and so many had perished?'

And all the while
her smile,
her hair
her eyes –
all beautiful –
her front intact
for all
the world
to see.[324]

PART THIRTEEN

ATOH-DACHAIA: GRATEFUL YET LONGING [325]

MAKE A JUST, LAWFUL AND SAFE WORLD WITH(OUT) GOD.[326]

The universe with all it contains is neither evil nor good.
What man makes of it by free choice creates evil.
Iron can indifferently be a plough or a sword. [327]

In the year of commemoration of the victory of Good over Evil, I celebrate my 50th birthday, November 1995. I declare, to my part of the world, that I have made it thus far, and to each guest I say, 'I am two times 25. This gets a laugh. During the year, I've put in much effort into the garden and, on the day of Christmas Eve 1995, contemplating the result of my labours, I am pleased. My garden – comprising a kaleidoscope of plants that having taken my fancy, jostle against their neighbours; evolving rather than pre-planned – the garden could give the impression of untidiness – but magic has entered to interweave the parts into a sanctuary of dappled delight: intricate, fragrant, vibrant, peaceful.

As I stand, grateful for this evidence that as nature's law is variety, so God surely loves diversity, something I've suspected for a long time becomes clear: order of an immaculate kind is not to my liking.

And I know why. Nature has not that kind of order; her fruits are not uniform and, though the same as the others of its kind, every flower is yet a little bit different. Only man seeks to create identical, inflexible, indelible entities and concepts: Rows of Barracks, Banks of Ovens,

Synchronised Goosesteps, Rules and Rituals with meaning and intent arcane or lost, unknown or no-longer-relevant, containers of toxic waste – our gift to the future.

Many aspire to a world lawful and coherent, that learns from the Angel of History, takes guidance from The Better Angels Of Our Nature[328] *and The Angel Of The Future.*[329] *Concerned with positive possibilities, it makes and follows just laws and systems with compassion that treasures and safeguards the planet and all its creatures. My hope: may all who believe in God, and all who don't, accept that, whether we have dominion or not, we are all responsible.*

As a precursor to the momentous celebrations of 1995, (shortly after their 50th wedding anniversary) in April 1993, along with hundreds of other survivors,[330] *my mother and father travelled to what had been their home, to commemorate the 50th anniversary of the destruction of the Warsaw Ghetto. A consideration that indeed some people had helped them at personal risk, such that money was inadequate motivation to answer a 'Why?' aided the decision to visit that once loved, then loathed, land.*

Basia and Heniek stand on Polish soil. Amid much commemorative ceremony and production, they listen to words that speak with emotion of regret and even apology from the lips of Lech Wałęsa.[331] Many dignitaries acknowledge the heroism of the fighters during those last days of the Warsaw Ghetto. The concentration camps of Treblinka and Auschwitz convey indelible horrors; for the first time since his parents' death, Heniek is grateful that their fate had been death by a quick bullet.

Basia seeks out the family cabin at Świder. Nothing recognisable remains; all has been cleared and subdivided. A Polish woman shouts at her to go away. Basia's companion assures the agitated woman that she has not come to take anything from her but only wants to stand a while and look. However, the Polish woman sees not the gentle woman Bella, but a Jew come again to cause trouble.

Many on this pilgrimage responded in kind towards the Poles with not a grain of forgiveness evident; mutual hatred and mistrust has not died; too soon for that.[332]

Heniek, seeking familiar landmarks, finds none; everything known is gone, leaving no places in which even the shadows of the vanished beloved could congregate. He wanders around in disbelief, sad and amazingly glad for the life he has known. Anger gone. Waves of awe at the phenomenon of remembrance. Poles commemorating Jews.

Too late! This should have been his home!

Memories long shut away came back to haunt his nights as had his wife's before. Surely there was something to learn out of all this?

'Never again!'

In that still poor land they stand on the blood-stained soil; symbols of survival. Voicelessly they shout to those who had sought their annihilation: '*You* wanted us obliterated, but *I* am here to tell you I've had a full and rich life. I have children and grandchildren. Nothing can replace what you took away but, despite the nightmares and grief, I know contentment and happiness. I have not come to threaten. I will not claim as mine the home that you now live in. It is you who are less, because you could not find a way to allow me to be.'

Back home, to the amazement of their family, they begin to argue out their differences. Rather, Basia argues; Heniek withdraws. Now Heniek has frequent nightmares; when he shouts in the night Basia wakes him, holds him safe.

On several occasions, he falls out of bed; his scarred forehead tells what his mute lips will not. On Friday nights he rarely speaks. Basia rages at him after the children and grandchildren have gone. Desperate to draw him out, fearful that his ill health – his diabetes – will take him away from her, she who had been mostly timid has become a paragon of forcefulness. He who had held his authority by storm – while holding a silent rage hidden even from himself – is now visibly affected, lost in thought, sometimes submissive, even depressed.

The daughters, enduring their various financial and emotional hardships, engage in heated Friday discussions – expressing differences to the point of being awful. Something keeps them talking and, just when it seems that all is truly too difficult, some pieces come together. After all, love has not died but has waited, and through all their differences, through the poles-apart nature of their characters and discussions, it has found some common ground upon which to nurture shared seeds of wanting to make some of it nice, and accepting that a bit is a lot.

And a year or so after that return to their destroyed home, one *Shabbat*, Heniek smiles at someone's joke; encouraged, they draw him in and a while later, in front of his daughters, he holds his wife in a warm embrace, speaking tenderly to her. She winks at her daughters. 'He's been like this all the time lately.'

And for now, it is good again.

A few years later in 1996 we uncovered a wondrous truth;
it has to do with the power of Kaddish.

Her words tumbling over themselves reduced me to monosyllabic responses as Janette told how a change had come over our father last night at second night Rosh Hashanah at her in-laws; softened by the four glasses of wine, he had articulated some of what we had guessed of the confusion in his soul.

'Oh, I'm sorry to talk so much but I wish you'd been there …'

I reassured my sister that I was glad to listen and she went on. 'It all began when I mentioned *beshert*, destiny … he talked as never before and when Mummy interrupted, I put my hand over her mouth. She complains that he doesn't talk then never lets him get a word in. Anyway, he talked about his youngest sister and her converted Christian husband whom he loved, and his religious uncle who prayed while bombs fell and stables burnt, about his father helpless in the wheelchair. And about faith and destiny … how one of his sisters was almost saved – safe in Russia – handing out propaganda with her husband, and then the town fell to the Germans. And how he was glad that his parents died by a merciful bullet. And he talked about himself and Mummy and his life and never making money and his sense of destiny … Our Father is so confused …' Janette paused.

'Yes, I know.' I said.

'It's like he is irreligious and in a way very religious – that sounds crazy …'

'No,' I smiled into the phone, 'that is how I am … I must get it from him.'

'But I can't stand it – I hurt so much inside I must be mad. I'm sorry.' She was crying. A choking embarrassed sound came from her, covering any slight sound accompanying my flowing tears.

'You're not mad,' I whispered. 'It's all right, you're allowed to cry.'

So we sat, the sixteen kilometres between us no barrier, pondering the too many twists, the shades of meaning and interpretations …

'Did you know? Daddy killed! My father-in-law asked him if he had and he said "Yes!" In the Polish Underground, they liked him so much they warned him not to go over to the resistance. "Heniek, you will find a bullet in your back."'

I smiled, – I already knew the saving story of his partisan-friend's warning – but Daddy had killed someone? He had never mentioned that. I'd have to ask him. And the converted brother-in-law, the stables burning, the sense of religion – all these things were new.

'Sara, he's old! No. He's not old! He's getting old!' I could hear her crying again. 'Did you know, in Poland during the 50th anniversary of the uprising visit last year he went to the cemetery?'

'No. I didn't.'

'Yes. He sent Mummy away – "Basia, I want to be by myself!" and then he went to the commemorative grave and he said Kaddish for his parents. You know he couldn't bring himself to do it before – I don't know why.'

In that moment, I knew why.

'Because Kaddish is not about death – it is a prayer in praise of God. That explains why he is a bit more at ease with himself.'

We sighed, relieved for him. She added, '
We are so lucky. They are such good people.'

Reluctantly we bid each other goodnight.

And I wrote: History being so complex, perpetrators and bystanders cope through willed ignorance, helplessness, reimagining their roles. The survivors omit and simplify; they tell a story easily grasped, and, in the way of such stories, they, and we, fall into archetypes.

The serendipitous and heroic bits emphasised, the incomprehensible reduced to oppositional pairs: we/they, good/evil, friend/enemy, gain/loss, victim/perpetrator; and to the personal: my pain, my family, mine. And in that process – all being black or white – all shades of the lived experience, are lost.

So no matter how careful the transition to written words,
there is always so much missing, that it seems not right.
But the terror is real; somewhere, sometime, another will rise.
It could be you; it could happen to yours …
It could be me; it did happen to mine.

Tired … I'm so tired. I must get up at six.
And still the night brings terrors. I am afraid … afraid to sleep …
The street is dark and narrow; tall walls on both sides tower.
Black dots on the ground menace … I must walk this street
without standing on a black dot or else fall forever. I run …
the black dots will take me … they are everywhere … I'm falling …
Frère Jacques … Frère Jacques … Dormez vous … Dormez vous …
Sonnez les matines … Sonnez les matines …
Ding dang dong … Ding dang dong …
My Mummy is so beautiful …
How? Why? Keep on going. Not the end …

The past really happened; can we who were not there know it?
From all this, what do *I* know?

Timothy Snyder alerts:

> *The history of the Holocaust is not over.*
> *Its precedent is eternal, and its lessons have not yet been learned.*[333]

A.H. had said:

> *The struggle for world domination is between me and the Jews. All else is meaningless. The Jews have inflicted two wounds on the world: Circumcision for the body and conscience for the soul. I come to free mankind from their shackles.*[334]

Avraham Burg points to where A.H. succeeded:

> *Hitler is no more. But we still suffer his evil legacy, and refuse to be comforted. It was easy for Hitler to take our lives away from us, and it is difficult for us to get Hitler out of our lives.*[335]

A.H. undeniably brought forth a terror that led men into the abyss.
But, by underestimating the small and great acts, he failed.
Indeed, as Herman Wouk declares,

Hitler is gone like a typhoon, leaving behind wreckage,
mass graves, crumbling crematoria and haunted minds …
He did not kill (all) the Jews. If we are God's witness, God still lives.[336]

Hannah Arendt's words remind:

… one man will always be left alive to tell the story.[337]

And so it is said: *Am Yisrael Chai* – The Jewish People Live.

I respond: Yes, and we remember our murdered dead.
Our murdered dead. In created mythologies they are clichéd:
victims or heroes. By individual testimony,
they are immortalised as ordinary individuals.

Everyman. Just like you and me.

It is also said:

May he who makes peace in the high places make peace for us,
and for all the people of Israel and say Amen.

These last two lines are from the Mourners' Kaddish.[338]
On 14 June 2011, at a minyan, in a prayer book used by liberal Jews,
I found an unambiguous clarification:

… May the One who causes peace to reign in the high heavens,
let peace descend on us, on all Israel, and <u>all the people of the world</u>,
and let us say Amen.[339]

By inclusion or omission, words hold power:
*'May **all** the people of Israel be forgiven, including all the strangers who*
live in their midst, for all the people are in fault.'[340]
Amen.

The Chai*, the essential ingredient of my*
father's Hebrew name Chaim,
is a symbol of Israel,
and also of the number eighteen.
Its meaning is to live, and,
as in l'chaim, *to life.*[341]
We know so much. We know so little.
Bella and Chaim are safe.

Their amazing story told.

I want to tell you a bit more.

AFFIRMATION: LIVING THE QUESTIONS

THE GOLDEN RULE

Rilke wrote to a young poet:

> *I … ask you … to show patience towards everything in your heart that has not been resolved and try to* cherish questions themselves, *like sealed rooms and books written in a language that is very foreign. Do not hunt for the answers just now – they cannot be given to you … What matters is that you live everything. And you must now live the questions. One day perhaps you will gradually and imperceptibly live your way into the answer.*[342]

Primo Levi wrote:

> *… be suspicious of those who seek to convince us with means other than reason, and of charismatic leaders: we must be cautious about delegating to others our judgement and our will. Since it is difficult to distinguish true prophets from false, it is as well to regard all prophets with suspicion. It is better to renounce revealed truths … (rather) … content oneself with more modest … truths, those acquired painfully … without shortcuts, with study, discussion, and reasoning …*[343]

This memoir, begun in 1992, in part as a response
to the rise of fascism and Holocaust denial,[344] *'completed' in 1996,*
for nearly thirteen years it lay in a box as if abandoned;
but not so. I knew a something was missing and kept searching;
the years had to pass for me to do more living and reading,
embrace despair and longing, and find a new well-spring
of delight and gratitude.
So, before we finish, four questions are posed
and recorded are the 'answers'.

ONE: Did I get it right, Daddy?
Heniek says yes.

A man of few words, my father.
Remembered are his periods of withdrawal and virtual silence.
But after I began writing, he began talking.
Not to me. To Janette – my younger sister. They shared time each
Friday afternoon while having a cigarette together.
I was glad. Not jealous? No! Glad!
I'd had my precious happy-past memories when it was him and me.

But now, I could not talk to him any more – not a conversation.
He rang me every day and we had our how-are-you-I'm-fine exchange.
It occurs to me – this project of mine, recording the smattering
of heroic saved in-the-nick-of-time anecdotes –
was this not in part an instrument for connection,
a substitute for conversation?

When Heniek read my 1996 draft, he asked, 'How do you know this?'

I replied: 'You told me, and I read it in books.'

'Mmm. But these names …'

'I got them from memoirs, history books and encyclopaedias. Are they right?'

He looked at me incredulously. 'This is written?'

'Yes. Are they right?'

He shook his head in disbelief … a long pause … then an emphatic, 'Yes.'

Years later in the winter of 1999, my parents went to Surfers Paradise.
With his final ordeal just weeks away,
this was to be Daddy's last holiday.
How did he manage to swim every day with just one leg?

Mummy and Daddy are back from Surfers. Mummy rings to tell me Daddy has reread my manuscript. Days pass with no comment.

Shabbat comes and he says nothing. I drop in on the Sunday and, over a cup of tea, I gather my courage and casually ask,
'Daddy, I believe you read my manuscript again.'

He looks at me intently, his lips pressed together.

'Did I get it right, Daddy?'

Silence. His amber eyes look steadily at me as if truly seeing me.
I remain quiet, respectful. I wait.
At last he says: 'Yes.' And he nods in affirmation.

Daddy, you'd progressively gone from
powerful, charismatic, to moody, withdrawn –
you who had mocked material things had come to see money
or rather lack of money as the marker of my success –
in this we nearly lost each other –
yet your last words to Branko and me resonate.

You, at 77, facing losing your other leg, ready to go, just days before your end; Branko, 57, a shrunken scarecrow with voice removed, desperately hanging on, just a few months before his.

We sit at your hospital bedside quiet, waiting.

Looking at Branko you say: 'I am proud of you.'

'You too.' His eyes include me. He continues, 'You never gave in …
I would have! But you never gave in.'

What did you mean?

Was it that Branko and I ignored condemnation to marry, at a time when inter-marriage was taboo, and stayed true to our vows while many around us did not? Could it be that, after all, you thought I had 'got it right'?

Turning to Branko, you add, 'I wish we could have one more smoke and a whisky together and talk a bit – maybe we would reach some understanding – maybe we would just enjoy the cigarette.'
You pause; we wait.
'Go now.' you say. 'I'm tired.'
We kiss you. Goodbye.

Just the next day, he declares to the gathered throng of family:
'No more cutting. No more medicine.

Let me go – I am happy with my life'.

In his eyes that had, to me, revealed terrifying anguish,
is a new warm contentment, a calm gaze of wonderment.

My father died a death to fear, and yet a death to wish for;
he died a happy man. With bits removed,
he'd suffered much but, at his end,
he was satisfied: with us, with his life, his achievements,
as if by living his life he'd found meaning.
In the hospital, just before he died, he said:
'God is love. God is inside everyone.'
An atheist all his life, this final statement was uncharacteristic,
reflecting back to me what I had written,
realisation of an extraordinarily lived life, with me always,
loving and loved, no more need to speak.
On his tombstone, we engraved:
A Man of Strength.

TWO: Why did such things happen? Live and let live: We are all the same.

In 2010, my mother, at 87, is shrunken and hunched. Her skin is still lovely, but her interior world has collapsed in concert with her body and her living space – which is now one room in my sister's rented home. Conversations commence with her medical problems, her current prognosis, how her many pills affect her, the various undignified dramas of being old.

We progress to updates and grumbles: who died, the various illnesses of her remaining band of friends (with whom she still lunches and plays cards), how she has to often catch taxis because her friends do not like to drive at night. (She never learnt to drive.)
I remind her they are nearly 90!

Her faculties are still sharp – not only does she remember every anniversary and birthday, but also, she has the love to remind me … Thanks, Mummy.

I do so love my mother; I also contend with things largely unspoken and unresolved that pain and grieve my consciousness. One is her inability to 'get' my husband Branko.[345] Another, her endless disappointment and litany of complaints; the core of this being our lack of financial success. 'It just wasn't given to us.' This aspect of bitterness she hid from the rest of the world behind a well-spring of platitudes – 'I am not wealthy, but I am rich in my family' – thus conveying a wise-woman persona that I find exasperating.

Third, she kept herself an absolute stranger – not in the sense of being one who has 'absolute desire to belong and absolute experience of rejection, always positioned in the eye of the other'[346] but neither longing to belong nor facing rejection, she held herself as one enduring suffering at every turn.

To that, add an overwhelming grief and fear: for much of our life Janette and I have known a weeping seemingly without end and a fear in every moment of every day: of loss, of losing, of imminent disaster. A question unanswerable: Why did such things happen?

Thankfully somewhere in the past few years – perhaps since we both lost our husbands, perhaps since I turned 60, perhaps since I became a grandmother, perhaps the way in which we remained a loving family despite the drama of the family money evaporating – somehow respect for each other emerged.

And, though she still has her litany of hurts, her counting of the blessings has expanded as she celebrates, from her two children, five grandchildren with their five spouses and many great-grandchildren.

In 2017, twelve great-grandchildren – ranging in ages from newborn to nearly twenty.

And she still has the ability to take me by surprise.

Take a typical Sunday a few years ago – on the way to a favourite café, she got into her love of things in the Jewish tradition as she experiences them through my sister's children. Both my children have married gentiles, as did I, and I take her comments to be provocative.

At this moment, as we try to make our points, our voices rise; conversation becomes argument. I should know better. I've long ago worked out she often falls into stereotype when trying to express her point of view. (I suppose I do too.) I should also take into account that she left school at sixteen, English is not her first language, and in her community, many of her generation, despite a 'nice' life in Australia, deal with their memories in a way that translates to fear and hatred of the 'they'. They being everyone who is not Jewish. And, these survivors are not so sure about Jews outside their own group either.

I do accept their right to their feelings; but she is my mother; from her I want more. So when her anecdotes include references to 'them' and 'us', I can't just let it go. Not with her. Her attempts to explain her 'hurts', when blocked by my 'logic', always trigger the same response from her:

The Holocaust.

They did this to us; you do not understand;

you cannot know.

This day she declares her ongoing terror that, because of my daughter's affiliation, the church will draw me in. Like all our discussions, we have gone over this ground before. I begin to tell her, yet again, not to worry … She interjects, 'I believe …'

She pauses, considering her words, continues with something I haven't heard her say before:

'I believe, everyone is just the same. I mean all people.'

She pauses again. 'There are good ones and bad ones.'

My hands on the wheel, glancing at her, I catch the affirming nod of her head as she agrees with herself. I give her a reassuring smile. She smiles back, her eyes sparkling, pleased with herself. I am pleased with her too.

'Watch the road,' she admonishes.

For good measure she adds, as if for the first time,
'Live and let live.'

Then she tells me of a recent vision: her Uncle Mayer had come to her. He sat on a chair in an alcove in his full orthodox garb and beckoned her to approach him. She dared not look directly at him; he was a *tzaddik* – a pious man – he would not look at her, yet, it was as if he had come to bless her. I glance at her; her eyes are full of tears.
'He blessed me,' she affirms.

And I have an insight – she who was denied a 'normal' period of youth, in a way remained ever youthful. Long may she live.
When she is gone, long may the memory of her live on.

All this is for Mummy.
And for my grandchildren and for those to come
so they may know something of her, and of all the people she loved.

And so they may know something of me.

THREE: *Desiderium.*[347] How may we meet?

With loved ones – they listen and mind me,
I pray for the God inside, to guide me,
And alone – in the indifferent flow –
To know when to say yes, when to say no.
The manner of your death an alert,
More than an object of destiny; more than beshert.
Always I bear witness to you alive.
Not flotsam, hear me! For this I strive.
Making a gift of words,
I write names of the murdered dead,
I open my eyes – banish fears; this testimony,
I wipe my tears; desiring synchrony,
Memorial Immemorial, with intent
As I still live, let me be extant.
as your trace, consecration, shroud.
I evoke your names; I say them aloud.
Aunts, uncles, cousins. All killed. Method of murder: unknown, or shot,
Laugh, sing, through the shames; across the void cry out,
From villages and towns near and far,
Forever out of reach, as if on a bright star.
Not in any records found. No trace. Book shut.
Assurance of G.O.D. as a Grand Organising Design
too hard for me yet.
Named and Unnamed. To the world lost.
Still praising God as Yahweh?
Surely, I must? Yes? No! I do not know.
Absorbing images via family lore, books, films – present and past.
From stardust we come to stardust we go.
May we one day all meet, if only as dust.

It is said we must name the names
and so I write names of the lost family:

The Grandfathers:

Yakov Heber, known as Jacob – the handsome jeweller.
Shot at 57. Murdered.

Pinkus Birenbaum, the worldly astute businessman.
Taken at 47. Murdered.

The Grandmothers:

Sara Heber nee Degenszajn, mysterious, ill, twirled her hair.
Shot at 55. Murdered.

Rena Birenbaum nee Czosnek, Racla in Yiddish, intelligent, book-lover.
Taken at 46. Murdered.

The Five Sisters of my Father Heniek:

Fella (Felicity), Frimit in Yiddish, beautiful, exotic.
Married to Moniek Kohn.
Taken at 34. Murdered. Moniek also murdered.

Franka (Francis), married to Natek Mann with a baby son.
Taken (with baby son) at 28. Both murdered.
Natek also murdered.

Marisa (Mary), Mania in Yiddish.
Shot, age 26. Murdered.

Dorka (Dorothy), married to Yacov Lebensold.
Yacov survived and went to Israel.
Taken (with baby son), age 25. Both murdered.

Inka (Regina), Rifka in Yiddish. Married to Stefan Tadeusz Drom Levich.
Taken, age 24. Murdered.
Stefan also murdered.

The Two Sisters of my Mother Basia:

Zosia (Sophia), Zysla in Yiddish, meaning wise.
The glamorous young woman. Married to Adam Poznanski.
Taken at 22. Murdered.
Adam, also murdered.

Celina, Tsirele in Yiddish, the clever child.
Taken at fifteen. Murdered.

Others whose names I know: Uncle Chilmier Heber, Tolla, Uncle Mayer Birenbaum and Leyele Birenbaum.

Cousins: Sara, Tseile, Gucia, Renia.

And the many whose names are lost …
All the people …
six million Jewish souls …
and all the other souls:
five million gypsies, gays, political prisoners …
All the men, women, children – Polish and others;
and all the soldiers on all sides.
An estimated total of over 60 million (range 50-80 million)
in a period of more than five years.[348]

And for them and us and those to come:

Though their story told, it is not my story,
yet, in the heart and soul of my raison d'être, it lives
as both unique and universal: a known mystery.
May the part we play, to future seasons give
footprints for a commonwealth that we hope will be
a shared reality for all who come to know and see.
Though their story told, is not my story,
may the part we play, to future seasons give.[349]

A work in progress.

FOUR: (How) may we know each other (?)

Insights into the tragedy of the human condition,
the I and Thou, pose a continuing dilemma.

Where one man's enlightenment is not necessarily another's,[350]
And loving all one's neighbours eludes the best of intentions.[351]
Neither selfishness nor selflessness are sufficient to resolve conflict,
How do we develop a space for goodwill so that we all can flourish?

Janusz Korczak implores us to work together.[352]

'We all are brothers and sisters, children of the same earth. We have been preceded by generations that shared a common destiny for good and evil – one long common path. We get light from the same sun and our crops are destroyed by the same hail. The same earth covers the bones of our forefathers. We have known more sorrow than joy, more tears than laughter, and neither you nor we bear the blame for this. Let us work together, let us educate ourselves together.

Sholem Asch solicits via his characters:[353]

When you are older you'll understand everything … for yourself.
Until that time … all you must strive for is to become a good man,
to love all men, do evil to nobody, keep straight and help others
whenever you can. That is … the religion of all men
whether they are Christians or Jews. Do you promise faithfully?

The Quran says:

O Mankind! (God) created you from a single pair of male and female
And made you into Nations and Tribes, that you may know each other
not that you may despise each other …[354]

And a plea for civility in public discourse:
from Israel's President Reuven Rivlin:

Each of us must ask ourselves, what is our part in this? Friends, we must not be silent. Silence is dangerous … specifically silence about the erosion of shared values. We have to find the way, the language and words whereby we deal with difficult tensions between us. I ask you, for us, for all of us, to find new meaning and think about your words.[355]

May more people of all faiths and none,
move beyond the justifying use of
any one or all of the names of God
where the good of the one
tramples on the good of the other,
and the tradition of tit-for-tat weds us unhappily to
failure,
reprisal,
divorce.

> Pastor Martin Niemöller[356] – writing as an indictment of inactivity of German Intellectuals during the Nazi regime:
>
> FIRST THEY CAME FOR THE COMMUNISTS,
> and I did not speak out—because I was not a communist;
> THEN THEY CAME FOR THE SOCIALISTS,
> and I did not speak out—because I was not a socialist;
> THEN THEY CAME FOR THE TRADE UNIONISTS,
> and I did not speak out—because I was not a trade unionist;
> THEN THEY CAME FOR THE JEWS,
> and I did not speak out—because I was not a Jew;
> THEN THEY CAME FOR ME –
> and there was no one left to speak out for me.

Ultimately, can you and I find ways beyond they and us?
What is it that makes a life good?
And how is that different from a good life?
Don't we yet long for a Better World?
Not a perfect world but one filled with the (im)possible.
A life worth living; mine *and* yours.
Ours and theirs.

How do we achieve all that? So far not much good for all.
In these uncertain times where any 'lessons' of the past elude
does it make any difference what we do?

Sometimes Yes; sometimes No.

Still we try.
Meanwhile we
live in the present, remember the past.
Interpret: for ourselves and for those to come.

Though in parts thirteen[357] *plus – what it means to be a*
human being of integrity and honour – a mensch
(this Yiddish word corresponds to Mencius,
the great Confucian sage of China,
he who asserted the innate goodness of the individual,
acted upon by society) –
remains an unanswered question,
and though I do not believe in any God –
I find through these pages that I discern a something beyond knowing.
John Caputo[358] *expresses it for me:*

> *… a dream, a desire, or a restlessness, a passion for the impossible … there is in Derrida, in deconstruction, a longing and sighing,*
> *a weeping and praying, a dream and a desire, for something non-determinable, un-foreseeable, beyond the actual and the possible …*
> *beyond the scope of what we can sensibly imagine.*

Yes, I do like the idea of a longing for the impossible.
A longing to love God whether He is there or not.
And if God is the infinite union of all contradictions including non-belief –
or if the right idea is God as a 'white page'
which writes itself as we evolve
or if there is '… a struggling divine essence … striving to merge with our hearts just as the mystic is striving to merge with God's',[359]
or some other wondrous (non)being
or some aspect we may never (dis)prove,
yet the complexity and the dimensions blow our minds and challenge us:
to dare to know, love our lives

and to strive to better be
as if there is a God,
and with(out) a formula for the good of the one
and the good of the other,
after all who is it we talk to
when we talk to God
if not our longing for a better world.

The Golden Rule is a good place to start.

The Golden Rule Across The World: Thirteen Sacred Texts + One More[360]

Bahá'í Faith: Lay not on any soul a load that you would not wish to be laid upon you, and desire not for anyone the things you would not desire for yourself. *Bahá'u'lláh*, Gleanings.	
Buddhism: Treat not others in ways that you yourself would find hurtful. *The Buddha*, Udana-Varga 5.18.	
Christianity: In everything, do to others as you would have them do to you; for this is the law and the prophets. *Jesus*, Matthew 7:12.	
Confucianism: One word which sums up the basis of all good conduct ...loving-kindness. Do not do to others what you do not want done to yourself. *Analects* 15.23	
Hinduism: This is the sum of duty: do not do to others what would cause pain if done to you. *Mahabharata* 5:1517.	
Islam: Not one of you truly believes until you wish for others what you wish for yourself. *The Prophet Muhammad*, Hadith.	
Jainism: One should treat all creatures in the world as one would like to be treated. *Mahavira*, Sutrakritanga 1.11.33.	
Judaism: What is hateful to you, do not do to your neighbour. This is the whole Torah; all the rest is commentary. Go and learn it. *Hillel*, Talmud, Shabbath 31a.	
Native Spirituality: We are as much alive as we keep the earth alive. *Chief Dan George*.	
Sikhism: I am a stranger to no one; and no one is a stranger to me. Indeed, I am a friend to all. *Guru Granth Sahib*, p.1299.	
Taoism: Regard your neighbour's gain as your own gain and your neighbour's loss as your own loss. *Lao Tzu*, T'ai Shang Kan Ying P'ien, 213-18.	
Unitarianism: We affirm and promote respect for the interdependent web of all existence of which we are a part. *Unitarian principle.*	
Zoroastrianism: (Persia) Do not do unto others whatever is injurious to yourself. *Shayast-na-Shayast* 13.29.	
And one more: ***Existentialism***: (Sartre)[361] What we choose is always the better; and nothing can be better for us unless it is better for all.	

STILL NOT THE END [361]

Clockwise from top: Heniek, Janette, Basia, Sara. Taken around 1985

FAMILY TREE

COLUMBIAN FAMILY
KOTT FAMILY
ARGENTINIAN FAMILY
TO FRANCE
mid 1930s
BIRENBAUM
CZOSNEK
MENAHEM HEBER
PESACH DEGENSZAJN
m
FRIMIT ROSENKRANZ
Zisa?
Eliakim
Renia?
Fella Kott nee (Heber)
Felix Heber
TO AUSTRALIA mid 1930s
PINKUS 1895 - 1942?
RENA 1886 - 1942
Mayer
Yechiel Meir Heber
JACOB 1885 -1942
SARA LEAH 1887 - 1942
ZEV
DEGEN FAMILY
FAYGALLEH
ROSENBLATT FAMILY
m
m
ZOSIA 1920 -1942?
CELINA 1926 -1942?
BELLA 1923 -
CHAIM 1922-1999
FELLA 1908 - 1942?
FRANKA 1914 -1942?
MARISA 1916 - 1942
DORKA 1917 -1942?
INKA 1918 -1942?
m
Adam Poznanski
m. 9 August 1942
HANNAH Sara's twin
m
baby son
Moniek Kohn
baby son
m
Yacov Lebensold
m
Stephan Taduesz Drom Levich
BRANKO VIDAL 1942 - 2000
SARA RENA 1945 -
JANETTE PAULINE 1951 -
DANNY RUBENSTEIN 1950 -
m. 1968
m. 1971
JADE b.1973
JESSICA b.1974
LEE HADASSA b.1982
ELLIOT JOSHUA b.1976
AMY PETA b.1972
BELLA & CHAIM'S GRANDCHILDREN
m. 2008
JACQUELINE b. 1979
m. 2006
JOEL b. 1977
m. 2008
ELI b. 1981
m. 2006
GEORGINA b. 1977
m. 1994
MARK b. 1967
Leon b. 2010
Atlas b. 2014
Jacinta Bella b. 2008
Jordan Levi John b. 2010
Marli Rose b. 2011
Oscar b 2014
Jack b. 2018
Isabelle Rose b.2010
Asher Henry b. 2013
Jude Mark b. 2017
Joshua Jacob b.1997
Brandon Chaim b. 2000
Corey Jude b.2004
BELLA & CHAIM'S GREAT GRANDCHILDREN

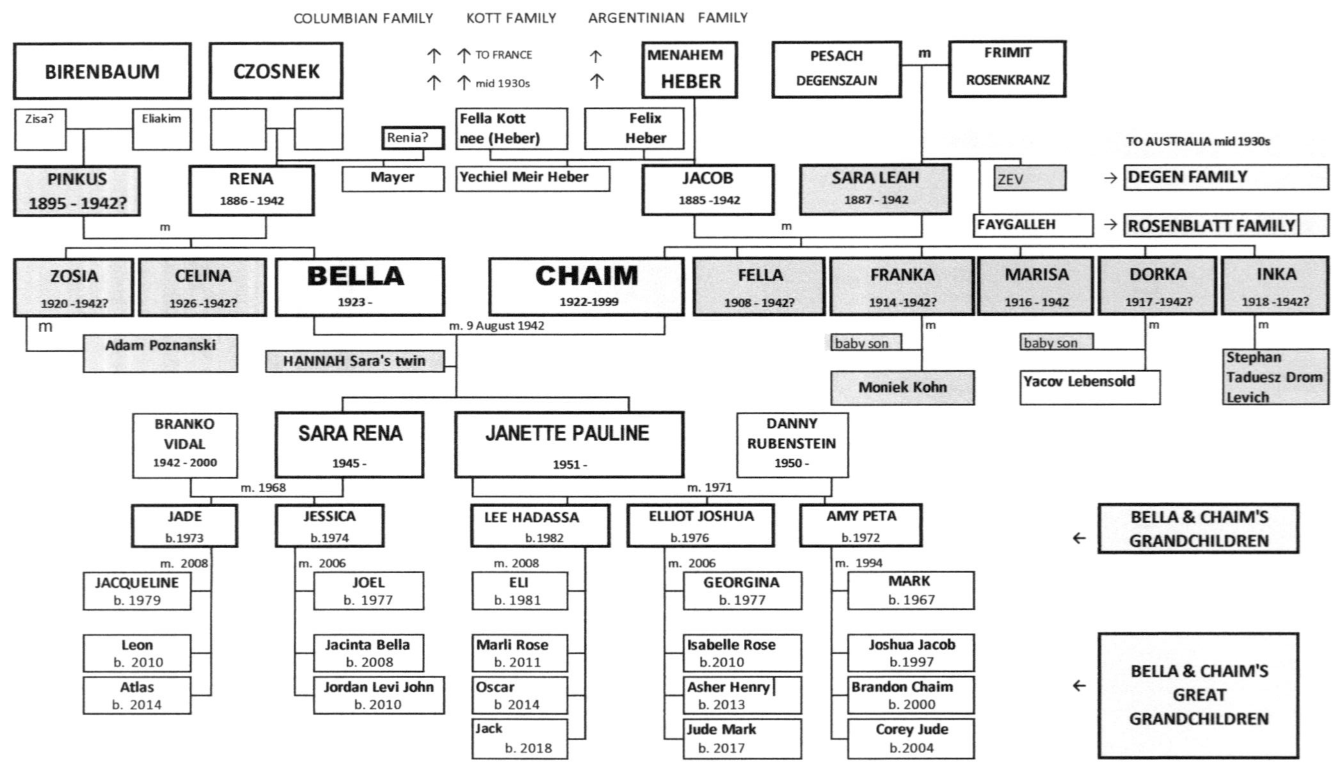

ACKNOWLEDGEMENTS

Thank you to the many people who have been part of making this happen including:

Dr Wesley Rouch for suggesting, in 1991, that I should write my stories;

Emma Kranz for linking me to Dorothea Cerruty and to Mark Baker (his advice led me to Yehuda Bauer's work) in 1996;

Dorothea Cerruty (Cerrie) OA, my inspirational mentor and friend during 1996–98;

Peter Bishop, director at Varuna, The Writers House, for the insightful handwritten feedback for an unsuccessful submission in 1997;

Professor John Rundell for his brilliant Social and Critical Theory subjects at Melbourne University in 2000;

Liliane Grace for her exceptional writing courses, encouragement, and manuscript review during 2009-11;

Gail Rockman, printmaker and art therapist, for guiding me on a liberating journey of self-discovery during 2009;

Leslie Rosenblatt, in 2011, for his enthusiastic praise and critical appraisal that I had two books in one and needed to separate them;

Leslie Cannold (via Writers Victoria) for her intensive writing course which resulted in a new introduction in 2012;

both Frank Peniguel (who serendipitously led me to Liliane Grace) and Arnold Sackville, for companionship, encouragement and for putting up with my unorthodox writing hours;

Kerry Chong, Jenifer Nicholls, Susan Balderstone, William Beasley, Howard Dosser, Mary Burbage, Helene Richards, and the members of the Williamstown Writers Group for reading, listening, discussing and commenting (and for their instructive body-language);

Nola Firth and Jane Yule, who both encouraged me to cut, cut, cut; Deb Robertson for guidance and for recommending Jane.

Over 120 people and organisations contributed to making this book possible by pre-purchasing books via a crowd-funding campaign. I thank you all. There were several awesome supporters: Greg Missingham, John Denton and Barrie Marshall, Kay Didenkowski, and others who wish to remain anonymous.

And for truly amazing encouragement and support, a very special thank you to all at the Rotary Club of Point Gellibrand, Ilga and Mareks Petrovs, Rene Eisner.

To my Publishers – Anna Rosner Blay and Louis De Vries – for finding value in this book and bringing it into being with patience and skill.

And to my family: my husband, Branko Vidal – in my family he was 'the other'; he believed in me and read, endlessly encouraged and loved my many drafts from 1992 to his death in 2000;

my mother Bella Heber and father Heniek Heber, for sharing their story, reading my drafts, and for being patient with my desire to know more and more;

my cousins: Jeff Degen, Rene Eisner, Norma Zandle, Aviva Stillman, and my nieces and nephew: Lee Green, Amy Wasbutzki and Elliott Rubenstein – who variously read multiple drafts, provided information and encouraged me to keep going;

Danny Rubenstein for being like a son to my mother;

my children Jade and Jessica for taking me seriously;

and my sister Janette Rubenstein for all our discussions and for her view: 'Well, if I wrote a book it would be completely different!'

GENERAL SOURCES

Guided by my parents' testimonies and supplemented by extensive research, my attempt to tell and verify their story brought me into contact with a vast body of historical record, memoir and analysis.

TESTIMONY OF HENRY HEBER

Interview conducted by Mr Philip Maisel at the Melbourne Holocaust Centre, as part of the Stephen Spielberg USC Shoah Foundation collection of testimonies. In 1995 my father gave his testimony. I was given a copy on tape which I have since had copied to DVD. The image and sound are poor. Though details and sequence of events occasionally differ from his sessions with me, I was able to confirm with him that I had recorded the events correctly. What is remarkable is being able to look at his face and hear his voice as he tells his story.

THE EARLY YEARS

Celia S. Heller's *On The Edge Of Destruction,* distilled from the memories and records of Jews pre-1939, parallels what I heard from my parents and their friends, and thus added depth to what my parents told me; through her musings, things I'd held in contempt were transformed. For example: the fact the Jewish synagogue is noisier than the Christian church is not a sign of disrespect (as I had taken it to be) but of being 'at-home'.

Chaim Bermant's T*he Walled Garden* presents an insightful array of Jews and Jewish life that goes far beyond victim or hero.

Both these writers evoke the family as central to Jewish life.

THE WARSAW GHETTO PERIOD

It is evident many people writing about the Warsaw Ghetto period draw on the found archival documents plus survivor accounts such as that of Marek Edelman, and Nazi records such as *The Stroop Report*.

Kermish's *To Live With Honor And Die With Honor: Selected documents from the Warsaw Ghetto Underground Archives* covers a huge range of topics from a program of a children's play to studies on starvation, copies of Nazi edicts and minutes of meetings. These outpourings of feelings, thoughts, diarised events and research by inhabitants of the Warsaw Ghetto speak to us with an intensity undiluted by applied historical or ideological bias. More reliable than recollective memory, their immediacy demonstrates a lack of knowledge of the outside; as such, they are an aspect but not the whole picture. (Refer also endnote 165.)

Notes from the Warsaw Ghetto: The Journal of Emmanuel Ringelblum, is rich in detail, knowledge and immediacy.

The Warsaw Diary of Adam Czerniakow. Before purchasing a copy in 2015, I accessed it online on 20/9/2014 at http://www.holocaustresearchproject.org/ghettos/acdiary.htm

Documents on the Holocaust is an invaluable and comprehensive collection of German, Polish and Jewish documents, ranging from The National Socialist Programme (a.k.a. the 25-point Programme or the 25-point Plan) of 1920 to the Nuremburg Trials in 1947.

Books by Yehuda Bauer and Israel Gutman contain much detail and many archival photos, some of which are now available online.

Of the recent histories, particularly thorough is the work of the Polish Center for Holocaust Research database and website: http://warszawa.getto.pl/index.php; and *The Warsaw Ghetto: A Guide to the Perished City* by Barbara Engelking and Jacek Leociak. It contains maps that locate known services, official and clandestine, which indicate and are a tribute to the vibrancy of the ghetto.

Black Earth: The Holocaust as History and Warning by Timothy Snyder: his approach to history and political theory is novel and controversial. He draws a distinction between occupation and colonisation. He warns that blaming ethnicity or the inherent nature of certain groups and applying collective responsibility, is a trap that leads to the 'abolition of political thought and the lifting of individual agency.' *Black Earth* (150). Rather, we need to maintain the State and civility for all.

Oxford Readers Nazism is a valuable overview and collection of extracts on National Socialism.

Neil Ascherson's *The Struggles For Poland*, a vibrant insight to Poland's spirit, takes the reader through its turbulent history: restoration of independence in 1918, horrors of Nazi and Soviet occupation, Warsaw uprising, the communist state, Solidarity.

GENERAL INTERNET SOURCES

The United States Holocaust Memorial Museum History site: https://www.ushmm.org/

Chicago, Illinois Newspaper Archives (1877–2000): https://newspaperarchive.com/us/illinois/chicago/

Yad Vashem, The World Holocaust Remembrance Center: http://www.yadvashem.org

Holocaust Research Project: http://www.holocaustresearchproject.org/

And the many Wikipedia sites are informative and give detailed citations.

THE DISPLACED PERSONS PERIOD

Yehuda Bauer's *Out Of The Ashes* and Mark Wyman's *DPs: Europe's Displaced Persons, 1945–1951* made my father's unbelievable anecdotes suddenly real. Despite minor variations in detail, their facts, figures, and dates (actual edicts, records and diaries) are consistent with his. Where there is variance in figures, I indicate the range or use the 'safer' reference such as the Polish Center for Holocaust Research database. Any discrepancies are unintentional.

THE HUMAN CONDITION

There are many writers whose ideas influenced mine, provided affirmation of my views, or invoked a negative reaction. In the context of this book, Primo Levi, George Steiner, Hannah Arendt, Peter Gay, Hermann Hesse, Thomas Mann, Sholem Asch, John Caputo, Leon Feuchtwanger, and Frederic Grunfeld, among others, illuminated.

RELIGION

Having borrowed it from a cousin's bookshelf in the early 1990s, I was surprised to discover, in *This is My God* by Herman Wouk, that much that I'd taken to be part and parcel of so-called New Age thinking can be found in the Jewish tradition.

BIBLIOGRAPHY

Andrews, Andy. *How Do You Kill 11 Million People? Why the Truth Matters More Than You Think.* New York; Thomas Nelson, 2011.

Arad, Yitzhak; Gutman, Yitzhak; Margaliot, Abraham. *Documents on the Holocaust: Selected Sources on the Destruction of the Jews of Germany and Austria, Poland, and the Soviet Union.* Jerusalem: Yad Vashem, 1981.

Arendt, Hannah. *Eichmann in Jerusalem: A Report on the Banality of Evil.* New York: Penguin, 1963.

Arnon, Joseph. *Who Was Janusz Korczak?* Booklet from Jewish Holocaust Centre (Melbourne), under the patronage of Yad Vashem Jerusalem for the World Federation of Polish Jews. (1977).

Asch, Sholem. *Three Cities.* New York: Putnam, 1933.

Ascherson, Neal. *The Struggles for Poland.* London: Michael Joseph, 1987.

Barker, Kenneth (ed.). *KJV Study Bible* – Large Print. Michigan: Zondervan, 1995.

Bauer, Yehuda. *A History of the Holocaust.* Revised Edition. USA: Franklin Watts, 2001.

Bauer, Yehuda. *Out Of The Ashes.* New York: Pergamon Press, 1989.

Bauer, Yehuda. *Rethinking The Holocaust.* USA: Yale University Press, 2002.

Benjamin, Walter. *Illuminations.* (Translated from the German Shiftren 1955) London: Pimlico, 1999.

Bermant, Chaim. *The Jews*. Great Britain: Weidenfeld and Nicolson, 1977.

Bermant, Chaim. *The Walled Garden*. London: Weidenfeld and Nicolson, 1974.

Borkin, Joseph. *The Crime and Punishment of I.G. Farben.* London: Andre Deutsch, 1979.

Burg, Avraham. *The Holocaust Is Over; We Must Rise Above Its Ashes.* USA: Palgrave Macmillan, 2008.

Caputo, John D. *The Prayers and Tears of Jacques Derrida.* Religion without Religion. Indiana University Press, 1997.

Des Pres, Terence. *The Survivor***.** New York: Oxford University Press, 1976.

Dombrowski, Daniel A., *Kazantzakis and God*. Albany: State University of New York Press, 1997.

Dudley, Will. *Hegel, Nietzsche, and Philosophy: Thinking Freedom***.** Cambridge: Cambridge University Press, 2002.

Elton, Zyga. *Destination Buchara***.** Australia: Dizal, 1996.

Engelking, Barbara & Leociak, Jacek. *The Warsaw Ghetto: A Guide To The Perished City.* London: Yale, 2009.

Facing History And Ourselves Foundation. *Holocaust and Human Behaviour.* Resource Book. Massachusetts. 1994. And online at www.facinghistory.org

Ferrone, Vincenzo. *The Enlightenment.* New Jersey: Princeton University Press, 2015.

Feuchtwanger, Lion**.** *Jew Süss.* London: Martin Secker, 1928.

Feuchtwanger, Lion**.** *Success: Three Years in the Life of a Province***.** London: Martin Secker, 1930.

Feuchtwanger, Lion. *Tis Folly to be Wise: Death and Transfiguration of Jean-Jaques Rousseau*. London: Hutchinson, 1954.

Forche, Carolyn. *The Angel of History*. Newcastle upon Tyne: Bloodaxe Books, 1994.

Gay, Peter. *The Cultivation of Hatred.* New York: Norton, 1993.

Ginzberg, Natalia. *The Little Virtues*. NY: Skyhorse Publishing, 2013.

Gregor, Neil. *Oxford Readers Nazism*. UK: Oxford University Press, 2000.

Grunfeld, Frederic V. *Prophets Without Honour*. London: Hutchinson, 1970.

Gutman, Israel. *Resistance: The Warsaw Ghetto Uprising.* United States Holocaust Memorial Museum: Miles Lerman Centre, 1994.

Gutman, Israel & Avital Saf (Eds.). *She'erit Hapletah*, *1944–1948*. Proceedings of The Sixth Yad Vashem International Historical Conference. Jerusalem, Oct 1985.

Gutman, Israel. *The Jews of Warsaw, 1939–1943: Ghetto, Underground, Revolt*. Bloomington: Indiana University Press, 1982.

Heber, Henry. *Testimony of Henry Heber.* Melbourne Holocaust Centre. Interview conducted by Mr Philip Maisel, 1995.

Heller, Agnes. *A Theory of History.* (First Edition) Routledge and Keegan Paul, 1982.

Heller, Celia S. *On The Edge Of Destruction: Jews of Poland between the Two World Wars*. Detroit: Wayne State University Press, 1994.

Hilberg, Raul. *The Destruction of the European Jews*. New York: New Viewpoints, 1973.

Hilberg, Raul; Staron, Stanislaw; Kermisz, Josef. (eds). *The Warsaw Diary of Adam Czerniakow*. New York: Stein and Day, 1979.

Hinchman Lewis P. & Sandra K. Hinchman. (eds). *Hannah Arendt: Critical Essays*. USA: State University of New York, 1994.

Hitler, Adolf. *My Struggle*. The Paternoster Library G.B: Hurst & Blackett, April 1937. (First published 1933)

Johnston, Paul. *The Holocaust.* London: Phoenix Abridged Edition, 1996.

Jones, Hugh (ed.) *Famous Front Pages of the 20th Century*. Victoria (Australia): Hardie Grant Books, 1999.

Joseph, Sandra (ed.) *Loving Every Child: Wisdom for Parents: Janusz Korczak*. New York: Workman Publishing, 2007.

Keneally, Thomas. *Schindler's Ark*. Great Britian, Hodder and Stoughton, 1982.

Kermish, Joseph (ed.). *To Live with Honor and Die with Honor: Selected Documents from the Warsaw Ghetto Underground Archive. 'O.S.' (Oneg Shabbat)*. Jerusalem: Yad Vashem, 1986.

Kugelmass, Jack. *Jews, Sports, and the Rites of Citizenship*. Urbana: University of Illinois Press, 2007.

Langer, Lawrence L. *Holocaust Testimonies: The Ruins of Memory.* London: Yale University Press, 1991.

Levin, Nora. *The Holocaust.* *The Destruction of European Jewry 1933–1945*. New York: Schocken Books, 1973.

Levy, Primo. *If This Is A Man and The Truce*. London: Penguin, 1979.

Mann, Thomas. *The Magic Mountain*. (First published 1924). G.B: Penguin, 1976.

Metaxas, Eric. *Bonhoeffer: Pastor, Martyr, Prophet, Spy.* Nashville: Thomas Nelson, 2010.

Miłosz, Czesław. *The History of Polish Literature*. Berkely and Los Angeles, California: University of California Press, 1983.

Miłosz, Czesław. *The Captive Mind*. New York: Vintage International Edition, 1990.

Mogilanski, Roman (ed.). *The Ghetto Anthology*. Los Angeles: American Congress of Jews from Poland, 1985.

Niewyk, Donald L. *The Holocaust*. New York: Houghton Mifflin Company, 1997.

Naor, Mordecai. *The Twentieth Century in Eretz Israel.* Cologne: Könemann, 1998.

Perl, William R. *The Holocaust Conspiracy.* New York: Shapolsky Publishers, 1989.

Pisar, Samuel. *Of Blood and Hope.* London: Cassell, 1980.

Plowman, Peter. *Australian Migrant Ships 1946-1977.* Australia: Rosenberg Publishing Pty Ltd, 2006

Quinion, Michael. *Ologies and Isms: A Dictionary of Word Beginnings and Endings.* USA: Oxford University Press, 2008.

Rauschning, Hermann. *Revolution of Nihilism: A Warning to the West.* NY: Alliance Book Corporation, First ed. August 1939.

Rilke, Rainer Maria. *Letters To A Young Poet.* Translated by Mark Harmon. USA: Harvard University Press, 2011.

Rundell, John (co-editor). *Critical Horizons: A Journal of Social & Critical Theory*, Vol 1 – no 1 2000. The Netherlands: Brill Academic Publishers, 2000.

Steinsaltz, Adin. *The Thirteen Petalled Rose.* New York: Basic Books, 2006.

Singer, Isaac Bashevis. *The Family Moskat.* Penguin, 1980.

Sloan, Jacob (ed.). *Notes From The Warsaw Ghetto: The Journal of Emmanuel Ringelblum.* New York: McGraw-Hill Book Company, 1973.

Snyder, Timothy. *Black Earth: The Holocaust as History and Warning.* New York: Tim Duggan Books, 2015.

Snyder, Timothy. *Bloodlands: Europe Between Hitler and Stalin.* New York: Basic Books. 2010.

Solnit, Rebecca. *Hope in the Dark. Untold Histories, Wild Possibilities.* Chicago: Haymarket Books, 2016.

Steiner, George. *A Reader.* New York: Oxford University Press, 1984.

Steiner, George. *The Portage to San Cristobal of A.H.* New York: Simon & Shuster, 1981.

Stern, Chaim (ed.). *Gates of Prayer for Weekdays: A Gender Sensitive Prayerbook.* New York: Central Conference of American Rabbis 5755, 1994.

Stroop, Jürgen. *The Stroop Report: The Jewish Quarter Of Warsaw Is No More.* Written 1943. English Translation US: Random House, 1979.

Trunk, Isaiah. *Judenrat: The Jewish Councils in Eastern Europe Under Nazi Occupation.* Boston: Scarborough Books, 1977.

Watt, Richard M. *Bitter Glory: Poland and its Fate 1918 to 1939.* New York: Simon and Schuster, 1979.

West, Morris. *The Tower of Babel.* New York: William Morrow, 1968.

Weizmann, Chaim. *Trial and Error: The Autobiography of Chaim Weizmann*. London: East and West Library, 1950.

Wouk, Herman. *This Is My God*. G.B: Abe Wouk Foundation, 1960.

Wyman, Mark. *DP: Europe's Displaced Persons, 1945–1951*. US: Associated University Presses, 1989.

Zuckerman, Yitzhak & Harshav, Barbara. *A Surplus Of Memory: Chronicle Of The Warsaw Ghetto Uprising*. University of California Press, 1993.

Zvielli, Alexander (compiler). *Front Page Israel: The Jerusalem Post*. Jerusalem: Jerusalem Post, Tenth Edition, 2012.

ENDNOTES

PART ONE: LIGHT IN THE DARK

1 Bella, meaning beautiful in French and Latin, is also God's Promise, from Isabelle, in Hebrew. The rose symbolises Beauty. Chaim means life, as in *l'chaim* – to life. The symbol is the Hebrew letter *chai* which means life and is also the number eighteen. Rose symbol viewed 18/7/2016 at: http://www.merry-christmas.com/traditions/symbols-of-christmas-and-christianity/rose. Chai symbol viewed 26/9/09 at http://en.wikipedia.org/wiki/Chai_(symbol)

2 This phrase is from Isaiah, chapter 56, verse 5; *memorial and a name* in Hebrew is *yad vashem*. This is the name taken by the the World Holocaust Remembrance Center in Jerusalem.

3 Andy Andrews, *How Do You Kill 11 Million People? Why the Truth Matters More Than You Think* (7).

4 Agnes Heller, *A Theory of History* (50).

5 The Commandment to 'Choose Life' is in Deuteronomy 30: 19-20: *I call heaven and earth to record this day against you, that I have set before you life and death, blessing and cursing: therefore choose life, that both you and thy seed may live …'* from Barker (ed), *KJV Study Bible* Large Print.

6 Exodus 20:2-3: 'I am, thus accept me' and/or 'I am, thus believe in me'.

7 *Shabbos* is the Yiddish word for Sabbath (*Shabbat* in Hebrew).

8 Found in the *The Dictionary of Obscure Sorrows* on 25/3/2016 at http://www.dictionaryofobscuresorrows.com/post/105778238455/anemoia-n-nostalgia-for-a-time-youve-never

9 I found *Hiraeth* when searching on 19/10/2014 for an encompassing word for loss and longing at http://www.theparisreview.org/blog/2012/09/18/dreaming-in-welsh/
Wikipedia informs: *Hiraeth* bears considerable similarities with the Portuguese concept of *saudade* (a key theme in Fado music), Galician *morriña*, Romanian *dor*, German *Sehnsucht* and Ethiopian *tizita* which is like the blues. Viewed 30/8/2016 at https://en.wikipedia.org/wiki/Hiraeth

10 Still searching for a word to encompass loss, longing, gratitude for life; finding none, make one: *Atoh-dachaia*, meaning gratitude for life encompassed in longing: for a past that was and was not, and for a future that is better for those to come. It is an amalgam of five words: TOH-DA from toh-dah, the Hebrew word for gratitude תּוֹדָה, used for thank you. Viewed 2/3/16 at http://ulpan.com/how-tosay-grateful-in-hebrew/. Plus CHAI meaning Life. The AI also relates to Eudaimonia (see endnote 268); the 'A' at the beginning is a nod to the non-word Anemoia – meaning nostalgia for a time you've never known (found in The Dictionary of Obscure Sorrows viewed 25/5/2016); and the 'A' at the end stands for things desired as essential as in Desiderata. ATOH-DACHAIA = GOOD LIFE.

PART TWO: PICTURE (IM)PERFECT

11 Found in Herman Wouk, *This Is My God* (154).

12 The names of Pinkus' half-brothers were Schmul and Gerszon Birenbaum.

13 The hat that religious Jews wore either originated from that worn by Polish or German gentiles or had beginnings shrouded in time. There is a photo of such a Warsaw Jew in Heller, On *The Edge Of Destruction: Jews of Poland between Two World Wars* (67).

14 The Nazi propaganda machine, with Goebbel's guidance, showed newsreels that succeeded in striking terror into the hearts of Germans. In the minds of Nazis and Germans, the Jewish connection was clear. Karl Marx, Vladimir Lenin and Leon Trotsky were all of Jewish descent. Communism was thus conveyed as a realisation of the Jewish desire for socialism to triumph over capitalism. Never mind that in point 24 of the National Socialists' NSGWP 25-Point Plan, the Jew is declaimed as being materialistic: 'The Party, as such … combats the Jewish-materialist spirit within and without us.' Yitzhak Arad et al., *Documents on the Holocaust* (18); A.H. would develop a 'Hunger Plan' (under Goering) to starve out 30 million superfluous human beings. See Timothy Snyder, *Black Earth: The Holocaust as History and Warning* (21), and Snyder, *Bloodlands: Europe Between Hitler and Stalin* (162-63, 416).

15 References for German angst, viewed 17/3/2106 http://www.bbc.co.uk/education/guides/zh9p34j/revision/6 and http://www.historylearningsite.co.uk/modern-world-history-1918-to-1980/weimar-germany/the-young-plan-of-1929

16 Volume 1, published in Vienna in 1925, and Volume 2 published in 1926.

17 For transcripts of the original mass pamphlet issued by the Nazis during the second round of the 1932 presidential campaign which presents Hitler as the only person able to save Germany, and in which A.H. addresses what he calls slander and lies, go to http://research.calvin.edu/german-

propaganda-archive/tatsachenundluegen.htm – viewed 15/10/2016.

18 http://ww2history.com/blog/ww2-controversies/why-do-so-many-people-want-to-think-hitler-was-mad-2/#more-96 – viewed 2/4/2016.

19 I borrow this from George Steiner's name for Hitler in *The Portage to San Christobal of A.H.*

20 National Socialist German Workers' Party (*Nationalsozialistische Deutsche Arbeiterpartei*, NSDAP) – 25-Point Plan – refer Arad, *Documents on the Holocaust* (15-18).

21 The evidence for the Reichstag fire points to the SA (*Sturmabteilung*, Storm Troopers) acting on A.H.'s instructions or perhaps on Göring's. The day after the fire Hitler asked for and received from President Hindenburg extensive powers. Thus enabled, he formed the Gestapo (contraction of *Geheime Staatspolizei*, the Nazi Secret State Police, incorporated into the SS in 1936), which suspended most civil liberties in Germany. http://911review.com/precedent/century/reichstag.html France and England knew Germany was re-arming in contravention of the Treaty of Versailles but made no protest. Poland, in 1934 – having renouncing the Minorities Treaty (the condition on which she was granted independence) – made no complaint. http://www.yivoencyclopedia.org/article.aspx/Minorities_Treaties – viewed 19/7/2016.

22 What is this National Socialism? Much has and will be written in an attempt to answer this question. The following are a sample of evolving views, in Gregor's *Oxford Readers Nazism*:
1939: Hermann Rauschning, writing in *Revolution of Nihilism: A Warning to the West*, said: '… what is this Third Reich in reality, a new order in the making or a holocaust, a national re-birth through the historic energies of the nation or a progressive, permanent revolution of sheer destruction …?' (24);
1941: Ernst Fraenkel, in *The Dual State,* identified National Socialism as a combination of two States: the Normative State (rational and legal) which enabled stable capitalism, and the Prerogative State (governed by the party) which exercised 'unlimited arbitrariness and violence unchecked by any legal guarantees'(146);
1972: Tim Mason discusses the rise of the economic ruling class from 1936 and the way in which the re-armament boom caused a shortage of materials such that the need for raw materials to keep up production made war a worthwhile risk. From 'The Primacy of Politics' (152-56).

23 Nazi is a portmanteau of *Nationalsozialist*, i.e. a supporter of National Socialism.

24 I was puzzled when I found quotes online and elsewhere that I had not seen in my copy of *Mein Kampf*; then I realised my copy (the Paternoster version) is abridged. I found confirmation at: https://en.wikipedia.org/wiki/Mein_Kampf – viewed 20/8/2016, which states: 'Houghton Mifflin's

abridged English translation [and thus Paternoster's] left out some of Hitler's more antisemitic and militaristic statements.' My copy is the Paternoster abridged version..

25 Hitler, *Mein Kampf*, Paternoster abridged version (138).

26 This quote is from *Mein Kampf*, Vol. One: A Reckoning, Chapter XII: 'The First Period of Development of the National Socialist German Workers' Party'. Found online at http://www.hitler.org/writings/Mein_Kampf/mkv1ch12.html – it is the last sentence of point 4, viewed 21/8/2016.

27 *Holocaust Encyclopedia*, THE GERMAN CHURCHES AND THE NAZI STATE: https://www.ushmm.org/wlc/en/article.php?ModuleId=10005206 – viewed 29/7/2016.

28 Bonhoeffer was a man of conscience who said: 'What is at stake is by no means whether our ... congregation can still tolerate church fellowship with the Jews ... (but) to say: here is the church, where Jew and German stand together under the Word of God ...' Quote found in Eric Metaxas, *Bonhoeffer. Pastor, Martyr, Prophet, Spy: A Righteous Gentile vs the Third Reich* (150).

29 Read the speech by Joseph Goebbels in *Holocaust Encyclopedia*, BOOKS BURN AS GOEBBELS SPEAKS: https://www.ushmm.org/wlc/en/media_fi.php?ModuleId=10005852&MediaId=158
See the film of it at: https://www.youtube.com/watch?v=JbLDrnnRBBM

30 In German: *'Dort, wo man Bücher verbrennt, verbrennt man am Ende auch Menschen.'*

31 18 May 1933 the *Chicago Daily Tribune* article on p. 3 described: '... a pact whereby each Nation would pledge itself not to send armed forces across its boundaries ...' http://archives.chicagotribune.com/1933/05/18/page/3/article/hails-roosevelt-proposal-as-aid-to-world-peace/ – viewed 7/3/16. And on the same day on p. 1, http://archives.chicagotribune.com/1933/05/18/page/1/article/germans-cheer-peace-vow are details of A.H.'s speech; here are some of its headings: Assails Versailles Treaty; Set Fears at Rest; Asks What France Wants; Praises Mussolini Plan; Germany Completely Disarmed; Calls Sanctions 'Monstrous'; Lays Blame on Others; Tells Harm of Reparations; Threatens Entire World; Pictures Peril of Bolshevism.

32 Banner of *The Herald* newspaper on 18 May 1933 found in Hugh Jones (ed): *Famous Front Pages of the 20th Century,* And similarly *The Chicago Tribune* on the same day: viewed 7/3/16. http://archives.chicagotribune.com/1933/05/18/page/1/article/germans-cheer-peace-vow 'Hitler Accepts Roosevelt Plan to End All War'.

33 Nuremberg Laws (*Nürnberger Gesetze):* A series of decrees first passed on September 15, 1935, that institutionalised Nazi racial theory, defined who was a Jew, deprived Jews of German citizenship, placed strict restrictions on their lives and employment, segregation of them from

German society, and forbade intermarriage between Jews and non-Jews; also established 'degrees of Jewishness' based on family lines. Source: http://www.holocaustcenter.org/glossary-terms – viewed 14/11/2016. Just a year earlier on June 30, 1934 in the 'Night of the Long Knives', A.H's order to purge the leadership of the SA and other actual or perceived opponents within the Nazi party had been enacted. *Black Earth* (40, 41, 80).

34 Industrialists that bankrolled the Nazis, include (allegedly):
• Hjalmar Schacht, Head of the Reichsbank, organised fund-raising parties;
• Fritz von Thyssen, German steel businessman;
• Alfred Krupp, owner of Krupp steel firm;
• I.G. Farben, the German chemicals firm, funded half the 1933 elections;
• The German car firm Opel (a subsidiary of General Motors);
• Schroeder Bank – on Jan. 3, 1933, Reinhard Schroeder asked A.H. to form a government.
And many foreign firms including:
• Henry Ford of Ford Motors. A.H. borrowed passages from Ford's book *The International Jew* to use in *Mein Kampf* and had a picture of Ford on the wall of his office;
• Union Banking Corporation, NY. George Bush's great-grandfather was president;
• WA Harriman and Co., American shipping & railway company. George Bush's grandfather was vice-president;
• Irénée du Pont, who served on the Finance Committee and the Board of Directors of General Motors (GM) and was active on DuPont's Board of Directors, was a strong supporter of eugenics and I.G. Farben, and advocated the creation of a super-race by spinal injections to enhance children of 'pure' blood.
Source: http://www.johndclare.net/Weimar7.htm – viewed 6/6/2015.

35 *Holocaust Encyclopedia*, KRISTALLNACHT. The shooting in Paris of German diplomat Ernst vom Rath by Herschel Grynszpan, a German-born Polish Jewish student (vom Rath died on 9 November 1938, coinciding with the anniversary of the 1923 Beer Hall Putsch) provided a pretext for a government-sanctioned coordinated reprisal throughout the German Reich on the night of November 9, 1938; known as *Kristallnacht* or 'The Night of Broken Glass'. For details see *Holocaust Encyclopedia*, *Kristallnacht*: https://www.ushmm.org/wlc/en/article.php?ModuleId=10005201. And in Zvielli, *Front Page Israel*, from the *Palestine Post* section, these front page headlines:
11 November 1938:
'NAZI HOOLIGANS VENT WRATH ON JEWS THROUGHOUT GERMANY' (35);
13 November 1938:
'NEW NAZI SAVAGERY SPELLS DOOM FOR JEWISH LIFE IN GERMANY' (36).

36 And even in Australia eugenics was and is taken very seriously: http://www.theage.com.au/victoria/melbourne-university-bows-to-pressure-removes-racist-professors-name-from-campus-20170321-gv2sjc.html – viewed 22/3/2017.

37 *My Struggle,* Paternoster (122).

38 ibid. (123).

39 While Palestine was under British administration, land in Palestine was owned primarily by absentee Turkish landlords. Both the Turkish landlords and Palestinian landholders profited by selling to Jews; Arab workers forced to leave the land were not welcomed elsewhere. The *Harvard Israel Review* has an excellent short paper on land ownership: 'The Myth of Jewish "Colonialism": Demographics and Development in Palestine' by David Wollenberg. http://www.hcs.harvard.edu/~hireview/content.php?type=article&issue=spring01/&name=myth – viewed 17/7/2016.

40 Britain's White Paper of 1931 limited Jewish immigration into Palestine, dashing Zionists' hopes, trapping them in Poland, and marking the beginning of a period of despair and disillusionment. *On The Edge Of Destruction* (7, 271, 273).

41 According to Celia Heller, 'the generational gap epitomised by the not un-common occurrence of Orthodox fathers ... and revolutionary sons and daughters ...' Heller, *On The Edge Of Destruction* (212).

42 In the fashion of the time, cousin Sara was quoting Nietzsche and Marx.

43 ibid. (148).

44 ' ... the Orthodox-traditional Jew was often perceived by Poles as laughable'. Heller, *On The Edge Of Destruction* (147).

45 ibid. (22).

46 *Compulsory Sunday Rest Law 1919*, an improvement for Polish workers, forced Jewish workers to work on Saturday. Heller, *On The Edge Of Destruction* (101-02).

47 Chaim Bermant, *The Jews* (7).

48 Heller, Bermant and others describe Jewish life in Warsaw and Poland. See Bermant, *The Walled Garden.*

49 We sang the 1937 hit version popularised by The Andrew Sisters.

50 In Zvielli, *Front Page Israel – The Palestine Post* front page of 16 March 1939, said: 'NAZIS ANNEX CZECHO-SLOVAKIA: Anglo-French Attitude "Calm But Not Complacent"' (37).

51 My mother remembered the address and said it was owned by her father's firm: 'Birenbaum and Hammer', Wool And Cotton Merchants at 16 Gesia Street, Warsaw. Her attempts to reclaim it in 1949 and subsequently, failed.

52 Most Jews talk of One God. This name for God – *Eloheinu* – is plural.

There are many names of God and 'El'. Some Kabbalist texts identify two aspects of God: male and female. Jews for Jesus draw out the Kabbalistic texts and acknowledge three. New Kabbalah talks of the *Ein-sof*; this embraces all aspects and ideas of God and creation including non-belief. Religious Jews believe in a hereafter. Resurrection, reincarnation, temporary (not eternal) punishment after death, are all within the range traditional of Jewish belief: http://www.jewfaq.org/olamhaba.htm (– viewed 15/7/2016) but my mother told me emphatically Jews do not believe in a hereafter. It seems that the general Jewish population was only given a simplified glimpse of Jewish thought – as if they would not cope with the whole mystery – that being the domain of rabbis – who at the time were all male.

53 Chaim Bermant identifies that the Jews are the choosing people rather than the chosen – they accepted God's conditional offered laws: Bermant, *The Jews* (7). Detailed and extremely specific, Mosaic Law has an abundance of differing interpretations; every family's observance varies within differing group consensus. Guilt, self-criticism and justification were and are constants.

54 Many tried to build bridges between the two religions. Notably Sholem Asch, in his book *The Nazarene* (*Der Man Fun Natseres*) (1938), hoped, by retelling the story of Jesus and portraying him as an observant Jew, to 'repudiate the calumnies heaped on Jews for centuries'. His depiction of Jesus as a Jew, 'which serialised appearance in Yiddish [and] coincided with A.H. institutionalising Jew-hatred in Germany,' shocked Asch's Jewish readers; Asch was attacked for encouraging conversion. Reference viewed 15/3/2016 at: http://www.yivoencyclopedia.org/article.aspx/Asch_Sholem

55 The ritual murder charges go back to before Christ, and early Christians faced the same charges. It came up in 1144 in Norwich, featured in Chaucer, and gained momentum throughout Europe. Despite Pope Innocent IV declaring the charge malicious in 1247, it became part of folklore. See Bermant's *The Jews* (31-33). *Jew Süss* tells of this 'blood libel' that was used in the early 18th century to incite, convict and execute an innocent man. See Lion Feuchtwanger, *Jew Süss*. This astonishingly good book was used by the Nazis as an antisemitic pejorative by associating the apostle Judas with Jews, and was grotesquely distorted in a 1940 film, notorious for its antisemitic propaganda. The re-issue of a publication of *The Protocols of Elders of Zion* in the 1930s fuelled ancient hatreds. Fabricated by the Czarist secret police in the early 1900s to divert grievances onto the scapegoat of Jew, this fiction perennially reappears as if newly discovered. Bermant in *The Jews* (33) describes the reactions to the *Protocols* in the 1920s and concludes: 'The criticism and fears voiced by Hitler were thus not singular, but he added to them … [bringing back] … fear of the Jew as a destroyer and poisoner …' The

blood libel persists.

56 The Second Commandment: Exodus 20:4-6: 'Thou shall not make unto thee any graven image, or any likeness of anything that is in heaven above, or that is in the earth beneath … Thou shall not bow down thyself to them, nor serve them: for I the LORD thy God am a jealous God. Visiting the inequity of the fathers upon the children unto the third and fourth generation of those that hate me; and showing mercy unto thousands of them that love me, and keep my Commandments.' See Barker, *KJV Study Bible*.

57 *The Angel of History,* a reference to Walter Benjamin's description of a Klee painting 'Angelus Novus'. In Walter Benjamin, *Illuminations* (249).

58 The notion of change, of everything changing, is often attributed in Western philosophy to Ovid but dates at least to Heraclitus of Ephesus c.535–c. 475 BCE. 'No man ever steps in the same river twice, for it's not the same river and he's not the same man.'

59 My mother was unsure of the name of the school. She says the principal's name was Cecelia Goldman. I have not found any record of this school.

60 O-Lan was the wife of Wang Lung, the Chinese farmer in *The Good Earth,* written by Pearl S. Buck, awarded the Pulitzer Prize in 1932.

61 This, the ethic of reciprocity, is upheld as the basis of Jewish teaching. It is told that when a gentile asked that the Torah be explained to him while he stood on one foot, Rabbi Hillel the Elder replied: 'What is hateful to you, do not do to your fellow: this is the whole Torah; the rest is commentary – go study.' It is also the Golden Rule: http://www.jewishvirtuallibrary.org/jsource/Quote/hillel.html – viewed 24/7/2016.

62 Zvielli, *Front Page Israel – The Palestine Post* front page (41). The pacts gave the Nazis Finland, Estonia, Latvia and half of Poland.

PART THREE: NAMES & EYES OF THE FATHER

63 The Third Commandment: Exodus 20:7: 'Thou shalt not take the name of the LORD thy God in vain; for the LORD will not hold him guiltless that taketh his name in vain.' *KJV Study Bible*. The insight viewed 25 April 2011 at http://atheism.about.com/od/tencommandments/a/commandment03.htm

PART FOUR: THE WHOLE THING

64 Found in Celia Heller's *On The Edge Of Destruction* (148-9).

65 Immanuel Kant, 'What is Enlightenment?' (1784) found in Ferrone, *The Enlightenment* (9).

66 From the play *Heauton Timorumenos* (*The Self-Tormentor*) a play written in 161 BC by Publius Terentius Afer, known as 'Terence' – a playwright of the Roman Republic. https://en.wikipedia.org/wiki/Terence – viewed

10/8/2016. Quote found in Ferrone, *The Enlightenment* (99). Ferrrone says this is the real motto of the Enlightenment.

67 My father's cousin – 'Auntie' Mania – conveyed her life to me on several occasions.

68 Most of this from Auntie Mania; Daddy and Mummy eventually contributed titbits.

69 This asserts direct descent from Levi, the third child of Jacob and Leah, he being one of Joseph's eleven brothers. It was my mother who first told me, and my father confirmed it.

70 The Fourth Commandment: 'Remember the Sabbath day, to keep it holy.'

71 More on Branko in future writings.

72 Conducted against the backdrop of the Suez crisis and the Hungarian Revolution, the Melbourne Olympics in October 1956, centred around the Melbourne Cricket Ground, were one of the most successful ever for Australian athletes. Television, introduced in Australia in time to broadcast the events, made sure their success became part of Australian sporting history. Fact Sheet 57 – National Archives of Australia. http://www.naa.gov.au/collection/fact-sheets/fs57.aspx – viewed 12/3/2016.

73 With the pool removed, it was used for sports and entertainment until, in 2002, the unique proportions and profile of this landmark building were restored. https://www.mopt.com.au/about/history/holden-centre/ accessed 5/2/18.

74 The *Haskalah*, meaning 'reason' or 'intellect', was the Jewish Enlightenment from the 1770s to 1880s. Evolving out of the hundred-year-old Christian piety-destroying European Enlightenment, which had arisen after massacres and terrors and famines, this force encouraged Jews to shed superstition and strengthen moral values through one's ability to reason. This meant one should study secular subjects, learn European languages, and participate in, even assimilate into, gentile society in dress, language, manners and loyalty to the ruling power. Young men were drawn to cities where they gave private lessons on the founders of science and philosophy: Galileo, Newton, Descartes, Bacon, Voltaire, Spinoza. Inspired and inspiring, their search for a new code for living was to influence both the Reform and Zionist movements. Refs and further reading: Celia Heller, *On The Edge Of Destruction* (29-31); Ferrone, *The Enlightenment* (100). http://www.jewishvirtuallibrary.org/the-haskalah – viewed 11/3/2107

75 Some of the views:
The World Zionist Movement, which sought establishment of a Jewish nation in Palestine while establishing the rights of Jews in the Diaspora, had many strands and greatly influenced Polish Zionism which, in September 1935, split into two opposing philosophies: Chaim Weizmann's Diplomacy (advocating persuasion of the British to

honour prior agreements to create a Jewish homeland, with the vision of living harmoniously with the Arabs under British rule), and Vladmir Jabotinsky's Revisionism (advocating in 1933 that Poland inherit the Mandate of Palestine from the British and initiate a rapid evacuation plan for Jews caused dismay in London. Revisionism tapped into para-military movements of youth. The largest was Betar. Betar's members, trained in weaponry by Polish army officers, espoused a secular messianism and included a very young Menachem Begin and Yitzchak Shamir. Reference: Snyder, *Black Earth*: Chapter 3 'The Promise of Palestine' (62-7).
The Bund, the Yiddish-speaking General Jewish Workers Union, was committed to secular Jewish nationalism within a Polish socialist state.
The Orthodox Party, The Yiddisher Agudath Israel, included many *Hassidic* groups and maintained meticulous observance of Jewish law, while mostly rejecting secularist Zionism.
The communists, ardent but guarded, thought man would not truly live in unity until all things were held in common.
Other Streams: these included:
Forbearers of our commoditised world engrossed with a profit/prosperity paradigm held a view that industrialisation and science would bring prosperity, hence happiness to the world. Others cursed industrialisation, fearing machines would crush human beings. Some people glorified the nobility longing to return to a not very distant past. The Positivists believed organic evolutionary progress of society paralleled nature: Miłosz, *The History of Polish Literature* (283). The Romantics' longing for a return to Eden (as in Rousseau's philosophy) is conveyed by Thomas Mann in *The Magic Mountain* (401) via the Jesuit Naphta: '... original state of man ... without government ... without force ... neither lordship nor service, neither law nor penalty ... no distinction of classes, no work, no property: nothing but equality, brotherhood ... moral perfectitude.' Additional references: Gutman, *Resistance* (26-7). Meanwhile in Bavaria ... (I recommend Lion Feuchtwanger's *Success*, a riveting roman à clef of the epoch.)

76 It has been said that paradoxically in a time of flourishing art and culture the people of Germany became a murderous amoral mob with a hive-mind. Historians attribute, hypothesise and disagree on the conditions that permitted mass subjugation and mass murder. Some of the key elements discussed: The Treaty of Versailles, June 1919, forced onto the new Weimar Republic for a war fought by the deposed Kaiser, was punitive (largely on the insistence of France); it had caused German anger at the Weimar Republic for signing the Treaty. Whether unfair and vengeful or no worse than prior treaties, it did not restore order to Europe; it was a cause for despair and provoked desire for revenge. With Germany's default on payment of reparations, France occupied the Ruhr, taking over coal, while Britain and America placed huge duties on German goods. The Weimar government, having instructed the Ruhr

workers to strike, printed money to pay the strikers; 'like in Weimar' remains a euphemism for the disastrous consequences of hyperinflation. In 1918, $US1 equalled 4.2 marks; on 16 November 1923, $US1 equalled 4,200,000,000,000 marks (4.2 trillion marks). Plans to help Germany, such as the Dawes Plan 1924 and then the *Young* Plan 1929, indebted Germany to American loans. With the currency stabilised, Weimar Germany (from 1924 to 1929) was a fledgling democracy; neither it nor Germans en masse supported the Social Nationalism of A.H. In the three elections held between 1924 and 1928, the Nazis gained fewer seats than the communists. With the Wall Street Crash in 1929, America called in its loans. German industries failed, unemployment rose to 6 million; as people starved, the Nazis gained support.
References: http://www.bbc.co.uk/education/guides/zh9p34j/revision/6 http://www.historylearningsite.co.uk/modern-world-history-1918-to-1980/weimar-germany/the-young-plan-of-1929/ https://www.facinghistory.org/weimar-republic-fragility-democracy/primary-sources/weimar-culture viewed 12/8/2017 Also see *Paper Money* by 'Adam Smith' (George J.W. Goodman) (57-62) at http://www.pbs.org/wgbh/commandingheights/shared/minitext/ess_germanhyperinflation.html (viewed 17/7/2016).

77 Two years prior, on 4 October 1957, the Russians launched Sputnik. On 31 January 1958, the Americans launched an earth satellite Explorer 1.

78 *Sapere aude:* Latin phrase meaning: Dare to know, dare to be wise, dare to discern. First recorded use was by Horace in his *First Book of Letters*, 20 BC. Claimed by Kant, in 1784, as the Enlightenment motto, Kant added: 'Have courage to use your own reason.' Ferrone (9).

79 Additional references for this chapter: Neal Ascherson, *The Struggle For Poland* (80); Heller, *On The Edge Of Destruction* (38, 82-3).

80 My father mentioned an organisation called VAT, but I have not found documentation for it. Heniek was emphatic about this name. In his testimony in 1995 he mentioned JUST (pronounced Joost). In 2016 I found an organisation called *Jutrznia-Morgnshtern*, Yiddish for 'Morning Star', sometimes also known by its Polish name Jutrznia. It was a Jewish sports organisation linked to the Bund. Its largest branch was based in Warsaw. Membership reached 1855 in 1938. Found at https://en.wikipedia.org/wiki/Morgnshtern – viewed 26/7/2016. See Brenner & Reuveni, *Emancipation Through Muscles* (119-20) and Jack Kugelmass, *Jews, Sports, and the Rites of Citizenship* (119-20).

81 The word Utopia, coined by Thomas Moore, is a pun meaning no place that exists, based on the Greek words *ou* and *topas* – no place. Utopia has come to mean an ideal place or good place (also an unrealistic place); dystopia means the opposite to utopia. i.e. not a good place; kakotopia means the worst possible place, http://www.thefreedictionary.com viewed 28/1/2016, from Quinion, *Ologies & Isms*. Also, kakistocracy

means government by the worst persons; a form of government in which the worst persons are in power: http://www.dictionary.com/browse/kakistocracy?s=t – viewed 2/4/2017.

82 Heniek called it the Labour Party. It was probably the Polish Socialist Party – Freedom, Equality, Independence (*Polska Partia Socjalistyczna - Wolność, Równość, Niepodległość*); this was part of the underground in WWII. https://en.wikipedia.org/wiki/Polish_Socialist_Party viewed 17/7/2017.

83 This street fight is as described by my father.

84 In October 1937 the separation and separateness encouraged by the Nazi Nuremberg Laws (which in 1935 had declared the Jews an inferior race) flowed into the Polish classrooms with the establishment of ghetto benches in most law and medical faculties. The student body and the teachers watched on as Polish militants armed with clubs, knives and sticks insulted and bodily attacked any Polish defenders brave enough to object; they reviled calls for moderation as treason. Jewish youth of all social classes, determined to repel treatment of themselves as a lower caste, and considering the ways of their parents as embarrassing or irrelevant, increasingly sought non-traditional solutions. Ref: Heller, *On The Edge Of Destruction* (118-25); Ascherson, *The Struggles For Poland* (80)

85 It was once a haven for Jews fleeing Tsarist Russia in the 1800s; allowed to develop their own communities and systems, they settled and flourished in Poland. Warsaw gradually acquired the largest Jewish population of any city in Europe. In 1926 Marshall Piłsudski, having retaken control, formed the *Sanacja* regime (from the Latin sanare, 'to make wholesome'); but by brutal crushing resistance, he took Poland from a fledgling democracy to a dictatorship. Roman Dmowski's National Democratic Party in 1928 became the National Party know as Endecja; it sought to rid Poland of hated minorities: Jews, Slavs, Ukrainians, Byelorussians. Though there were Poles who wanted to let Jews emigrate, Palestine was closed, no country wanted large numbers of Jewish immigrants, and with the split of the *Sanacja* government (following Marshall Pilsudski's death in 1935) into two rival factions, the right-wing Endecja took ever increasing action against the Jewish population. See Gay, *The Cultivation of Hatred* (421). Other references: Heller, *On The Edge Of Destruction*. (53-7, 89-92, 94-7); Watt, *Bitter Glory. Poland and Its Fate 1918 to 1939* (305-66); Ascherson, *The Struggles For Poland* (39-77).

PART FIVE: (DIS)HONOUR, (DIS)GRACE, (DIS)BELIEF, DIFFERENCE

86 Exodus 20:12.

87 'Life is not meant to be easy, my child; but take courage: it can be delightful.' George Bernard Shaw.

88 With the demolition of the Berlin Wall in November 1989, East and West were no longer divided – celebration; Freedom Triumphant. The end of the cold war was termed *The End Of History* – Francis Fukuyama's famous term. Democracy, having 'won', basked a mere moment; the pendulum's swing brought a deluge, visual and aural: young men assertive in black shirts, banners of swastika and eagle, trumpeting of vile slogans; re-emergence of the extreme Right.

89 The Pledge: 'I love God and my country; I honour the flag; I will serve the Queen, and cheerfully obey my parents, teachers, and the laws.'

90 No less than one who follows the 613 *Mitzvot* – those much disputed and discussed commandments or rules of conduct governing dress, food, marriage and divorce, on matters trivial and profound, some relevant today, some archaic, with no distinction between the sacrosanct and the petty; entrapment endless. They were formulated in the 3rd century BCE, and were integral to the belief that such following – by each and every Jew – will bring the messiah. http://www.chabad.org/library/article_cdo/aid/756399/jewish/The-613-Commandments.htm. http://www.hebrew4christians.com/Articles/Taryag/taryag.html – viewed 20/5/2016.

91 The Old Testament tells: 'Heber, grandson of Asher, is the great-grandson of Jacob; the Heberites are a clan of the Tribe of Asher.' In Numbers 26:44–45: 'Of the sons of Asher according to their families: … Of the sons of Beriah: of Heber, the family of the Heberites …' And in Genesis 46:17: 'And the sons of Asher; … Beriah … the sons of Beriah; Heber.' And if the unknowable truth be that my ancestors chose this name out of a need in law to choose a name, nevertheless my parents said that grandfather Jacob was a Levi.

92 A.H.'s decree to make identification easier. Sara for the women, Israel for the men. Ref: *The Weekend Australian*, 30-31 Dec 1995. Review 1: 'Passion at War' by Peter Millar.

PART SIX: WITH(IN) WAR

93 Facing History And Ourselves Foundation, *Holocaust and Human Behaviour* (189). And online at www.facinghistory.org

94 Additional references for this chapter: Kermish, *To Live With Honor* (214); Watt, *Bitter Glory* (419, 432-44); Ascherson, *The Struggles For Poland* (90-100).

95 A.H. to Chief Commanders and Commanding Generals, 12 August 1939 regarding the genocide by the Turks of two million Armenians during WWI. And online at: http://www.armenians.com/genocide/index.html – viewed 12/9/2009, this quote: 'Perhaps if Turkey was punished at the time by the "civilized world", the Armenian Genocide would not have become a blueprint or instruction manual for the Jewish Holocaust, the Somalian massacres … and … Kosovo.'

96 http://www.telegraph.co.uk/history/world-war-two/6105782/Second-World-War-Why-we-delayed-declaration-of-war.html – viewed 11/6/2017.

97 Falling on his knees is significant as Jews do not kneel.

98 Bitter Enemies: the Ukrainians. From them had come the Cossacks – free descendants of serfs – who retaliated in extreme violence against Polish masters and against those who they saw as agent of the Poles: the Jews. Many Ukrainians died during twenty years of Polish rule. Ref: Snyder, *Black Earth* (182).

99 Arad, *Documents on the Holocaust* (173-8).

100 Quote found in Ascherson, *The Struggles For Poland* (100).

101 Additional references for this chapter: Kermish, *To Live With Honor* (5, 9, 135-6, 142, 220-31); Johnston, *The Holocaust* (3, 43); Ascherson, *The Struggles For Poland* (108); Gutman, *Resistance: The Warsaw Ghetto Uprising* (54-60, 76); Sloan (ed.), *Notes From The Warsaw Ghetto*; Arad, *Documents on the Holocaust* (189). Also http://warszawa.getto.pl/index.php?show=kalendarium&lang=en – viewed 5/01/2010.

102 Raul Hilberg et al., *The Warsaw Diary Of Adam Czerniakow* (21).

103 Withdrawals were limited to 2,000 złoty – approximately $US200. (One złoty was worth approx. 20c.) Value in 2017 approx. $US3,120.

104 This came in force by an order issued on 23 November 1939: Arad, *Documents on the Holocaust* (178). After 1939, categories of prisoners were identified by a marking system combining a colored inverted triangle with lettering. Generally, green: criminals; red: political prisoners; black: 'asocials' (including nonconformists and vagrants); brown: Roma (gypsies); pink: homosexuals; purple: Jehovah's Witnesses. From 1938 Jews were required to wear the yellow Star of David throughout most of occupied Europe. *Holocaust Encyclopedia*, CLASSIFICATION SYSTEM IN NAZI CONCENTRATION CAMPS: https://www.ushmm.'org/wlc/en/article.php?ModuleId=10005378 – viewed 13/3/2016.

105 Swastika: an ancient symbol from *svastica* (Sanskrit) meaning auspicious, it has many meanings.

106 $US20,000 in 1939 (based on 1 złoty or guilden being worth US 20 cents) equals approx. $US312,000 in 2017.

107 A.H. saw Jews as a spiritual pestilence to be eradicated, because they had brought the knowledge of good and evil. And he believed both capitalism and socialism were Jewish. He also believed Christianity was Jewish but did not say this in public. A.H.'s aim: to rid Germany of the Jews by encouraged and enforced emigration; he had not yet developed 'The Final Solution'. Snyder, *Black Earth* (3-10) and A.H.'s *Mein Kampf*.

108 William Perl, *The Holocaust Conspiracy*. (19-20). Note: America had taken in 120,000 Jews between March 1938 and September 1939.

Holocaust Encyclopedia, REFUGEES: https://www.ushmm.org/wlc/en/article.php?ModuleId=10005139 – viewed 21/7/2016.

109 The Madagascar Solution: A.H. formed the ghettos as a holding-pen pending deportation of surviving Jews. His ally Russia refused to take the requested two million. As far back as 1938 A.H. had suggested Madagascar (in French colonial possession) to the Polish leaders. The Vichy government support this scheme but Britain remained in the war. With Madagascar impossible, A.H. planned to crush Russia quickly and send the Jews to Siberia. See Bauer, *A History of the Holocaust* (209) and Snyder, *Black Earth* (114-15). A.H. was not alone in seeking a homeland for Jews – there were many schemes, including notably the Kimberly Plan to relocate one million Jews in the Northern Territory in Australia: http://guides.naa.gov.au/safe-haven/chapter2/kimberley-scheme.aspx – viewed 29/6/2016. In November 1940 a memorandum requested the banning of Jewish emigration from the General Government, as it reduced opportunities for emigration of Jews from Austria, Moravia and Bohemia, and because immigration of religious Jews (such as those in Poland) posed the risk of regenerating Jewish religious life in the USA. See Arad, *Documents on the Holocaust* (219-20).

110 Heniek used the word 'carrier' and told of this event – I have not found it elsewhere. Gutman, in *The Jews of Warsaw (*27) described similar events.

111 For more, refer to Hilberg, *The Warsaw Diary of Adam Czerniakow* (187-212).

112 Arad, *Documents on the Holocaust* (206) and Gutman, *Resistance* (87).

113 Auschwitz was not used for Jews at this stage.

114 This map is from a brochure entitled 'They Lived Among Us: Polish Judaica' published by the Polish Tourist Information Centre (undated). My parents received it when they went to Poland for the 50th Commemoration of the Destruction of the Warsaw Ghetto in 1993. For more maps go to: http://www.siger.org/warsawghettomaps/

115 Additional references for this chapter: Sloan, *Notes From The Warsaw Ghetto*; Gutman, *Resistance* (92-3, 122); Kermish, *To Live With Honor* (xxvi, 60, 146-94, 195, 262, 267, 274, 627, 651); Hilberg, *The Warsaw Diary of Adam Czerniakow* (40, 206-24). http://www.holocaustresearchproject.org/ghettos/acdiary.html
http://warszawa.getto.pl/index.php?show=kalendarium&lang=en – viewed 5/01/2010.
http://www.holocaustresearchproject.org/ghettos/warsawghetto.html – viewed 5/01/2010.
Also there are summaries of events online at: http://www.local-life.com/warsaw/articles/warsaw-ghettohttp://www.local-life.com/warsaw/articles/warsaw-ghetto – viewed 27/8/2016 and at http://www.johndclare.net/Nazi_Germany3_WarsawGhetto.htm – viewed 7/6/2015.

116 Gutman tell in *Resistance* (86): Germans 2,613 calories, Poles 699 calories, Jews 184 calories, and the Jews pay more for their 'share'. An extract from Ringelblum's diary, in Arad, *Documents On The Holocaust* (228), identifies the rations as 10 per cent of normal requirements, and has a description of smuggling efforts thus necessitated.

117 Sloan, *Notes From The Warsaw Ghetto*. (66, 86-89). See endnote (164) for more on Dr Emmanuel Ringelblum.

118 Hilberg, *The Warsaw Diary of Adam Czerniakow* (40-1).

119 Chaim Kaplan. Found in Engelking, *The Warsaw Ghetto: A Guide To The Perished City* (74).

120 There is a Polish film *Ulica Graniczna (Border Street) (*set in the street that Heniek lived in) made in 1948; told through the eyes of several children, it chronicles the creation and destruction of the ghetto.

121 From David Graber, in Kermish, *To Live With Honor* (60).

122 Engelking's maps in *The Warsaw Ghetto* show the ghetto abuzz with activity (plates in the centre of the book, following p. 402).

123 Arad, *Documents On The Holocaust* (229).

124 Sloan, *Notes From The Warsaw Ghetto* (217).

125 Image is of *Czerniakow's Diary* found 7/10/2014 at http://www.holocaustresearchproject.org/ghettos/acdiary.html

126 Additional references for this chapter: Kermish, *To Live With Honor* (xxvi, 60, 195, 262, 267, 274, 627, 651); Steiner, *A Reader* (10-11); Gutman, *Resistance* (122). Also http://warszawa.getto.pl/index.php?show=kalendarium&lang=en – viewed 5/01/2010.

127 Czerrniakow's diary entry for 5 December 1940. Found in Joseph Arnon, *Who Was Janusz Korczak?* Booklet from Jewish Holocaust Centre (Melbourne) under the patronage of Yad Vashem, Jerusalem. For Federation of Polish Jews (no date) (21).

128 Under the inspired leadership of Emmanuel Ringelblum, this group was formed to record all that was happening; the records of their endeavours is the ghetto archive.

129 Bashenka was Heniek's affectionate name for Basia.

130 Hilberg, *The Warsaw Diary of Adam Czerniakow* (53, 220, 228-31); Sloan, *Notes From The Warsaw Ghetto* (213); and http://www.holocaustresearchproject.org/nazioccupation/polishforthnigtreview.html – viewed 25/8/2016.

131 ibid., entry November 4, 1940. (212).

132 Arad, *Documents on the Holocaust* (170).

133 Kermish, *To Live with Honor* (544-5).

134 House-Committees: some 2,200 with 10,000 workers – established to deal with the inflow of the desperate and starving – varied enormously

in quality, finances, commitment and ability. The *Judenrat* controlled resources; all funds came from donations (voluntary and coerced) within the community and from the Joint Distribution Committee centred in America. Of the ghetto population, swollen to some 460,000–520,000 (estimates vary), some 240,000 were in need of social funds. See Arad, *Documents on the Holocaust* (208).

135 Kermish, *To Live With Honor* (743). (Answers to a questionnaire by Dr Milejkowski.)

136 ibid. (519-29).

137 Since 1911, Korczak's orphanage was a kind-of-a-republic for children with its own small parliament, court and newspaper. Korczak was a WWI military doctor awarded the Silver Cross, a traveller to Palestine, a contributor to Polish radio, and he even gave a lecture at a Berlin conference in 1929. His books' titles speak volumes: *How to Love a Child (Jak kochać dziecko)*, Warsaw 1919; *The Child's Right to Respect (Prawo dziecka do szacunku)*, Warsaw, 1929. And fairy tales as a vehicle for learning, including a story of a boy-wizard, *Kaytek The Wizard* – truly he was a man ahead of his time. Revered by all, he was a humanitarian, a believer that improvement of the human being was necessary for the future of society. His many articles and diary notes tell us of his thoughts and life. References: Arnon, *Who Was Janusz Korczak?* http://www.jewishvirtuallibrary.org/jsource/biography/Korczak.html – viewed 31/8/2016. His will and curriculum vitae, written 9/2/1942, is in Kermish, *To Live With Honor* (488).

138 Approximately $US156,000 in 2017.

139 For years I found no record of my father's account of this college. Verification came through a chance meeting with Holocaust survivor Zyga Elton in 2004 in his capacity as a volunteer at the Melbourne Holocaust Centre. Zyga, the author of a memoir *Destination Buchara*, knew Heniek in Warsaw. He told me he also went to this college and confirmed that it was a school of sorts. Zyga also believed it was a 'show-piece' to demonstrate to the Red Cross, and to the world, that the Jews were being treated humanely. He gave the address as 26 Grybowska Street. Googling this address in 2016 – twelve years later – brought a surprise; it is the address for the *Judenrat* (Council). Czerniakow, before he was *Altester*, was an engineer and before that he was a trade school teacher. Online, it seems the Nazis allowed trade schools. So it seemed to be an initiative of the *Judenrat* to protect some young men. The link for the information that this was probably the Council offices viewed 20/5/2016 is: http://www.holocaustresearchproject.org/ghettos/judenratgal/The%20Judenrat%20building%20in%20the%20Warsaw%20ghetto%20at%2026-28%20Grzybowska%20Street.html

Then in the early hours of 8/7/2016, looking for something else, I opened my copy of Hilberg's *The Warsaw Diary of Adam Czerniakow* which I had not yet read – and there on p. 20, in a paragraph listing some of the things he was proud of, two items stand out for me: 'the prohibition of confiscation of technical school equipment' (entry of 21 October 1940) and 'permission to open vocational training courses …' (not dated), and a reference (diary entry 24 May 1941) to a meeting to discuss vocational schools (242). Also a map of the ghetto in Gutman, *Resistance* (149) shows at location 16 *'Center For Vocational Training'*.

140 Additional references for this chapter: Kermish, *To Live With Honor* (277, 730-1); Engelking, *The Warsaw Ghetto* (397).

141 The Sixth Commandment: Exodus 20:13. The *KJB* says: 'Thou shalt not kill'. Yet many sites say this is 'Do not murder' and argue that it prohibits killing of the innocent, but sanctions war and other killing.

142 Isaiah 2:4.

PART SEVEN: (A)SHAMED.

143 The Seventh Commandment: Exodus 20:14: 'Thou shall not commit adultery.' In the context of this book I substitute 'Do not cause shame'.

144 Comedienne Gracie Allen, with her husband George, known as Burns and Allen.

145 Quentin Tarantino's 2009 film *Inglorious Basterds* postulates revenge-gratification as the Basterds hunt and indelibly knife-mark Nazis with a swastika on the forehead. What do those that do not know the context for this revenge make of this?

146 The Memorial Cross on Mt Macedon in Victoria is 21 metres high and was built to commemorate those who died in World War I.

147 It wasn't until 2014 that I learnt that Ricky Nelson's eyes were a startling blue.

148 Theodor Herzl, author of *Der Judenstat* (*The Jewish State*) published in in 1896, had a profound effect in furthering the current ideas on Zionism. Refer Weizmann's memoir, *Trial and Error* (61).

149 The Balfour Declaration 1917. This landmark letter from Arthur James Balfour, the United Kingdom's Foreign Secretary, to Walter Rothschild, 2nd Baron Rothschild, for transmission to the Zionist Federation of Great Britain and Ireland, says: 'His Majesty's government view with favour the establishment in Palestine of a national home for the Jewish people, and will use their best endeavours to facilitate the achievement of this object, it being clearly understood that nothing shall be done which may prejudice the civil and religious rights of existing non-Jewish communities in Palestine, or the rights and political status enjoyed by Jews in any other country.' Found in Weizmann's *Trial and Error* – plate 80 (2 pages before p. 257).

150 Israeli songs popular at the Habonim Youth Group: sung with gusto while

dancing and holding hands:
David Melech Yisrael, chai, chai, vekayam – 'David, King of Israel, lives forever' (Talmud – Rosh Hashanah 25a);
Hava nagila v'nis'mecha – 'Let us rejoice and be happy.' Written 1918, based on a Ukrainian folk song;
Tzena, tzena, tzena. I got a surprise when I learnt the meaning of the words of *Tzena Tzena*: 'Go out, go out, go out girls and see soldiers in the settlement / Do not, do not, do not hide yourself away from a virtuous man, an army man.'

151 Our parents' yearning for us is reflected in 'Somewhere Over the Rainbow', 1939. Lyrics by Yip Harburg, born to Russian Jewish immigrants, real name Isidore Hochberg; Music by Harold Arlen, a cantor's son, real name Hyman Arluck, parents from Lithuania.

152 This film may have been the State Zionist Council's *Fog (Mist) In The Night*. Source: Eddie Balfour – my *madrich* (leader) at Habonim in 1960 who I met again in 2011.

153 Adolf Eichmann – SS Colonel whom Israeli agents captured earlier in the year. The trial commenced on 12/5/1961 (the same day as the broadcast of Yuri Gagarin's triumph and the CIA's failed invasion of Cuba (the Bay of Pigs). Screened all over the world, it is credited with being the event that enabled survivors to finally be believed, and thus enabled the telling of their stories. Eichmann's testimony would provide information on Wannsee (refer endnote 195). A TV film *The Eichmann Show* (2015) documenting the trial was screened on SBS TV on 11/8/2016. An online review called the film 'absolutely enthralling': http://www.telegraph.co.uk/culture/tvandradio/tv-and-radio-reviews/11355086/eichmann-show.html – viewed 12/8/2016. Consider the following exchange from the film:

Eichmann: I am not responsible.
Prosecutor: Then who is responsible?
Eichmann: NOT I!
Prosecutor: Then who?

PART EIGHT: ALL THE PEOPLE

154 The Eighth Commandment: Exodus 20:15: 'Thou shall not steal.'

155 Additional reference for this chapter: Kermish, *To Live With Honor* (60-1, 277, 730-1). Also http://warszawa.getto.pl/index.php?show=kalendarium&lang=en – viewed 5/01/2010.

156 Arad, *Documents on the Holocaust* (236): Ringelblum identifies that the Gestapo agents were busy looking for rich Jews and were not interested in what the other Jews were doing among themselves.

157 Footbridge, connecting the two parts of the Warsaw Ghetto 1942: https://www.jewishvirtuallibrary.org/jsource/Holocaust/Chlodna.html – viewed 24/8/2016.

158 Ringelblum says this was done in part to avoid the occurrence of a Jewish area being directly adjacent to a Polish area to reduce the opportunities for smuggling. Sloan, *Notes from the Warsaw Ghetto* (222).

159 Source: Engelking, *The Warsaw Ghetto* (79-96) and http://www.siger.org/warsawghettomaps/ The brick walls sealed in; only a handful of workers were brought in and out daily to work in factories fringing the ghetto. Engleking's supplementary map entitled 'Borders before the great liqudation action' shows a total of 27 gates with 21 of these being through the wall. These were reduced progressively to nine in 1942. After the great liquidation, there were four gates. Photos in Engelking show the barbed wire down the middle of streets (Fig 1.4, p. 81) and entry via a factory (fig 1.6, p. 88). Heinz Auerswald, Kommissar (March 1941–Nov 1942) was intent on making the ghetto self-sufficient – even productive; Czerniakow communicated with him regularly and negotiated for 'improvements'. But being fanatical about the spread of typhus, Auerswald sealed the ghetto more and more, confounding attempts for the smuggling essential to lift inadequate supplies. Sources: http://www.yadvashem.org/odot_pdf/Microsoft%20Word%20-%205780.pdf – viewed 26/8/2016; Engelking, *The Warsaw Ghetto* (90-1); Gutman, *The Jews of Warsaw* (98-100). For map of gates refer http://www.siger.org/warsawghettomaps/ – viewed 26/8/2016; Arad, *Documents on the Holocaust* (244-6). Auerswald's report, dated 26 September 1941, gives an account of: soup kitchens, smuggling, numbers of deaths, typhus.

160 Sloan, *Notes from the Warsaw Ghetto* (201).

161 Kermish, *To Live With Honor*; quote is on p. 279 – the rest of this section (277, 730-1).

162 Shalom Asch, in his book *Kiddush Hashem,* describing pogroms of ancient times, writes, ' … we have not described everything the Tartars … did to the Jews so as not to shame the species man which was created in God's image.' Found in Kermish, *To Live With Honor* (277).

163 CENTOS – Society for the Care of Orphans and Abandoned Children – and TOZ – Society for the Protection of Health – initially gave aid and stemmed disease but now could not cope.

164 When the Germans invaded Poland, Dr Ringelblum, as a 39-year-old history teacher and on the staff of the Joint Distribution Committee, was safe in Geneva, Switzerland, as a delegate at the twenty-first World Zionist Congress. His decision to return to Warsaw made him part of history. He refused the opportunity to escape to England in late 1943, was captured with his wife and son in the ruins of the ghetto in March 1944, and executed.

165 The *Oneg Shabbat* (OS) operated with funding from the JDC (the American Jewish Joint Distribution Committee – know as the Joint). The work of this OS gave us the found archive: the source of written first-

hand real time events. Buried in milk cans and metal boxes, the recovered contents, found after the war in the ghetto rubble, provide source material for many works: historical and history-based fiction. Also see Arad, *Documents on the Holocaust* (235-6), and an article at: http://www.spiegel.de/international/europe/the-hell-of-polish-jewry-chronicling-the-holocaust-from-inside-the-ghetto-a-707506.html viewed 21/7/2017.

166 The *Judenrat*: Central and infamous, the council of 24 was established on 4 October 1939 to replace the social and religious *Kehilla* (congregation). With self-imposed responsibility for community services in the areas of health, housing, schooling, postal services and food, they transitioned from being respected as the authority, to reviled as conspirators. In 1941, 500 employees let contracts for services, issued decrees and edicts, and actioned these edicts on behalf of the Germans. See Kermish, *To Live with Honor* (292-3). Czerniakow's diaries indicate his desperate struggle to meet the needs of his community; such leaders were to be accused of being tools of the Nazis by Hannah Arendt. Refer to her *Eichmann in Jerusalem: A Report on the Banality of Evil*; others such as Engleking in *The Warsaw Ghetto* identify views which varied from contempt to seeing Czerniakow as a tragic hero (160).

167 Who are these men? Gutman in *Resistance* (144) says: 'As a rule, they were not ordinary inhabitants of the ghetto.' 580 volunteers formed a Ghetto police force in 1940; their task was, under instruction, to assist the German force of 150 to carry out Gestapo orders. Grown now to 2,000, operating under the orders of the Polish police, they served ostensibly to keep community order, minimise disruption, minimise distress for one's own. The leader was Jozef Szerynski, formerly a colonel in the Polish police – a convert to Catholicism. Who put their hands up for these posts? Lawyers, refugees from smaller cities and towns, also the educated and even young rich men, and the poor, the desperate, the criminal, the cruel. See Kermish, *To Live With Honor* (63); Gutman, *Resistance* (58-60,144) and https://en.wikipedia.org/wiki/Jewish_Ghetto_Police – viewed 24/8/2016.

168 Akiva was a Zionistic Youth Group named in honour of Rabbi Akiva, renowned scholar of the *Mishna* which is the entire body of Jewish religious law developed before 200 CE.

169 Refer: Niewyk, *The Holocaust* (107); Bauer, *A History of the Holocaust* (186); Trunk, *Judenrat* (43, 143, 451); Arendt, *Eichmann in Jerusalem* (121-3); Hilberg, *The Destruction of the European Jews* (665, 662-3).

170 Additional references for this chapter: Kermish, *To Live With Honor* (721); Mogilanski, *The Ghetto Anthology* (312).

171 From David Graber in Kermish, *To Live With Honor* (60).

172 Kermish, *To Live With Honor*, Economic Dynamics (533-52).

173 Found in Sloan, *Notes From The Warsaw Ghetto* (40).

174 Arad, *Documents on the Holocaust* (204).

175 Gutman, *Resistance* (144).

176 Engelking's map (Warsaw ghetto trade, service, production – map 7, plates in centre of the book following p. 402, in *The Warsaw Ghetto*) shows this to be workshops so perhaps the flat was above.

177 In 1996 I found my father's name in *Oneg Shabbat* documents in Kermish, *To Live With Honor.* (The index under 'H' lists Heber.) This (on page 416) turned out to be the minutes of a 'conference' to discuss the problems of providing more kosher lunches to meet the demands created by the influx of religious refugees. The minutes record the date as the day of the Fast of Esther 5701. I estimate this date was the 2 March 1942. Mr Heber was listed here as the Director of Nowolipie 15. I asked my father; he said, 'Yes that was me.' He was nineteen years old.

178 Such acts of decency are also described in Kermish, *To Live With Honor* (312).

179 Pejorative Yiddish Polish slang word from the Polish *Szmalcownik.* Also spelt '*Shmaltsovnikes*'. For more on exploitation of Jews living in disguise as Christians see Arad, *Documents on the Holocaust* (330).

180 Yisrael Gutman in *The Jews of Warsaw* (143) discusses the 'existential enclave' that was the youth movement, their 'consciousness of being part of human society', and the haunting realisation that they had not foreseen A.H.'s aims and prepared earlier.

181 http://www.newyorker.com/science/maria-konnikova/the-secret-formula-for-resilience – viewed 17/2/2016.

182 My father told me of this but I have not found confirmation elsewhere.

183 Shades: Every merchant, intellectual or social group had its Polish benefactor. Mean acts, insults and humiliation on the one hand – benefaction, kindness and sometimes empathy on the other. Despite almost universal hatred of the Germans and considerable mistrust of the Russians, there were Poles who, while worshipping their risen Jew, his Jewish mother, and following the teachings of the group of Jewish Apostles, still harboured the archaic 'Christ-killer' grudge against all present Jews. Some thought nothing of ignoring the pitiful plight of the Jews or, even more shamefully, in pointing out Jews trying to pass themselves off as Aryans. Others defied the Germans for financial rewards – 'Jewish gold'. This could vary from extortion to reasonable compensation; some simply took a particular individual or family to their hearts while still having mistrust or dislike for Jews in general. Yet others believed Jesus would have approved of acts of mercy to people in need and accordingly risked themselves. Some just thought it was the right thing to do. See Snyder, *Black Earth,* Chapter 12: 'The Righteous Few' (298-318); Kermish, *To Live with Honor* (619); Ascherson, *The Struggles for Poland* (112).

184 The first Jewish Underground organisation was formed in the Vilna

Ghetto on 1 January1942, under the leadership of Yitzhak Wittenberg with Abba Kovner. Their proclamation was prescient: *'Hitler aims to destroy all the Jews … Let us not go as lambs to the slaughter!'*

185 http://www.holocaustresearchproject.org/ghettos/warsawghetto.html – viewed 29/1/ 2010.

186 The offer came via Irene Sendler of Żegota. (refer endnote 261). Referred to in Sloan, *Notes from the Warsaw Ghetto* (336-8).

187 Though martyrdom does exist – for example the siege of Masada in 72CE, where 960 Jews, finding themselves trapped, suicided rather than being taken back into Roman slavery.

188 Of some 300 institutions in Poland, 189 are credited with taking in at least 1200 Jewish children. Statistics are contested and difficult to ascertain, as Jewish children entered convents with false papers identifying them as Catholic. https://www.yadvashem.org/yv/en/righteous/pdf/resources/nachum_bogner.pdf – viewed 25/4/2016.

189 Sloan, *Notes from the Warsaw Ghetto* (250).

190 The name of this hotel is confirmed in Engelking, *The Warsaw Ghetto* (581).

191 Ringelblum – in Sloan, *Notes from the Warsaw Ghetto* (249) – refers to this nightclub in the Hotel Britannia as being owned by 'the thirteen', a special group of police reporting to the Gestapo.

192 Eichmann in his trial used a figure of 10.3 million. The figures vary; discussions on who counted as a Jew are unresolved. Snyder, *Black Earth* (223).

193 Bauer, *A History of the Holocaust* (220-39); Arad, *Documents on the Holocaust* (410, 427-30).

194 Eichmann in his trial would claim he suggested the words 'final solution' to mean marching the Jews out of Europe. See Bauer, *A History of the Holocaust* (227).

195 **Wannsee Conference**: One copy of the Wannsee Protocol was found by Robert Kempner, a US prosecutor in the Nuremberg trials. Participants who were brought to trial at Nuremburg and elsewhere testified as to the proceedings. Online sources both viewed 22/5/2016 are: http://germanhistorydocs.ghi-dc.org/sub_document.cfm?document_id=1532; http://www.ghwk.de/fileadmin/user_upload/pdf-wannsee/texte/eichmanns-testimony.pdf. Arad, in *Documents on the Holocaust* (249-61), has the protocol (minutes) headed 'Reich Secret Document – 30 copies' which identifies eleven million Jews to be dealt with in 'the coming final solution of the Jewish question.' Bauer, in *A History of the Holocaust* (220-27) includes maps that show distribution and numbers of Jews (222) and selected sites for concentration camps (223). The award-winning 2001 TV movie *Conspiracy*, based on the found protocols, tells

of a secret session organised by Adolf Eichmann under the direction of Reinhard Heydrich, where discussion is quashed, dissidents (concerned with rule of Law or other matters such as availability of a labour force) are coerced, and a unanimous secret agreement is 'reached' by the fifteen participants, to achieve A.H.'s goal of a '*Judenrein*' Europe ('cleansing' Europe of eleven million Jews) by 'evacuation' – euphemism for annihilation; the gas chambers were already under construction. Wannsee House, the site of the conference, became a Memorial and Educational Site in 1992; the documents and photographs of the attendees are on display at https://www.berlin.de/museum/3108697-2926344-haus-der-wannseekonferenz.en.html – viewed 11/3/2017.

196 More recently the judgement of the German as 'evil' is being questioned. Under similar or the same set of conditions, would not most of us act the same?

197 Heinrich Himmler, on 4 October 1943, addressing SS generals, said: 'I also want to talk to you frankly on a grave matter ... "The Jewish people is going to be annihilated" says every party member. "Sure, it's in our program, elimination of the Jews, annihilation – we'll take care of it." And then they all come trudging, eighty millions [sic] worthy Germans, and each one has his one decent Jew. Sure, the others are swine, but this one is an A1 Jew. Of all those who talk this way, not one has seen it happen, not one has been through it. Most of you know what it means when 100 corpses are lying side by side, or 500, or 1000. To have stuck it out and at the same time – apart from exceptions caused by human weaknesses – to have remained decent fellows, that is what made us hard.' This version viewed 26/10/2010: http://akimel.net/himmler.html

198 Bauer, *A History of the Holocaust* (276).

199 Kermish, *To Live With Honor* (529-32).

200 Additional references for this chapter: Kermish, *To Live with Honor* (34, 63); Engelking, *Warsaw Ghetto* (various and 798); Sloan, *Notes from the Warsaw Ghetto* (278-80, 295, 320); Gutman, *The Jews Of Warsaw* (199-208). And http://www.shoaheducation.com/warsawtimeline.html – viewed 10 May 2010.

201 Some of the things A.H. got wrong: He denied all morality, denigrating it as a Jewish invention. He declared food shortages as the reason for trying to turn other countries into food bowls for Germany – but there was enough productive land in Germany. His fantasies about American space morphed into *Lebensraum* – living space. He believed Poland would support Germany against Russia, England would withdraw once France fell, there would be peace with England with both of them remaining world powers, and Madagascar would be a 'solution' to the removal of eleven million Jews; more people would take up antisemitic rhetoric, and he believed the Judeo-Bolshevik myth that with Russia being Jewish, thus inferior, the Soviets could be used, fooled, defeated, subjugated.

202 The terrors of the Soviets were not revealed until much later – destroyers of lives and ways of life on a grand scale; and in more recent times: Pol Pot in Cambodia, Rwanda, horrors and hate continue seemingly unabated – arguing about which is worse is not productive.

203 Opposition from youth in Germany: the Meuten: working-class teenagers and young adults sympathised with socialist ideology; the Swing Kids wore long hair and fashionable clothes, and listened to swing music, which was seen by the Nazis as Black music; the White Rose students at Munich University published anti-Nazi leaflets and they were executed in 1943; the Edelweiss Pirates painted anti-Nazi slogans, sheltered deserters and beat up Nazi officials. In 1944, the Cologne Pirates killed the Gestapo chief. http://www.bbc.co.uk/education/guides/zn8sgk7/revision/8 – viewed 17/7/2016.

204 Hilberg, *The Warsaw Diary Of Adam Czerniakow* (53); Kermish, *To Live With Honor* (281).

205 Arad, *Documents on the Holocaust* (171).

206 Kermish, *To Live With Honor* (671).

207 Arad, *Documents on the Holocaust* (275-6).

208 Gutman, *The Jews of Warsaw* (199); Kermish, *To Live With Honor* (699). David Graber says it was the 20th; ibid. (63).

209 Arad, *Documents on the Holocaust* (281-2).

210 Gutman, *Resistance* (152-3) and Arad, *Documents on the Holocaust* (293-4) have reports by Yizhak Cukierman and Hirsh Berlinski on these events.

211 Engelking, *The Warsaw Ghetto*, lists 80 major bunkers. (796-800).

212 Sloan, *Notes from the Warsaw Ghetto* (356).

213 Kermish, *To Live With Honor* (2, 66).

214 From The *Desiderata* (Latin: 'things desired as essential'). Previously cited as 'by anonymous', it is now attributed to Max Ehrmann, Methodist attorney from Indiana, apparently of Jewish origins on his father's side, written in 1927 or before. See more at: https://www.poetryfoundation.org/features/articles/detail/70274 – viewed 30/8/2016.

215 References: Kermish, *To Live With Honor* (96, 759-60); Arnon, *Who Was Janusz Korczak?* (28). Also see Wikipedia: Janusz Korczak.

216 Codename for the Polish Council to Aid Jews – *Rada Pomocy Zydom*.

217 Arnon, *Who Was Janusz Korczak?* (23).

218 Both Basia and Heniek tell of an escapee. It is unclear if this was the same person.

219 Hilberg, *The Warsaw Diary of Adam Czerniakow* (43).

220 David Graber in Kermish, *To Live With Honor* (64).

221 Even Inka, Heniek's youngest sister, is present. In 1939, with her husband

Stefan Tadeusz she'd escaped to Russia then to Rome to study. Returning to Russia they'd travelled by truck, filming documentary/news footage on behalf of the Soviet government. Inka, with her carrot-red hair, and Stefan, being uncircumcised and born Christian, were not of Jewish appearance. Believing themselves safe, they'd moved about openly. However, when captured by German soldiers, something gave them away. Sent to Warsaw with other gathered Jews, they were now 'home'. Arad, in *Documents on the Holocaust* (191) confirms that borders were open until the end of 1939.

PART NINE: LONGING FOR THE (IM)POSSIBLE

222 Carolyn Forche, *The Angel of History* (51).

223 Lion Feuchtwanger, *Tis Folly to be Wise: Death and Transfiguration of Jean-Jacques Rousseau* (89). Feuchtwanger tells of Henry Rousseau's last days and the aftermath of the varied interpretations of his words and ideas.

224 I was inspired by Matthew Henry's expanded expansion of the Ninth Commandment, Exodus 20:16. In summary: 'Do not equivocate, plan or scheme to deceive; unjustly prejudice another's reputation, charge him with things that he knows not, either judicially, upon oath or extrajudicially, in conversation, slander, gossip, and in any way seek to raise one's own reputation upon the ruin of another's.' (Matthew Henry, *Concise Commentary on the Whole Bible*) viewed on 15/8/2016 at: https://en.wikipedia.org/wiki/Thou_shalt_not_bear_false_witness_against_thy_neighbour

225 Andy Andrews, *How Do You Kill 11 Million People?* (21).

226 George Steiner points to the brutal paradox that '… "the big lie" had it's base … in the heartlands of western culture … Men could come home from their day's butchery … to weep over Rilke or play Schubert … How could this be?' Steiner, *A Reader* (11).

227 https://en.wikipedia.org/wiki/Big_lie – viewed 15/8/2016.

228 Check out Plato's *Allegory of the Cave* (with the Matrix), on-line.

229 This became *More Than Lament* and will be in Vidal, *Just Be Happy.*

230 https://en.wikipedia.org/wiki/Immanuel_Kant – viewed 16 April 2106.

PART TEN: BESHERT?

231 *The Moving Finger* by eleventh-century Persian mathematician, philosopher, astronomer, physician and poet Omar Khayyám, made famous in the West by the Edward FitzGerald (1809–83), translation in *Rubáiyát of Omar Khayyám.*

232 Shown on the map in Engelking, *The Warsaw Ghetto* (map area 7 (District 3) plates in the centre of the book (following p. 402).

233 Gentiles who risked their lives to save Jews during the Holocaust are honoured by Yad Vashem (The Holocaust Martyrs' and Heroes' Remembrance Authority). I searched the Yad Vashem Righteous Gentile Register but found no Countess Felix listed. Googling eventually gave me a society snippet referring to a Countess Felix Von Luckner which led me to Ingeborg (nee Engestrom), wife of the famous Count Felix Von Luckner known as the Sea Devil. They visited Melbourne in 1938! In addition, a photo of them both at http://cas.awm.gov.au/photograph/044903 – viewed 24/8/2009. In Engelking's *The Warsaw Ghetto*, there is a reference (486) to an Anna Melita Feliks and her 'shop' next to Kurt Roerich which was liquidated during the first *Aktion* (486). That would be the 'January' *Aktion*: 18 January 1943. Is it possible Countess Ingeborg Von Luckner, wife of Count Felix Von Luckner, and Anna Feliks were the same person? According to my parents, the factory Felix was on the boundary with part inside, part outside, the ghetto; they did not tell me of it being liquidated; where they were between the January *Aktion* and leaving the ghetto in April is unclear.

234 *Mishnah*, Sanhedrin 4:5.

235 In *Rethinking the Holocaust* (190), this is Rabbi Irving Greenberg's hypothesis.

236 Timothy Snyder in *Black Earth* sets out the how and why such ruthlessness was possible – and postulates that these men killed in response to a carrot offered by the Nazis: kill Jews – get statehood, kill Jews – defeat communism (136, 142). Photos online show these men were just boys. https://www.pinterest.com/pin/472033604664030699/ – viewed 16/2/2016.

237 *Einsatz Reinhard*: *Aktion* (Operation) Reinhard: code name for the Nazi plan to seek out and murder Poles (gentiles and Jews) in the General Government. Two million Poles were killed by these task forces, of which 1.3 million were Jews.

238 Militiaman is what my father called the Jewish policeman when recounting this event. He told it with bullets flying and much noise; my mother insists the courtyard was strangely empty and she led the charge. In any event, a blessing on that unknown man who pointed the way.

239 Most recent figure viewed 13/7/2016 at *Holocaust Encyclopedia*, WARSAW GHETTO UPRISING: https://www.ushmm.org/wlc/en/article.php?ModuleId=10005188. The figures show 265,000 were exterminated in Treblinka and other camps, 11,580 taken to work camps, 200 suicided, 10.000 shot. Total killed in this action was 275,000.

240 No other occupied country was subjected to such an edict.

241 http://www.savingjews.org/bekanntmachung3.htm – viewed 16/1/2010.

242 Kermish, *To Live With Honor* (280).

243 Gutman, *Resistance* (155-60).

244 Jan Karski (1914–2000). One of the first to deliver eyewitness accounts, of what was happening to Jews, to Allied leaders during the war. Gutman, *Resistance* (175); *Holocaust Encyclopedia*, JAN KARSKI: https://www.ushmm.org/wlc/en/article.php?ModuleId=0008152 – viewed 14/4/2016.

245 Extraordinary in its detail (I viewed it on 15/7/2016) it can be read in full at: http://www.holocaustresearchproject.org/nazioccupation/polishforthnigtreview.html

246 Found in Weizmann, *Trial and Error*: 'England Pays Tribute to the suffering of European Jews' (plate 156, opposite p. 505). This is an extract as reported in *The Daily Telegraph* and *Morning Post* on Friday, 18 December 1942.

247 It is not clear whether this was the factory Felix. My father is long gone and my mother is unsure of this detail.

248 Hotel Polski – Scam or Saving Scheme? In 1942, the Germans promised to allow Jews from Warsaw holding foreign passports of neutral countries to leave the General Government for South America. In May 1943, after the last deportation from the Warsaw Ghetto, a network of Jewish collaborators sold documents to Jews hiding on the 'Aryan' side of Warsaw. The South American governments refused to recognise most of the passports. Of 2,500 who came out of hiding, about 350 Jews who held Palestinian affidavits survived. This was thought to be a German trap to lure the richer Jews out of their hiding places and steal their possessions. But new Polish research identifies that, if the South American governments had recognised these passports, more could have survived. Reference: Engelking, *The Warsaw Ghetto* (745-8); also Yad Vashem: Hotel Polski at http://www.yadvashem.org/odot_pdf/Microsoft%20Word%20-%206430.pdf – viewed 12/8/2009.

249 Approximately $US1.4m in 2017.

250 Marek Edelman. Bund Leader. Anti-Zionist. Polish Hero. Member Solidarity. Wikipedia: *Marek Edelman*. Viewed 13/5/ 2010.

251 Additional references for this chapter: Kermish, *To Live With Honor* (587-600); Gutman, *The Jews of Warsaw* (121); Gutman, *Resistance*; Mogilanski, *The Ghetto Anthology* (317). Also at http://warszawa.getto.pl/index.php?show=kalendarium&lang=en – viewed 5/01/2010.

252 Numbers of arms are unclear – correspondence and reportage between the ghetto fighters and the Polish AK conflict – refer to Arad, *Documents on the Holocaust* (304-09).

253 In *A Surplus of Memories*, Yitzhak Zuckerman (known as Anton or Antek) relates that the ZOB discovered that several *Judenrat* members had been giving the SS advice on tactics to manage the Jewish population. Zuckerman et al., *A Surplus of Memory: Chronicles of the Warsaw Ghetto Uprising* (434).

254 A fifth column: a group of people who undermine a larger group from within.

255 Arad, *Documents on the Holocaust:* 'Call to resistance' (302).

256 *Zydowski Związek Wojskowy* (ZZW), numbering 250, organised by the Betar Zionist Youth Movement and the Revisionist Zionist Movement, formed primarily of former officers of the Polish army in late 1939; they are largely unsung because so few survived. In Israel, this was and is the Irgun: http://www1.yadvashem.org/odot – viewed 6/12/2009. Also Gutman, *Resistance* (169).

257 Zivia Lubetkin would fight in the Warsaw Ghetto Uprising of 1943 and the Warsaw Uprising of 1944, be part of *Brichah* (refer endnote 301), marry Yitzchak Zuckerman (commander ZOB), emigrate to Israel, be a pioneer on a kibbutz, and would give crucial evidence at the Eichmann trial.

258 This account is from my father – Gutman in *Resistance* (177-88) gives a very full account. Documents of these notices are in Kermish, *To Live With Honor* (588-91) and Arad, *Documents on the Holocaust* (302).

259 Heniek was not alone in the misconception of the 'outside' as Aryan. To Jews (and to Poles themselves), Poles were Aryan like the Germans. Aryan is derived from a Sanskrit word meaning 'noble', the term construed according to Nazi doctrine to refer to a 'master race' or *Übermensch* of blond northern European perfection. To the Nazis, Poles, being Slavs, despised and designated as a filthy vermin race only second to Jews and gypsies, were *Untermenschen* - subhuman all. See Ascherson, *The Struggles For Poland* (99).

260 **Warsaw Ghetto Massacre** (April 19 to May 16, 1943). The Germans' conduct of a selection on the eve of A.H.'s birthday – which coincided that year with Passover – was greeted by intense resistance led by ZOB and ZZW; this was just days after Basia and Heniek's escape. In response, the Gestapo levelled the ghetto with 2,000 troops and full battle array, including tanks against 60,000 men, women and children armed with nine rifles and 59 pistols, hand grenades and homemade incendiary devices. See Gutman, *Resistance,* Chapter 11 'The End' for a description of these four weeks that have transformed the image of a Jew from being submissive, passive and pious to warrior (255). In this operation to suppress the uprising, commanded by SS Brigadier-General Stroop, SS and Gestapo units killed 56,065 Jews. (*The Stroop Report* – entry dated 16 May 1943.) Many ghetto-fighters, not killed in battle, killed each other to avoid capture. *The Stroop Report*, in horrifying pictures and narrative detail, presented A.H. with documentation of the desired news: 'The Warsaw Ghetto is no more.' While the ghetto was being destroyed and smoke filled the air – on the other side of the wall on 25 May 1943 there was festivity to mark Easter: carousels, laughter, music. Source:

Kermish, *Resistance* (233). Arad, *Documents on the Holocaust* contains Polish reports on the destruction with praise for heroism (316-21), to denigration by the Polish Workers Party (Communist Party) claiming supply of a great many arms (322-3). Also see Engelking's map (2 pages before p. 403) in *The Warsaw Ghetto*. Stroop, sentenced to death by an American court at Dachau, was hanged on 8 September 1951, at the scene of his crime in Warsaw. Viewed 26/7/2016 at: http://www.holocaustresearchproject.org/nazioccupation/jurgenstroop.html

261 Zofia Kossak (code name Weronica), an author and conservative nationalist, and Wanda Krahelska-Filipowicz, a socialist activist married to a former ambassador to the USA, drew together a consortium of Polish Catholic and democratic circles charged with the sole purpose of rescue. Zegota is credited with saving up to 28,000 Jews. And Irene Sendler, a Catholic social worker in charge of the children's section of Zegota – between 1942 and 1943, with 20 helpers – posing as a nurse, entered the ghetto on the pretext of checking on the typhus epidemic, and smuggled out 2,500 babies and children: in ambulances, on trams and as packages. Severely tortured by the Gestapo, rescued by Zegota, in hiding in the forests, she survived eventually to receive many honours. http://www.raoulwallenberg.net/saviors/others/keepers-flame/ – viewed 25/6/2015. Also for more on Wolinski and Zegota see Gutman, *Resistance* (172-5), and Arad, *Documents on the Holocaust* (327-8).

262 Primo Levi, *If This Is A Man / The Truce*. This quote from *The Truce* (235).

263 Czesław Miłosz, writing in the early 1950s, movingly conveys how the Poles of Warsaw – caught in a trap between the furious Germans destroying-all-in-their-retreat and the ruthless advancing Reds – in a no-win situation without any clear sense of what they were dying for, nevertheless were prepared to fight and die. Miłosz, *The Captive Mind* (92-101).

264 Additional references for this chapter: Bauer, *Out Of The Ashes* (1); Wyman, *DP* (38, 46, 107, 116, 160); Levin, *The Holocaust* (704-08).

265 The numbers are contested. This figure is on the high side; from Frank Golczewski's 'Polen' in W. Benz (ed.), *Dimensionen des Volkermords*, found in Gregor, *Oxford Readers Nazism* (331).

266 Watt, *Bitter Glory* (449-53) and Ascherson, *The Struggles For Poland* (130-8). Indeed, the Soviets 'fooled' everyone on a scale such that at his end A.H. declared that they, not the German people, were the master race: '... the future belongs entirely to the stronger people of the East.' Snyder, *Black Earth* (242).

267 http://www.google.com.au/images?sa=3&q=photo+of+destroyed+warsaw+ghetto&btn – viewed on 22/03/2010.

268 Eudaimonia, happiness and/or human flourishing; a belief that right

action leads to wellbeing (Aristotle) https://en.wikipedia.org/wiki/Eudaimonia. Viewed 28/7/2017.

269 The Tenth Commandment: Exodus 20:17: 'Thou shalt not covet thy neighbour's house … nor any thing that is thy neighbour's.' Some consider this Commandment, 'You shall not covet', to be the most important and the most difficult to follow. Joel Hoffman, author of *The Bible Doesn't Say That*, suggests that this has been misinterpreted and is not so much about wanting what one's neighbour has but not actually taking it. (At a Limmud Oz Conference in Melbourne 27/6/2016.)

270 Also found in Wyman, *DP* (143).

271 Leviticus 19:34: 'The foreigner residing among you must be treated as your native-born. Love them as yourself, for you were foreigners in Egypt.' Also, Romans 13:9 and elsewhere, and in the gospels of the New Testament, 'love thy neighbour' is the most important wisdom attributed to Jesus together with love of God.

272 "What will I tell him, I, a Jew of the New Testament, / Waiting two thousand years for the second coming of Jesus? / My broken body will deliver me to his sight / And he will count me among the helpers of death: The uncircumcized." Milosz, *The History of Polish Literature* (460)

273 Wyman, *DP* (142-5).

274 In honour of the children of the Warsaw Ghetto, the poem 'The Little Smuggler' can be found in Engelking, *The Warsaw Ghetto* (448).

275 Peretz Heim: an asylum and soup kitchen established by Zionist leader Emil Sommerstein for the Soviets and Polish Committee of National Liberation in July 1944. Bauer, *Out of the Ashes* (2).

PART ELEVEN: AMOR FATI?

276 Nietzshe's words affirming his pursuit of life: *Amor Fati*. In Dudley, *Hegel, Nietzsche and Philosophy* (201).

277 Dharma: Hinduism & Buddhism, the basic principles of cosmic or individual existence: divine law, conformity to one's duty and nature (Merriam Webster definition).

278 Karma, meaning action, work or deed, refers to the spiritual principle of cause and effect where intent and actions of an individual (cause) influence the future of that individual (effect). Found at https://en.wikipedia.org/wiki/Karma on 8/3/2016.

279 Determinism is a 'belief that all events are caused by things that happened before them and that people have no real ability to make choices or control what happens' (Merriam Webster definition).

280 Dudley, *Hegel, Nietzsche and Philosophy* (201).

282 Research suggests: 'Malnourishment in the womb causes genetic changes that can still be seen when people reach middle and old age'. Health

effects of this genetic change are being studied. Viewed 16/5/2001 at http://www.timesonline.co.uk/tol/news/uk/health/article5029679.ece

PART TWELVE:(UN)WELCOME

283 Earl G. Harrison, the Dean of the University of Pennsylvania Law School, was sent in August 1945 to investigate the DP camps, reporting to President Harry S. Truman. Viewed 6/12/09 at: http://geography.about.com/od/populationgeography/a/displacedjews.htm

284 The term – unknown to the Nazis – stems from the Ancient Greek *holokauston* which derives from the Hebrew *olah* meaning a sacrificial offering consumed by fire. It refers to the mass murder of 6 million Jews, 5 million Sinti-Roma, Slavs, and other unwanted persons under the Nazi regime during the period 1941–45 throughout occupied Europe. *Shoah,* the Hebrew word meaning 'Desolation', is the preferred term by many Jewish scholars. http://www.huffingtonpost.com.au/entry/the-word-holocaust-history-and-meaning_n_1229043

285 Found in Wyman, *DP* (160).

286 The Hebrew word *ger*, meaning stranger or, in our terms, immigrant, appears 92 times in the Old Testament. http://welcomingthestranger.com/wp_welcoming/learn-and-discern/scripture-and-immigration – viewed 23/3/2017. A selection: Exodus. 23:9: 'Also thou shall not oppress a stranger: for ye know the heart of a stranger, seeing ye were strangers in the land of Egypt.' Leviticus. 19:34: 'But the stranger that dwelleth with you shall be unto you as one born among you, and thou shalt love him as thyself; for ye were strangers in the land of Egypt: I am the Lord your God.'

287 It is thanks to Irka we have some photos of Basia's family.

288 These agencies included UNRRA (United Nations Relief and Rehabilitation Administration), JDC (Joint Distribution Committee), Red Cross, and CARE (Cooperative for American Remittances to Europe).

289 Displaced Person (DP). There were an estimated 6.34 million to 8 million DPs in the zones of Allied occupation after May 1945: https://www.holocaustcenter.org/glossary-terms?

290 Snyder, *Black Earth,* in particular Chapter 5: 'Double Occupation'.

291 Labelled by the authorities for easy identification: Polish workers wore an insignia with a large 'P' on a yellow square, Ukrainians and Russians an 'O' for *Ost* – east – on a blue square.

292 Legal Classifications produced by SHAEF, The Supreme Headquarters Allied Expeditionary Force, as set out in Wyman, *DP* (25) included: evacuees, war refugees, political refugees, political prisoners, forced or voluntary workers, transfers of population, civilian internees, ex-prisoners of war, and stateless persons.

293 I.G. Farben was the most powerful German corporate cartel in the first

half of the 20th century and the single largest profiteer from the Second World War. I.G. (*Interessengemeinschaft*) stands for 'Association of Common Interests': It included BASF, Bayer, Hoechst, and other German chemical and pharmaceutical companies. I.G. Farben built a giant plant at Auschwitz and was intimately involved with the human experimental atrocities committed by Josef Mengele (Angel of Death). They also had their own concentration camp, Monowitz, where 30.000 slave workers died. Josef Borkin writes: 'I.G. reduced slave labor to a consumable raw material which was recycled into the German war economy: gold teeth for the Reichsbank, hair for mattresses, and fat for soap'. Borkin, *The Crime and Punishment of I.G. Farben* (126).

294 The Nazis had deported between 7 and 9 million Europeans, mostly to Germany. More than 6 million displaced people were repatriated to their home countries within months of Germany's surrender in May 1945. Between 1.5 million and 2 million DPs refused repatriation. From the *Holocaust Encyclopedia*, POSTWAR REFUGEE CRISIS: https://www.ushmm.org/wlc/en/article.php?ModuleId=10005459 – viewed 27/7/2016.

295 ibid.

296 Pisar, *Of Blood and Hope* (98-9).

297 Wyman, *DP* (133).

298 Levi, *The Truce* (188).

299 Detailed statistics of casualties at https://en.wikipedia.org/wiki/World_War_II_casualties – viewed 27/8/2016.

300 Naor, *The Twentieth Century in Eretz Israel* (241).

301 *Brichah*: Yehuda Bauer, in *Out of the Ashes* (2, 73) explains that *Brichah*, meaning flight, was an alliance formed in December 1944 between Abba Kovner (head of Polish ex-partisans) and Yitzhak (Antek) Zuchermann (deputy commander of the Warsaw Ghetto Uprising) to enable young ex-fighters and returnees from the Soviet Union to get to Palestine via Romania. Officially established in Lublin, Poland, in January 1945, Kovner led men who had fought in forests with the Lithuanian partisans; Zuckerman led Zionists who, having fled to Russia, now returned to help get survivors out of Europe. Later when this route became closed, it was changed to be via Hungary, Austria, and Italy.

302 *Aliyah,* meaning 'Return' or 'Going Up', is the name for this journey of Jewish refugees to Palestine. They planned to take out 5,000–10,000 in small groups but 65,000 wanted to go.

303 Referred to in Bauer, *Out of the Ashes* (57) and in Wyman, *DP* (156).

304 Total equivalent to around 400 $US in 2017.

305 Naor, *The Twentieth Century in Eretz Israel* (241).

306 *Remember,* a 2015 Canadian-German film, brilliantly illustrates this identity theft.

307 see endnote 301 – *Brichah.*

308 Source of quote: Zvielli, *Front Page Israel – The Palestine Post* front page of May 2, 1945 – under the heading of 'Palestinian Policy Attacked' (63). Other references: Naor, *The Twentieth Century in Eretz Israel* (238); Bauer, *Out of the Ashes* (57); and *Holocaust Encyclopedia*, 'Postwar Refugee Crisis': https://www.ushmm.org/wlc/en/article.php?ModuleId=10005459– viewed 21/7/2016.

309 Bauer in *Out of the Ashes* (57) identifies that 15,000 DPs came into Italy by this route until stopped by British obstruction. *In Rethinking the Holocaust* (251) Bauer confirms President Truman – though not sympathetic to Zionistic aspirations – took up Earl G. Harrison's appeal to permit 100,000 Jews entry into Palestine, and says that if the British had granted entry, Israel might never have been.

310 Additional references for this chapter: Bauer, *Out of the Ashes* (46-59); Gutman, *Sher'erit Hapletah* (519-20); Wikepedia: *Brichah* – viewed 12/10/2009.

311 Ezekiel, 37:25.

312 More recent histories point out that Germans within Germany were cushioned during the war from events elsewhere by 'celebration-of-life' rituals. Extract in Gregor, *Oxford Readers Nazism* (216-19) from Klaus Vondung's *Magic and Manipulations.*

313 Refer to https://www.ushmm.org/outreach/en/article.php?ModuleId=10007722 for details of those tried. Also there is an excellent 1961 film *Judgement at Nuremburg.*

314 Agnes Heller, in an interview with John Rundell, says Hannah Arendt, in thinking that evil is an unthinking act, misunderstood Eichmann and thus got it wrong. Agnes Heller says: 'the modern problem is … to maintain the possibility of distinguishing between good and evil.' Rundell, *Critical Horizons* (137).

315 Mummy later told me that the collar had been her sister Zosia's and had come to her from Zosia's sister-in-law Irka with whom they had stayed in Łódź.

316 George Moore.

317 This account is Heniek's version; I have not been able to confirm his description of the officers and camp.

318 The *Exodus* loaded at Sète near Marseilles with 4,200 women, men and children brought by the *Brichah* from Germany in 1947. Ordered back to France by the British, the Jews refused to disembark and the French officials refused to use force. The British then ordered the *Exodus* passengers to Germany to camps in the British zone.

319 On 14 May 1948, the last British forces had left Haifa; the Jewish Agency, led by David Ben-Gurion, declared the creation of the State of

Israel, in accordance with the 1947 UN Partition Plan.

320 The *Continental* – claims to fame: built 1902 in Maryland for the Boston Steam Company, this ship had many names and roles: *Shawmut* – (freighter) → *Ancon* (the first ship carrying guests to go officially through the Panama Canal; then cargo; then rebuilt as a 200 passenger ship) → *Exancon* (carrying cement); → *Permanente* (she took war brides from Australia to America); → *Tidewater* (refitted to take approx. 350 people); → *Continental* (migrants from Europe and phosphate to NZ and several trips from NY to Antwerp). My parents came on its second trip to Australia carrying migrants in 1949 – it made three more trips with migrants before being turned into scrap. Plowman, *Australian Migrant ships 1946-1977* (16).

321 Source: Passenger Lists of Public Record Office Victoria. *Continental* 24/2/1949. Passenger listed as: British, Greek, Polish, Italian, Swiss, Latvian, French, Albanian, Stateless.

322 Norma was Auntie Mania's middle daughter.

323 The order of events is unclear. But it is certain that Mr Roth helped my parents and others like them.

324 From photo of family 1949. Back row from left: Mania Fish (Heniek's cousin, my 'Auntie' Mania); Basia, here 26 years old; Esther Munz (Mania's sister). Front row: Martin Munz; Rebecca Fish; Sara (me); Barbara and Norman Rosenblatt.

PART THIRTEEN: ***ATOH-DACHAIA***

325 Refer endnote 10 – *Atoh-dachaia* (pronounced a-toh-da-hi-a). I searched for a word to encompass and, finding none, created one: longing encompasses gratitude; built on knowledge and understanding.

326 This is my Thirteenth Commandment: Make a just, lawful and safe world with(out) God. Where 'just', incorporating reasonable and fair, dovetails with compassion, and is akin to 'the space between' as in Part Nine. Environmental responsibility, strong throughout the Bible, is compellingly conveyed in the *Midrash* [ancient Rabbinic commentary on the oral law given to Moses] Kohelet Rabbah 1 on Ecclesiastes 7:13, where God says to Adam and Eve: 'Look at my works! See how beautiful they are … For your sake I created them all. See to it that you do not spoil and destroy My world; for if you do, there will be no one else to repair it.' http://www.jlaw.com/Articles/environmentbible2.pdf

327 Herman Wouk, *This Is My God* (169).

328 Steven Pinker's highly recommended book *The Better Angels of Our Nature* arrived mid-August 2016 and is on my to-read pile.

329 There is an inspiring exposition of 'The Angel of Alternative History' found in Solnit, *Hope in the Dark* (70).

330 From Melbourne this return was organised by Betar – a Zionist youth movement.

331 Lech Wałęsa, co-founder of the Solidarity trade union movement in the 1980s, presided over Poland's transition from communism to a post-communist state. He also apologised in Israel in 1992. https://en.wikipedia.org/wiki/Lech_Wa%C5%82%C4%99sa – viewed 11/4/2016.

332 On 14/4/16 I attended a forum as part of The Jewish Museum of Australia (in Melbourne) called 'Can We Talk About Poland'. The conversation has begun.

333 Thinkers, researchers and writers identify that we are too close to the events. Timothy Snyder in *Black Earth* (xii) says more time and research are needed to come to some understanding. At the Jewish Writers' Festival in Melbourne on 22 June 2016, Israeli author Nir Baram said: 'The Holocaust is on a par with the collapse of the Roman Empire … it is too soon for "lessons" … we need much more time to understand.'

334 Hitler, *Mein Kampf* (64).

335 Burg, *The Holocaust Is Over; We Must Rise From Its Ashes* (44).

336 Wouk, *This is My God* (283).

337 Arendt, *Eichmann in Jerusalem,* found in Des Pres, *The Survivor.* (211-12).

338 Found at http://www.jewfaq.org/prayer/kaddish.htm – viewed October 2009.

339 Stern, *Gates of Prayer for Weekdays: A Gender Sensitive Prayerbook.* My underline – found in Reform and Liberal Judaism, I heard 'all the people of the world' in a prayer at my grand-nephew's barmitzvah in an orthodox synagogue on 5 August 2017.

340 Numbers 15:26. http://biblehub.com/numbers/15-26.htm – viewed 11/6/2015.

341 Symbol viewed 26/9/09 at http://en.wikipedia.org/wiki/Chai_(symbol)

AFFIRMATION: LIVING THE QUESTIONS

342 Rilke, *Letters To A Young Poet* (45-6).

343 Levy, *The Truce* (396).

344 In particular David Irving.

345 There is a happy postscript to my sentiments towards my mother for her antipathy to my husband. My sister's contribution after looking through a draft in June 2016: 'Sara, I just want you to know way back just after I got married, when my in-laws invited Mummy and Daddy for *Pesach,* my in-laws said they didn't want to have Branko there – him being not Jewish. Well, Mummy told them in no uncertain terms that if you and he

weren't welcome then she and Daddy wouldn't come either.' Hmmm – I didn't know that.

346 Reference to Agnes Heller's 'Absolute Stranger' found in Rundell, *Critical Horizons* (5).

347 *desiderium*: an ardent desire or longing; especially: a feeling of loss or grief for something lost (Merriam Webster definition).

348 For a graphic representation of the millions killed, see 'Jaw-Dropping Visualization Will Give You New Respect For The Sheer Number Who Died In WWII' at http://www.huffingtonpost.com.au/entry/world-war-two-fatalities-visualized_n_7526390.html?section=australia – viewed 5/4/16.

349 My poem was inspired by Francis R. Scott's (1899–1985) *Villanelle For Our Times* which was first sung by Leonard Cohen in 1999. He included it in his 2004 album *Dear Heather*.

350 In an article on *I and Thou*, Sarah Scott explains that 'the self becomes either more fragmentary or more unified through its relationships to others.' http://www.iep.utm.edu/buber/ Morris West in *The Tower of Babel* examines this dilemma in a story set in the Middle East on the eve of the 1967 War, where events unfold through the eyes of an Israeli spy living in Syria, a Palestinian leader, a Lebanese banker, and an Israeli military adviser (157). In this situation, with neither Jew nor Arab prepared to renounce their claim to the land, no solution is in sight. Still we try.

351 Natalia Ginzburg in *The Little Virtues* (80) says we cannot love our neighbour (this injunction is in Leviticus and Mark) because he despises us and we cannot even love ourselves.

352 Joseph, *Loving Every Child*, about Janusz Korczak (70). Also see *How to Love a Child*, http://www.januszkorczak.ca/legacy/3_How%20to%20Love%20a%20Child.pdf – viewed 18/5/2011.

353 The fictional character Gabriel Mirkin to his son Zachary, who at age twelve has just learnt he is Jewish. See Asch, *Three Cities* (67).

354 Sura 49:13 at http://www.wiamep.org/resources/aprogressivejewsdilemma.htm – viewed 12/10/12.

355 http://www.bridgesforpeace.com/il/news/article/israels-president-we-are-losing-our-ability-to-speak-with-one-another – viewed 28/10/2014.

356 Protestant Pastor Martin Niemöller (1892–1984), though a German nationalist, refused to recognise the state claim to supremacy over Christians; he sought and gained the release of arrested clergymen. He was imprisoned in Sachsenhausen and Dachau concentration camps 1937 to 1945. The Nazis murdered 4,000 priests. See Bauer, *A History of the Holocaust* (143). And https://www.ushmm.org/wlc/en/article.php?ModuleId=10007392 – viewed 28/3/2017.

357 The Ten Commandments plus one amendment and three more:

1. I am the lord your God

2. No God but Me
3. Do not take the name in vain
4. Remember the Sabbath
5. Honour your father and mother
6. Do not murder
7. Do not commit adultery (Do not cause shame)
8. Do not steal
9. Do not bear false witness
10. Do not covet
11. Choose life
12. Make the stranger welcome
13. Make a just, lawful and safe world with(out) God.

Yehuda Bauer in a speech to the Bundestag (the German House of Representatives) on 27/1/1998 also suggested three more Commandments to the Ten. In summary his are: 'never become perpetrators; never allow yourself to become victims; never be passive onlookers'. In *Rethinking The Holocaust* (273).

358 Caputo, *The Prayers and Tears of Jacques Derrida* (333).

359 Daniel Dombrowski, writing of Kazantzakis's theism, also relates this to the Tao in Dombrowski, *Kazantzakis and God* (87).

360 Acknowledgement: The English version of 'The Golden Rule Across the World's Religions: Thirteen Sacred Texts' was prepared by Paul McKenna. Permission to reproduce received by email on 22/10/14. Published by Scarboro Missions (Toronto, Canada) Copyright © Scarboro Missions 2000. http://www.scarboromissions.ca/Golden_rule/sacred_texts_en.php
There are many non-religious expressions of the Golden Rule. I have replaced the star and crescent, contemporary symbol of Islam, with the ancient one meaning 'Allah' in Arabic. The symbol for the one more – Existentialism – is Leonard Cohen's beautiful unified heart of reconciliation and harmony.

361 And at the bottom of the email regarding the Golden Rule from Paul McKenna, one more rule –

'You will always have what you desire for others.'
–The Dalai Lama

INDEX

C

H

T

U

V

W

www.ingramcontent.com/pod-product-compliance
Ingram Content Group UK Ltd.
Pitfield, Milton Keynes, MK11 3LW, UK
UKHW041950190726
13854UKWH00004B/1882

9 781925 272659